Masters of Madness

Social Origins of the American
Psychiatric Profession

Constance M. McGovern

Masters of Madness

Social Origins of the American Psychiatric Profession

Published for University of Vermont
by University Press of New England
Hanover and London, 1985

University Press of New England
Brandeis University
Brown University
Clark University
University of Connecticut
Dartmouth College
University of New Hampshire
University of Rhode Island
Tufts University
University of Vermont

Printed in the United States of America

Library of Congress Cataloging-in-Publication Data
McGovern, Constance M., 1938–
  Masters of madness.

  Revision of thesis (doctoral)—University of
Massachusetts at Amherst.
  Bibliography: p.
  Includes index.
  1. Psychiatric hospital care—Social aspects—
United States—History—19th century. 2. Psychiatrists—
United States—History 19th century. 3. American
Psychiatric Association—History—19th century.
I. Title.
RC443.M38 1985   362.2′0425′0973   85–40491
ISBN 0–87451–352–9

Frontispiece: Bloomingdale Asylum, New York, 1806.

To my mother and to the memory of my father

Without their encouragement of a child's curiosity and their support of a young woman's career aspirations, it is doubtful that this book would exist at all.

Contents

Preface

It has been a century and a half since Americans first concerned themselves with the building of asylums for the therapeutic care of the insane. In response to this rising wave of
humanitarianism, a number of men who had been trained in general medicine became medical superintendents of asylums. They
did not originate the concept of institutionalization; they embraced it and molded the details of asylum design and management. Their program of "moral treatment" called for both medical attention and diversionary therapeutic activities; central to
its success was the administrative role of the physician as medical
superintendent. To create and sustain recognition for their expertise, these institutional psychiatrists fashioned a professional
organization to protect themselves and their emerging specialty.
They took on the responsibility for the mentally ill, convinced
themselves they could manage and cure the insane, and set out
to persuade everyone else.

Their optimism was the result of more than belief in the spirit
of progress or a sense of social responsibility. The psychiatrists
had much at stake as well. Both personally and professionally,
they felt compelled to succeed. These medical superintendents
were after all rather ordinary men seeking to make a living,
among other diverse goals, and as with men of every generation,
the sources of their professional behavior preceded their emergence as professional men.

This study is an exploration of the reasons why the American
asylum took the form it did and an analysis of why psychiatrists
adhered to their plan of therapy and asylum organization after it
no longer worked. This is neither exclusively a study of the
Association of Medical Superintendents of American Institutions
for the Insane (now the American Psychiatric Association) nor

merely one of the origins of the asylum. It is the story of the men themselves. The personalities and experience of this group of 115 antebellum doctors-turned-psychiatrists are important for what they reveal about the institutional forms of nineteenth-century American psychiatry. While the way in which these men reacted to the exigencies of their professional lives reveals much about the complexities of life choices in early nineteenth-century America, their behavior clarifies the reasons why institutional psychiatry particularly, and the broader modern profession as well, has taken the shape so familiar to us.

In the last few decades, theories about the functions of mental illness, mental hospitals, and psychiatrists have proliferated. Critics of the medical model of mental illness, like Thomas Szasz, Thomas Scheff, and Erving Goffman, have adopted the labeling theory. Claiming that mental "illness" is culturally defined and aberrant behavior a learned response, these critics stress the repressive nature of the entire psychiatric profession.[1]

Less extreme critics still emphasize the social control functions of mental institutions. David Rothman finds that Jacksonian Americans devised asylums in an attempt to restore order to a peculiarly frayed social fabric. Michel Foucault, more wide-ranging in time and culture, attributed the changing definition of madness to a seventeenth-century shift in cultural values. With the development of bourgeois values, madness became an "incapacity for work" and resulted in the "great confinement" and, ultimately, the asylum, which alienated mad persons from their formerly "free" status.[2]

Other scholars have broadened the issues. Richard Fox rejects the social control view that "flattens out" many "vital structural developments by positing an abstract conflict between a group of controllers and their victims." Criticizing those who "reify the 'controllers'" and equate them with "a homogeneous elite" or "society as a whole," Fox examines the interconnections of the social, institutional, and professional structures of the commitment process.[3]

Nancy Tomes moves beyond the sometimes heated debate between the labeling theorists (or interactionists) and more traditional approaches and investigates the asylum as a social institution. Using the voluminous records of a nineteenth-century asylum, she brings new dimensions to the interplay of culture and mental illness. She stresses the interactions of patients and staff, the relationships of patients with one another, and the consensus between doctors and families of patients about definitions of insanity and expectations about the asylum.[4]

Gerald Grob, the most prolific writer on the history of American psychiatry, has brought considerable insight to the question of social policy and the mentally ill. Grob suggests that "much of the contemporary debate" among revisionists "rests upon an ahistorical analysis of medicine and disease." Grob acknowledges that both nineteenth-century and present-day psychiatric thought and practice are influenced by "external and nonmedical factors." But to ignore nineteenth-century medical theory, which used symptoms to define disease and made little distinction between physiological and behavioral processes, Grob says, is to misjudge psychiatrists as "engaging in a unique practice" when they "identified symptoms as pathology." Additionally, he warns that viewing asylums as monolithic, repressive institutions obscures the many uses that patients, psychiatrists, and the larger society made of the asylum. Examining the actions of the Association of Medical Superintendents of American Institutions for the Insane, Grob dismisses social control interpretations and characterizes the medical superintendents as a group of humanitarians whose good intentions did not survive the onslaught of large numbers of lower-class patients or the encroachments of state boards of charity.[5]

Accepting the existence of a broad social movement that dictated asylum building (for whatever complexity of reasons), my analysis of the lives, characters, and motivations of these medical superintendents suggests an additional perspective on the uses of asylums. The men of this study, who were to become the medical superintendents, initially had set their sights on careers of service as doctors. A conjunction of their benevolent interests with their social concerns and personal and professional frustrations, however, led them into asylum administration. The asylum movement and the emergence of medical authority over the insane, of course, were not merely American phenomena. Men in Britain and France, many of them doctors, devised most of the new techniques for treating the insane.[6] Like their European counterparts, American doctors learned the principle of institutionalization, and the plan of moral treatment quickly and garnered public support by claiming high curability rates. With a zeal arising from their demonstrated success in curing the insane and in keeping with their needs for professional success, they shaped a professional organization to sustain their new careers. They set criteria for membership in the specialty by restricting full participation in the association to medical superintendents, exercising personal and professional persuasion to gain consensus on their essential and powerful role in the asylum.

It was by this insistence on the essential role of the medical superintendent that they shaped American institutional psychiatry. For them "a military camp, nor a man-of-war [did] not more require the rigid observation of regulation and discipline under a single head"; he, and only he, was necessary for "all proper discipline and good order and good management."[7] They adamantly opposed all other plans. In fashioning this particular brand of moral treatment based on their positions as medical superintendents, they not only elevated their own status but also left their distinctive mark on the American asylum system and on the American psychiatric profession.

In an earlier form, this study was my doctoral dissertation at the University of Massachusetts at Amherst. I am deeply grateful to those teachers, friends, and, now, colleagues for their encouragement, conversation, confidence, and intellectual criticism. My director Leonard Richards, Mario De Pillis, and Paul Boyer, gave unstintingly of their suggestions for organization and style, and their always perceptive questions prodded me along new paths of inquiry. Not only did Mario De Pillis start me on the path of social history, but his abiding faith in me has meant more than even he can imagine.

I owe a special debt to Eric T. Carlson, M.D., of the New York Hospital and Cornell Medical School, who was an early reader and who, despite his manifold responsibilities as psychiatrist, historian, and teacher, continues to encourage my work. I am grateful, too, to my former colleague at the University of Arizona, Leonard Dinnerstein, whose advice has always been tempered with the generosity and warmth of friendship, and to Charles Rosenberg of the University of Pennsylvania, who gave generously of his time and expertise in reading the manuscript and made always astute suggestions.

Two of my colleagues at the University of Vermont have been invaluable critics. Samuel Hand's suggestions, delivered with inimitable wit and grace, helped to clarify issues. Marshall True's editorial comments and our long exploratory conversations sharpened the focus of this study.

Like most historians, I realize that our books would not happen without the services of librarians and archivists. I am indebted to the skillful staff of the Ohio Historical Society and the American Antiquarian Society, as well as to Hobart Hansen, former director of the Western State Hospital in Staunton, Virginia. I especially appreciate the dedication, generosity, and friendship of Caroline Morris, the medical librarian and archivist at the Pennsylvania Hospital in Philadelphia and of Jane Rand, the medical librarian and director of library services at the Brattleboro Retreat. Special thanks to Carol McGovern; her patience with the early scribblings of this historian and the speed and accuracy with which she turned that into fine copy deserve deep respect.

Burlington, Vermont   C.M.M.
July 15, 1985

Masters of Madness

Social Origins of the American Psychiatric Profession

Introduction: October 1844

It will be a great gratification to me to meet so many of my
fellow laborers . . . although little may be done by the conven-
tion as a body, I am sure that . . . getting to know each other,
indeed, cannot fail to prove beneficial in many ways.

Kirkbride to Stribling
28 August 1844

On the evening of 16 October 1844, conversation and warm
laughter drifted across the grounds of the Pennsylvania
Hospital for the Insane. The Association of Medical Superintendents of American Institutions for the Insane gathered in
the parlor of "The Mansion," the home of Thomas Kirkbride,
superintendent of the hospital. That morning thirteen superintendents had met at the Jones Hotel in downtown Philadelphia
to organize not only what was to become the first national medical organization but also what was to be for decades a powerful
professional association. Since ten o'clock that morning they had
worked on the agenda for the next four days of meetings, and
now they had retired to Thomas Kirkbride's parlor for an evening of sociability. Some were meeting for the first time although
they had exchanged numerous letters; others were old friends.[1]

Just six months before, Samuel Woodward of Worcester, Massachusetts, Francis Stribling of Staunton, Virginia, William Awl
of Columbus, Ohio, and Thomas Kirkbride of Philadelphia had
decided it was time to act. They harbored little doubt that a

meeting of the medical superintendents of insane asylums would "prove beneficial in many ways"; indeed, each of them had written about the need for cooperative action in their annual reports for years. In the last few months notes had gone back and forth among the nine others with news of this planned first meeting. A few hesitantly queried of their colleagues, "What do you say to it?" but most welcomed the news and presumed that "good would come of it to the cause." They looked forward to an event that they believed would be not only enjoyable but also of value professionally.[2]

Samuel Woodward, the patriarch of this group and of American psychiatry, had taken leave from his duties at the Worcester State Lunatic Hospital in the spring of 1844 to visit some of his fellow administrators in Virginia, Pennsylvania, Ohio, New York, and Connecticut. A year before, Woodward had suggested to Francis Stribling, the young and energetic superintendent of the Western Lunatic Hospital in Staunton, Virginia, that American heads of asylums exchange annual reports with their colleagues in England and Europe. And now both were convinced that the British Association of Medical Officers of Lunatic Asylums (founded in 1841) should serve as a model for American asylum administrators.[3] As the two men talked, Stribling advocated getting together as soon as possible, and they agreed upon a meeting in the fall. Promising to contact others, specifically William Awl, superintendent of the Ohio Lunatic Asylum, and Thomas Kirkbride, the new and promising superintendent in Philadelphia, Woodward headed north.

Woodward missed Kirkbride in Philadelphia but soon reported Stribling's ideas about the proposed gathering to him. Delighted because Woodward suggested Philadelphia as the likely spot for the meeting, Kirkbride took control. He spread the word to others and wrote to Stribling to ensure that even the southern superintendents would be invited, only to find that Stribling had taken care of that already. Because Woodward, seemingly happy to be rid of the details of arrangement, mentioned that he would stay at the Jones Hotel on Chestnut Street, that hotel became the obvious place for the others to gather, and Kirkbride contacted the manager to reserve the rooms. Pleased at the opportunity to

exhibit his own work, Kirkbride (only four years a superintendent) readied his hospital for their inspection and opened his
home for this evening of relaxation and conversation.

For these thirteen medical superintendents of American institutions for the insane, meeting to found their professional organization, the idea of hospitalizing and offering therapeutic care
for the mentally ill was paramount. Eleven of the twenty-six
states supported at least one asylum (Virginia had two), philanthropic groups financed six hospitals, New York City provided
two public hospitals and Boston one, Baltimore had a church-
supported institution, and at least three individual doctors ran
private asylums.

The general medical profession increasingly acknowledged the
expertise of these men in treating the mentally ill by sending
patients to the asylums, by adopting their views when testifying
in court cases, and by reading their articles published in medical
journals and almanacs. Moreover, the popular press had gradually accepted the special role of asylum doctors. Newspapers and
popular journals published excerpts from their annual reports,
described activities at the hospitals, urged the building of more
asylums, reported legislative hearings, accepted news items from
the superintendents, and editorialized about the statistics of insanity.

By 1844 the men gathered in Kirkbride's parlor had amassed
an impressive body of evidence to support their claims of restoring the mentally ill to health. As early as 1827, Eli Todd at
the Hartford Retreat for the Insane had cured 91.3 percent of
his recent cases, and in 1834, Samuel Woodward at the state
asylum at Worcester had discharged as recovered 82.25 percent of
his patients suffering from recent illness. Throughout the 1830s
and 1840s, other superintendents made similar claims. Although
doctors held out less hope for the chronically ill and the claims
for recent cases were exaggerated, doctors continued to be optimistic. Pliny Earle still thought that with "proper curative treatment," from "75 to 90 per cent recover," and Samuel Woodward
believed that "under judicious treatment" the mentally ill had
as much chance for recovery as a person sick "from any other
acute disease of equal severity."[4] State after state (sometimes

prodded by the new crusade of Dorothea Dix; sometimes by legislators, governors, medical societies, or lay reformers) built asylums for the treatment of the insane, and the public had responded by bringing their mentally ill to the hospitals in increasingly larger numbers.

Each of these "Original Thirteen" members had much to celebrate, but there is no doubt that Woodward dominated the group. Over six feet tall and weighing 260 pounds, Woodward had a carriage that was "majestic" and "commanding," and his movements were "quick and graceful." Eyes turned upon him everywhere, but in this room his professional reputation alone made him a center of attraction. For a dozen years he had been deeply involved in the building and supervising of the Hartford Retreat in Connecticut, and for nearly another dozen he had administered the Worcester State Lunatic Hospital. Already recognized as the American expert on the treatment and management of the insane, Woodward was eager to share his knowledge and experience with others.[5]

Pliny Earle and John Butler, longtime associates of Woodward and men who had learned their first lessons about the mentally ill at his side in Worcester, joined the gathering. Earle, a native of Leicester, Massachusetts, had traveled to Philadelphia from New York, where he was resident physician at the Bloomingdale Asylum. In later years, he fondly remembered that Woodward's affability and enthusiasm about his work "were well-calculated to fascinate a neophyte in the profession." Butler, while practicing general medicine in Worcester during the 1830s, had often stopped at the asylum to chat with Woodward, and now he was in charge of the institution at Hartford that Woodward had worked so hard to establish.[6]

Butler, one of the two superintendents who had changed asylum positions, had begun his psychiatric career at the Boston Lunatic Hospital. Remaining deeply interested in Boston politics and in the vagaries of asylum administration in the Bay State, he had much to share with Charles Stedman, the current superintendent at Boston. Amariah Brigham, the other peripatetic superintendent, made similar inquiries of Butler about Hartford, having served there for three years himself before moving on to the

New York State Lunatic Asylum at Utica. Brigham, an inveterate politician, shared interests with Samuel White as well. White was the owner of the most successful private institution in the country, at Hudson, New York, and had earned high praise from several state legislative committees for his advice about the establishment of the hospital at Utica. He was delighted to hear Brigham extol its merits. Nehemiah Cutter of Pepperell, Massachusetts, was the only other representative of private asylums at the meeting, and both he and White had been in the "crazy business" (as Cutter frequently referred to it) longer than any of the other superintendents.[7]

Professional concerns, however, more than self-congratulation brought these men together. These superintendents had led the crusade to build hospitals and to turn mere custodial incarceration into therapeutic care. They had argued both for the need to isolate insane persons from the social environment that had precipitated their illness and for the curative benefits that accrued from a heavy dose of their plan of treatment. Merely asserting the advantages of their plan of treatment, they knew, was not enough; they had to bolster their claims with substantial proof of success. In the early years, they carefully kept track of their results. In their annual reports, they recorded in detail the statistics of the hospitals, drawing special attention to the large percentage of patients whom they restored to health. Such displays of the statistical evidence of curability rates, they presumed, would guarantee the financial support necessary for long-term backing of their ideas about therapy.

Unfortunately, straightforward amassing of numbers did not always prove the success claimed. With quality care available for the first time (considerably more humane than that provided by almshouses and jails and in attics and sheds), the patients flooding the asylums were generally those who had been virtually without treatment for years. The prognosis for these people was clearly dismal and their presence in the statistics bothersome. In an attempt to emphasize the optimistic prospects for cure, each superintendent came up with his own solution to eliminate such long-standing, hard cases from his enumerations of success. Woodward, particularly pressed as the head of the first state hospital to offer therapeutic rather than merely custodial care, calculated only the cases he discharged in any one year (rather than taking into account the total hospital population or even the admissions for that year) and, in 1834, exulted over a recovery rate of 80 percent. Soon others outdid him. Such assertions were possible because superintendents continually manipulated figures. Many inflated their discharge statistics by separating long-standing cases of insanity from "recent" cases. It was a crucial move and one that only initiated further problems. What was "recent"? One year from the onset of illness, nine months, six months, three? Every administrator had his own answer depending on his previous statistics, the publicity about them, and his relationship with his board of trustees at the moment he wrote his annual report.

The record-keeping system in vogue called for each person upon admission to receive a case number. If discharged during the year, that number was retired. Not infrequently an individual patient left the hospital, discharged as cured or improved, and then reentered during the same fiscal year. The superintendent assigned a new case number and, although once again institutionalized, the patient appeared among the cured or improved for that year. Superintendents' talk of cases, not persons, contributed to the murkiness of the curability issue.

These men did not mean to be deceitful; rather they adopted such measures out of near desperation at coping with the politics involved in carrying out their work, and because they truly believed that a case of recent insanity had a full chance for recovery. With these patients lay their hope for eradicating insanity, and so, though unconsciously manipulative, they saw themselves as merely carrying on their crusade.

The keeping of curability statistics was the main thrust of these first meetings in Philadelphia. Woodward and Stribling had discussed the issue at length during their meeting at Staunton in April, and both had written to Awl in Ohio. Each had already struggled with the problem because it was closely related to their desire to keep hospitals small so that doctors could work their therapy on individual patients. Woodward, in his eleven years at Worcester, did all in his power to resist the Massachusetts legislature's propensity to expand the size of the hospital. He knew that providing beds for more patients without additional staff appointments would undermine the individual care essential for maintaining restorative therapy and recording its success. But, delighted that so much good was being done by Woodward, the legislators wanted more. Woodward knew that the principle of close doctor-patient relationships escaped them, and he fought every move to expand the facilities; he was in the midst of such a battle at the moment.[8] William Awl, meanwhile, had adopted techniques similar to Woodward's, listing only the percentage of discharged cases cured and redefining "recent" cases as those whose onset of illness had occurred within three to six months of admission. By 1842 he had claimed the ultimate success of curing 100 percent of all recent cases discharged. He was not as successful in the following year, however, and as Ohio legislators pushed for expansion of facilities, Awl sought both theoretical and professional reassurance that his administration was well conceived and well run.[9]

Few of these men remained untouched by this drive to illustrate success statistically, and the competitiveness inherent in the situation created ill will between at least two of the founders. Both Francis Stribling's and John Galt's attitudes about curability rates were exacerbated by their peculiar situation in Virginia, the only state with two publicly supported asylums. Thus Stribling and Galt not only felt compelled to produce figures that were on a par with those of other superintendents, but they also competed with each other for legislative attention and funds. By 1844 feelings between the two were tense and their relationship strained. Galt had petulantly found fault with Stribling's plans for the meeting; the season of the year and the location were "unsuitable and inconvenient," he wrote. Behind his complaints, however, lay the fact that Stribling had outmaneuvered Galt in numerous encounters with the legislature in the Old Dominion.[10]

At this Philadelphia meeting, Stribling, moreover, already had many acquaintances among these men. Attracted by his genial manner and even temper, most of his colleagues also grew to respect his competency as an administrator. Woodward had come all the way to Staunton to visit, Kirkbride had consulted him regularly in the six months before the conference, and both credited him with initiating this meeting.[11]

Galt, though he tended to be withdrawn and introspective at any type of gathering, still had plenty of opportunity for conversation and exchange of ideas with others. He shared, after all, a certain inherited prestige with Kirkbride: Galt headed the oldest asylum in the country, whereas Kirkbride administered the insane department of the oldest general hospital. They both were young and inexperienced when they came to such positions of power, and, although they both had assumed the responsibilities with some hesitation, they had revised their initial career plans and thrown themselves wholeheartedly into their new specialty.[12]

Isaac Ray, unlike Galt, enjoyed the company of others and delighted in regaling small gatherings with lively conversation. Ray's relaxed conversational manner frequently belied his earnestness when expounding his own views or querying others as to their opinion on a variety of issues. Ray took particular interest in the classifications of insanity and regularly debated legal principles with those who had recently appeared as psychiatric experts in court cases. In 1838, with no practical experience in the field of psychiatry, Ray had written a study of the relationship of the law and psychiatry. So thorough was this work that it became the focus of discussion in the famous M'Naghten trial of 1843 and a standard text throughout the nineteenth century, establishing Ray as the leading legal authority in this group.[13] On this evening of 16 October, Ray's reputation made him one of the centers of attraction for Luther Bell, who had published widely in medical journals and enjoyed a short political career in New Hampshire before becoming superintendent of the McLean Asylum in the Boston area.

At this moment both men were intent on the role of the expert in the courts and on the real possibilities of curing insanity if hospitals were kept to a reasonable size, interests shared by all their colleagues. On the issue of statistics, however, Ray and Bell disagreed with the others. They questioned the necessity of keeping uniform statistics and even the usefulness of any reliance on statistics at all. They held their tongues for the moment, but it would not be long before others in private exchanged comments about these two being "too dictatorial," domineering, and outspoken in their antistatistical views.[14]

Fascination with the power of statistical evidence, on the other hand, marked Pliny Earle, the young Quaker head of Bloomingdale, who already had served four years as resident physician at Friends' Asylum for the Insane in Frankford, Pennsylvania, and who had visited numerous European asylums in the late 1830s. Physically, he appeared in sharp contrast to both Ray and Bell. Ray's iron gray hair and stooped shoulders and Bell's well-known negligence of dress pointed up Earle's neat Quaker attire and meticulous grooming. Earle shared Ray's fascination with courtroom procedures, but he challenged Ray and Bell about their views on statistics. In 1844, Earle avidly believed in the curability of insanity and its statistical validity. A man of strong convictions, Earle easily held his own against opponents while displaying his analytic abilities and retentive memory.[15]

Earle was particularly close to William Awl and never missed the chance to chat or exchange anecdotes with him. Each had a keen wit and at this point in their careers could still see humor in many situations and even joke about themselves. Awl, for instance, often recounted the story of his early education by noting that he had attended school in Pennsylvania, which "was taught in the mode common at that time," laughingly adding, "and it was *common enough!*" Or he might narrate the tale of his hike from his Pennsylvania hometown to Ohio, with only a knapsack on his back and very few dollars in his pocket, and set everyone chuckling by adding, "and not much sense in my head!"[16]

Earle also had a repertoire of anecdotes, but he particularly loved puns and shared many of his stories with his patients. He liked to repeat a story he and his charges at Friends' had shared. One patient, a Quaker, he mentioned, was singularly impressed by William Penn's tract, *No Cross, No Crown,* and this patient steadfastly refused to shake hands with anyone. A friend offered his hand one day and was ignored. "'What is the matter?' inquired the acquaintance, 'thou seems very *cross* to-day.' 'Ugh!' abruptly and dryly exclaimed the maniac, 'No *cross,* no crown.' "[17] Earle knew his patients well and worked closely with them—a characteristic of this relatively new method of handling the mentally ill.

These men regarded themselves as a vanguard; they had the latest answers about insanity. They were confident that the insane could be cured and that their therapeutic program, popularly known as "moral treatment," could cure them. Moral treatment was relatively simple. The sick person had to be hospitalized in order to remove him or her from an environment that doctors believed had been both the precipitating and a contributing cause of insanity. In the hospital the doctors' individual attention, firm but kind treatment, and reluctance to use physical or mechanical restraint gained the confidence of the patient. Doctors then put into effect a program that interjected stability into the patient's life by its very regularity. Each asylum had a daily schedule of rising, eating, exercising, and socializing that varied only according to summer or winter hours.[18]

Next the doctors had to break up the "wrong association of ideas" of the patients and help them to form "correct habits of thinking as well as acting." They did this by planning a series of activities including manual labor, religious activities, and recreational and intellectual pursuits. Manual labor was especially important. Doctors believed that it not only diverted the mind and exercised the body but also instilled a sense of discipline and accomplishment. Thus Friends' Asylum required the male patients to work for three or four hours on the asylum farm each day and the women to participate in the household chores. Gardening, the sawing of wood, carpentry, and the making of brooms or baskets were other suitable occupations for men, and embroidery, sewing, knitting, and work in the laundry room for women. While some of these activities obviously benefited the asylum, in the doctors' minds their therapeutic value was primary. Indeed, the Belknap Sewing Circle at the McLean Asylum illustrated the potential of manual labor for reconstructing the patients' lives. These women patients, meeting weekly at the home of the superintendent under the direction of the wife of the steward, fashioned or mended the clothing of the other patients, but they also did fancy work, which they sold. They used their profits to subscribe to the *New York Mirror* and put aside funds for the purchase of a pianoforte for their own use and entertainment.[19]

Diversion and physical exercise were also the objects of the asylums' recreational programs. Every asylum had its horses and carriages for the patients' use and bucolic paths and picnic areas for their outings. Patients played chess, checkers, and backgammon, threw quoits, flew kites, played ball, used the swings, and bowled. Friends' built a 400-foot circular railway with a car that two patients could pedal by foot, and it kept rabbits and other small animals on the grounds for the patients' amusement. McLean's, taking advantage of its location on the Charles River, offered rowboat rides, harbor excursions, and chowder parties on the islands.

Equally important in the scheme of moral treatment was the effort to direct the patients' minds along new and healthy avenues of thought. While wary of religious fanaticism, these doctors never totally rejected the idea that some form of religious exercise would benefit their patients. Some asylums had separate chapels; others invited ministers to preach. But most settled for the reading of the Scriptures during evening gatherings rather than risk exciting some of their more impressionable charges with enthusiastic preaching.

On the question of intellectual pursuits there was more unanimity. Every asylum had its library of books, newspapers, and magazines; many included maps, drawings, or natural history specimens. Evening lectures were another favorite, and superintendents frequently purchased stereoscopes to enhance their presentations on the beauties of the island of Malta, the architectural splendor of London, Egypt and its antiquities, or scientific presentations about acoustics, meteorology, botany, or optical illusions. Believing that the "primary object" of moral management was to treat the patients "as if they were still in the enjoyment of the healthy exercise of their mental faculties," Pliny Earle, for one, conducted a school for his charges at Bloomingdale. And, as their patients showed signs of improvement, superintendents like Amariah Brigham of the New York State Lunatic Asylum at Utica and William Rockwell of the Vermont Asylum for the Insane encouraged their patients to publish their own newspapers. At Friends', the resident physician initiated the Restorative Society for his convalescent patients. The members played ball or fished together during the week and conducted a debate or presented a lecture every Friday evening.[20]

Even Nehemiah Cutter, somewhat eccentric and believing that a "good shaking up" of the physical system was all most patients needed, implemented these principles at his small private asylum in Pepperell, Massachusetts. Luther Bell, John Butler, Pliny Earle, and Thomas Kirkbride were particularly optimistic about the benefits of moral therapy because they headed corporate hospitals, asylums supported by philanthropic groups generally able to be more selective in their patient population than state-financed hospitals. The appeals for funds to build these institutions had been made not only on the grounds of restoring mental health and lessening the social cost of insanity, but especially on the premise that it was the humane thing to do. The others were confident about the system, too, but they had the task of convincing sometimes recalcitrant legislators and economy-minded voters that their work was indeed saving the taxpayers' money, making useful citizens of the formerly ill, and preventing potential harm to the public.[21]

Although moral treatment was in full swing, by the time of this meeting in Kirkbride's parlor the moral therapists shared a number of problems generated by their success. Even the more autonomous superintendents of corporate hospitals remained dissatisfied with the inadequacies of their buildings or with weaknesses in administrative structures. Thomas Kirkbride, for instance, was intrigued with the possibility of establishing uniform standards for hospital architecture and asylum administration. He found a sympathetic audience in Pliny Earle, who chafed under the directives of his trustees because they forbade him to coerce patients to work. Outraged by this interference from amateurs, Earle often expressed his dismay by explaining that if patients refused to eat they would be force-fed, and no one would object. How, then, he wondered, when manual labor was clearly essential to the plan of moral treatment and to recovery, could these laymen be so bull-headed in their misconceptions and arrogant about meddling in his work.[22]

Samuel Woodward, Francis Stribling, William Awl, John Galt, Amariah Brigham, and Isaac Ray shared the problems endemic to state-supported asylums and understood that the willingness of state governments to build and support such institutions was not an unmitigated blessing. They exchanged complaints about niggardly legislatures that would not always provide enough funds to upgrade facilities and sometimes did not even vote enough money to complete construction to their standards. Legislators simply did not understand the full implications of moral treatment. Awl, in particular, had given up entirely on his legislators, calling them all "blackguards."[23] There remained as well the potential for political interference in the running of the asylums; the threat that the increasingly larger patient populations attracted by the publicity about cures could undermine the asylum doctors' ability to implement a therapy based on close doctor-patient relationships; and the concern that well-qualified men might be in short supply to administer the growing numbers of asylums.

A handful of other men, many of them already interested in psychiatry although not present this October night in 1844, soon joined the ranks of the founders, became involved in their professional concerns, and carried on and expanded the work of the "Original Thirteen." John Curwen was so influenced by Thomas Kirkbride while he was his assistant at the Pennsylvania Hospital for the Insane that, upon his appointment as superintendent at the Pennsylvania State Lunatic Hospital at Harrisburg, he modeled himself upon his mentor, mirroring Kirkbride's administrative and organizational concerns and his dedication to the organization. He even stepped into Kirkbride's place as the association's long-term secretary. Dorothea Dix sponsored Charles Nichols's career, rescuing him from an unpleasant and frustrating position at a New York hospital by choosing him to supervise the construction, and later to superintend the operation, of St. Elizabeths, the only hospital for the mentally ill supported by the federal government. Unlike Curwen and Nichols, Horace Buttolph pursued his own sponsors. Early in his career, although interested in psychiatry, he had not made contact with anyone else of similar concerns. He was, however, well aware of the leaders in the field and unabashedly sought their recommendations for his initial appointment as an assistant physician in an asylum and, later, used their network for gaining a superintendency. Moreover, he courted the favor of Dix so successfully that she chose to spend her retirement years at his hospital.[24]

Edward Jarvis pursued his own career as a synthesizer of psychiatric theory and statistical analysis. Although always considered something of an outsider by the members of the association, Jarvis gained their respect for his humanitarian concerns, his contacts in high places, and his effective theoretical work, which frequently buttressed their position, especially on statistics. So keen was his interest that Jarvis seldom missed a meeting of the association until 1880, when his health so deteriorated that he could no longer get around. Jarvis's extensive attendance record was not unlike that of the other practitioners. Only Stribling and Galt came sporadically while they were still in office; the others rarely missed a meeting.[25]

Even the short associational life of some of the founders (White would die within the year and Woodward and Brigham within five, and Awl and Stedman would retire in 1851) did little to hinder the growth of their ideas about the treatment of the insane. Men of similar thought filled the ranks. Joshua Worthington of Friends' Asylum, William Chipley of the Kentucky Lunatic Asylum, and John Tyler of the New Hampshire Asylum for the Insane and later McLean's, took up the crusade and regularly discussed the issues that had led the founders to Philadelphia in 1844. Clement Walker took on Stedman's mantle at the Boston Lunatic Hospital and with William Stokes sought to clarify new issues that emerged, like the role of the psychiatric expert in the courts. And men like William Rockwell of the Vermont Asylum for the Insane, who had been trained by Eli Todd at the Hartford Retreat; Edwin Van Deusen of the Michigan Asylum for the Insane, who served under John Gray at the New York State Lunatic Asylum; and Merrick Bemis, who benefited from the successes of his predecessors at the Worcester State Lunatic Hospital

(Samuel Woodward and George Chandler) continued to promote moral treatment while addressing the issues of their mentors of 1844 and anticipating new problems that arose as the idea to institutionalize the insane spread.

In October 1844 these thirteen asylum doctors began to lay the groundwork and establish the rules by which any new problem concerning the treatment of the insane would be solved for the next several decades. The solutions they devised, however, did not arise out of a purely scientific, altruistic, or even simply pragmatic approach. Their professional decisions were as much responses to a changing American society as they were attempts to influence the shape of that society and find their own niche within it.

In chapter 1 I start the reader on the long journey of events that led the insane into asylums and these men to Philadelphia in 1844. In the world of the fathers and grandfathers of these asylum doctors, the mad had been viewed neither as sick nor in need of confinement or treatment. Their grandfathers had lived in a God-centered world characterized by unity, order, and surety of place. Young men followed in their fathers' footsteps, and the mad, even the poor, were integral members of the family and community. It was a world, through the course of the eighteenth century, that their fathers saw buffeted by intellectual challenge, economic expansion, and political revolution. As the potential for personal autonomy widened the horizons of most Americans, madness became threatening rather than harmless, and the mad suffered loss of liberty as communities increasingly confined them on poor farms or in almshouses or jails.

These young men came into adulthood with an ambiguous legacy from their fathers' world. The persistence of the old values that once had seemed to assure order and predictability clashed with the allure of unprecedented opportunity if one risked setting off on a path of ambition and individualism. In chapter 2 I illustrate that for most of these men the choice of a career in medicine solved the dilemma, if only for a time. They could satisfy their ambition to rise in the world by taking advantage of widening opportunities to pursue a profession and simultaneously retain the essence of traditional values by committing themselves to serve others. The world of medicine was in flux, however, especially on the American scene, where the spirit of egalitarianism permeated even the traditional professions; nothing stopped anyone from claiming to be a doctor. It was in flux, too, for the mad because of the Enlightenment's legacy about the promise medicine offered for human progress. When that promise converged with the enthusiasm of the revivalist drive toward removing impediments from the paths to perfection of even the most downtrodden, the mad, already confined, were perceived as sick and in need of treatment and their institutional environment in need of reform. For a number of doctors, acting out of a variety of motivations, these changed attitudes toward the insane created a new clientele.

Becoming an asylum doctor in the 1820s and early 1830s meant practicing a plan of moral treatment consisting of individual attention and a variety of religious, recreational, and occupational activities with a small clientele of middle-class patients in what these doctors described as a "home" atmosphere. The new approach of building asylums for the treatment of the insane proved so successful that it was not long before states took responsibility for their insane poor, offering them the advantages of moral treatment in publicly supported asylums and raising yet another set of problems for the doctors who had become institutional psychiatrists. In chapter 3 I trace, through the lives of four men, the impact of the changing world, the unfulfilled promises of medical practice, and the challenges created by American society's willingness to institutionalize and treat the insane at state expense. For a number of years each of these men had struggled alone to persuade families to hospitalize their insane at the first signs of mental illness, to thwart legislators' adventitious attempts to enlarge asylums or undermine budgets, and to stabilize his position as medical superintendent. They were the four, in that propitious moment of 1844, who organized the founding meeting of the Association of Medical Superintendents of American Institutions for the Insane.

Those who joined them in 1844 and in the ensuing years formed a receptive audience. They had lived through similar experiences in their youth and had been equally torn by the promises and disappointments of medical practice. They had struggled with the tensions created by a commitment to disinterested benevolence and a compulsion to impose an old order on a seemingly turbulent society. As they brought these insights to the specific problems of asylum administration, they, too, realized the need to create collegial strength and to forge a professional world that would enlarge their authority and assure the best treatment for their patients. The plan of treatment as encompassed in moral therapy was not the problem; that had gained ready acceptance. The means by which they would extricate themselves from ordinary medical practitioners, shape the new psychiatric profession, and control the care of the insane needed more attention and are subject matter of chapters 4, 5, and 6.

In chapter 4 I suggest that, despite the appearance of informality of their professionalism at times, they understood the potency of organizational techniques for creating consensus and generating professional clout. They pursued those techniques with a passion remarkable in the nineteenth century, and, as I illustrate in chapter 5, they focused their fervor on the asylum and their sway within it. Emerging from a world over which they had exercised little control, and still strapped in their new profession by the limits of public policy decisions, these asylum administrators hoped to use the moral force of their professional association to shape the world within the asylum walls. For them, the very quintessence of the asylum rested in the medical superintendent. The outside world, while receptive to the idea of treating the insane humanely, nonetheless was less concerned about the means by which this was accomplished. In chapter 6 I explain how asylum administrators tried to convince the public of the righteousness of their plan of management and, in the process, gained a balance between professional self-interest and altruistic commitment to their patients' welfare. Through the process of seizing every opportunity to publicize their work and anticipating sources of negative publicity about their asylums, they forged a public image that encouraged families to commit their insane to the asylum so that doctors could treat them effectively and humanely.

The intensity with which these asylum doctors formed their

professional organization, formulated policy about the internal operations of the asylum, and promoted their work had long-range effects. What becomes clear in chapter 7 is that these men, although well-intentioned, became so certain about the legitimacy of their claims to expertise and the validity of their solution to the social problem of mental illness that they remained largely unaware that they were slipping into an increasingly rigid position. Never questioning the concept of confinement nor receptive to suggestions for altering their own plan of asylum management, they determined the nature of institutional psychiatry for the next century. Over the course of that century, however, the public's use of asylums and the growing concentration of state bureaucracies altered the nature of their asylums and of their institutional role. Simultaneously, developments in medicine and psychiatry outside the asylum ultimately led to a total rejection of their asylum world.

1   A Changing World

We find the cultivators of the soil becoming traders, patient mechanics becoming manufacturers, the small trader enlarging his business to that of a wholesale merchant, the working man turning speculator.

Edward Jarvis
1858

In 1844, when these thirteen men met in Thomas Kirkbride's parlor, they brought with them a relatively new ideology about insanity. The notion that insanity was not only "manageable" but "curable" was rapidly gaining acceptance. To a man, however, they knew that at the beginning of the nineteenth century the insane had been "considered as lost to themselves and the world." In that world, the insane suffered incarceration in poorhouses or jails, enduring cold, neglect, or abuse. Some of them lived "in chains"; others were left emaciated and provided only with "a few filthy and tattered garments" to cover themselves. These pioneers had helped to shape a new world for the insane by participating in the move to build asylums for the humane treatment of the mentally ill and by convincing many that the insane, under a plan of treatment they had "conclusively and incontrovertibly established," could be "restored to their social and civil relations 'every wit whole.' "[1]

The insane had not always been confined, however, and people had not always been prone to active intervention or optimism as approaches to life. Understanding how these superintendents responded to a changing world explains why Americans changed their attitudes toward the mad and why these men adopted institutionalization and medical and social intervention as a way of life and as an approach to madness. The self-perceptions of these doctors were deeply rooted in the values of their ancestors, and thus their commitment to their careers and their attitudes toward their insane charges have a history that reaches beyond their own generation.

The Colonial World

These asylum administrators, born between 1775 and 1815, grew up in a social, political, and economic order markedly different from that of their grandfathers. Their ancestors stretched over at least three generations in America, and, whether they had lived in Puritan New England, Quaker Pennsylvania, or the Anglican South, these earlier generations had experienced a world characterized by culturally prescribed behavior patterns, structured political and economic relationships, and a sense of connectedness with a supernatural order of things.[2]

In New England at the beginning of the eighteenth century, the Puritan belief system, which had been shaped by a "series of stern fathers who stood over [individuals] in the homes of their childhood, in the church, in society, and in the state," still carried considerable weight. Parents taught their children self-restraint and self-abnegation and fostered ties to family and community through fathers' reluctance to turn over title to lands and through the encouragement of marriage by birth order. The vast majority of New Englanders lived out their lives in the towns of their birth, where ministers dictated the standards of personal behavior and perceived themselves as public officials equal to the local magistrates. The blurring of lines among family, church, and community allowed town leaders to exercise a consensus in politics that called for deference and clothed town meeting decisions with an "ethical significance all were bound to respect."[3]

Southern society shared neither the homogeneity of population nor the religious imperative of New England communities, nevertheless the interplay of slave, poor white, small farmer, and landed gentry produced a system of values and behavior remarkably similar in its emphasis on authority, deference, and hierarchy. Of its nature, slavery created limits on autonomy for Afro-Americans and determined the structures of white Southern society. Planters of the late seventeenth century had been singularly successful in acquiring land, in producing children, and in maintaining the influence of their families over a rapidly expanding and increasingly stratified populace. Rearing their children to value self-assertion, they left them a legacy of economic wealth, political power, and social status. Poor whites, frequently tenants of the gentry, became accustomed to differentiating between themselves and "what were called the gentle folks," people they thought of as "beings of a superior order." Small planters were equally deferential as they accepted the gentry's social authority and acquiesced in the decisions of "their betters."[4]

The inherent egalitarianism of Quaker theology did not preclude their rearing their children in an atmosphere permeated by prescription, structure, and hierarchy. Quaker families allowed their children fuller autonomy than New Englanders did by acquiring vast amounts of land and deeding it outright or selling it to their sons at marriage and providing cash for their daughters' dowries. This autonomy, however, carried with it an obligation on the part of children to contribute to the welfare of their younger siblings and a theologically enforced imperative to live an upright life to assure the religious and community status of their parents. Successful Quaker parents emerged as community leaders who were expected to provide the "same charismatic, loving authority for Quaker adults" in Monthly Meeting as they had for their children. Indeed, the Monthly Meeting added still another level of authority, structure, and rank to the Quaker culture, one enhanced by their practice of "holy watchings," which subordinated individual choices and family affairs to communal ideas about acceptable behavior.[5]

Wider economic activities permeated early eighteenth-century Quaker society and communal politics much as they did those in New England and the South. The staple crop economy of the South, which fostered large investments in land and labor, dif-

fered substantially from the small-scale agricultural interests of
New England and the mercantile diversity of the middle colonies;
nevertheless, the economic lives of the vast majority of whites in
each region were marked by freehold property ownership, a
household mode of production, and limited economic possibilities. Despite the entanglements of the imperial trade system, productive work was centered in the family; economic considerations
were tied to family and communal relationships; and business
transactions were ordinarily based on personal knowledge of
one's neighbors. Even in their economic lives, colonists had devised an intricate net of private and public expectations that
fixed the individual in the natural order of things.[6]

In the supernatural order of things, an other-worldly *mentalité*
played a similar role in the development of a central tendency of
consciousness. Puritan theology, with its emphasis on a corrupted
nature, the subjection of the individual will to God's, and religious rebirth, was the most intense. The rewards, however, were
the assurance of a fixed place in the covenanted community of
earth and the prospect of a place among the elect in the kingdom
of God. Quakers were no less ambitious in pursuing God's will,
but their belief about the presence of the divine "inner light" in
each soul led them along a more moderate path to salvation as
they designed an earthly system to prevent believers from stray-
ing into "carnal conversation." Neither dissenters nor utopians,
Anglicans had no theological ax to grind in the New World.
While the hierarchical structure of the Anglican church in the
colonial South veered sharply from its English model, Anglicans
remained comfortable with a transplanting of the traditional
church tenets and confident in their church's time-honored promises of salvation. The differences among church structures, theological doctrines, and religious temperaments were less important
than the religious experience the congregations shared. God's
plan for his people on earth and their strivings to gain salvation
were universal assumptions of that religious experience, as was
the colonists' sense of connectedness with that supernatural order.[7]

Over the course of the eighteenth century, cracks in the surface
of this unified, authoritarian world began to appear. Sparked by
the Great Awakening, which left in its wake a rising emphasis on

individual choice, a splintered ministry, dissenting sects, and a weakened community authority, the social fabric simultaneously was rent by the force of the Enlightenment. Rejecting tradition and revelation, Enlightenment writers placed their faith in the use of reason and natural law to understand, control, and improve human life and institutions. The basic premise of the individual's freedom to make choices about the future encouraged an optimistic attitude that, by the end of the eighteenth century, found a receptive audience in the changing social, political, and economic scene of the American colonies.[8]

Eighteenth-century economic activities contributed to the rifts in the colonial world because a large, but fluid, merchant class emerged, and farmers, both in the long-settled areas and in newly opened hinterlands, increasingly participated in a market economy. Those with surplus capital invested in commercial enterprises, land speculation, or bonds, but they pressed for expanded opportunities in manufacturing and bristled at imperial restrictions on the market. While the family remained the basic unit of production, by the end of the century these entrepreneurial activities of merchants and speculators had altered the structure of the marketplace and had focused the aim of production on profit.[9]

At the same time, a sustained population growth began to alter family and community life and disrupt cultural homogeneity. The settling of non-English peoples on the frontier introduced a diversity into the population in some colonies that was exacerbated by the frontier peoples' challenge of the traditional distribution of political power and stability. In other communities, the practice of partible inheritance created population pressures on land, leaving some parents to think about finding new ways of establishing homesteads and livelihoods for their children in distant places, a move they knew would interrupt their sway over their offsprings' social and sexual behavior. Communities, whose moral authority had arisen from the interconnectedness of family, church, and community, then faced incipient population depletion and, ultimately, diminished social control.[10]

These accumulating intellectual, economic, demographic, and social forces laid the basis for political revolution. And in the process of justifying resistance to British authority, colonists created an ideology whose principles of self-determination and political equality derived from and added to this changing American society.

The Mad in the Colonial World

This rising sense of opportunity and individual responsibility experienced by most Americans changed their worldview and affected their attitudes toward the mad. Early in the eighteenth century, the insane had evoked a response that emerged from and was consistent with the colonists' supernatural belief system, the homogeneity of their society, and the personal nature of their community life. Colonists had linked madness to supernatural actors, believing that the devil drove people to madness or, more often, that God tested the insane persons' piety or punished their sins. This belief reduced the mystery of the behavior and placed it within a divine scheme that fostered an attitude of inculpability for the insane. In the natural world, colonists considered rationality less important than conformity or belief because they enforced that external control system of family and community power that deemphasized the individual's capacity for consent. Indeed, madness was less threatening than apostasy, rebellion, witchcraft, or religious heresy, all of which more clearly challenged the social order. Moreover, the intimacy of colonial communities, where the "distracted" person was a neighbor and where friends were familiar with lifelong patterns of behavior, encouraged tolerant reactions and supported the belief that madness was periodic rather than permanent.[11]

Whether the mad person was a minister like Samuel Checkley of Boston, who wept constantly during the sermons he delivered to his congregation for thirty years, a schoolteacher like Samuel Moody of York, Maine, who wandered through town every night in his flannel nightgown and stocking cap, or an "eccentric spinster" of a prominent family who "guarded" the gates of the town of Winchester, Massachusetts, the insane lived out their lives without interference well into the eighteenth century. Indeed, one Savannah, Georgia, schoolmaster, although removed from his position because "his behavior has been so bad that he has but few Scholars," was nevertheless given the choice of continuing in the colony as a "Planter." Many continued in their "gibberish," "wild gestures," or similar disruptive behavior, and others moved in and out of their professional and community activities in periods of regained sanity.[12]

Reactions to the mad of lesser social status were no different as long as they eked out a living. One "mad woman" of Hopkington, Massachusetts, for instance, spent her life roaming the town as a beggar but was "well-liked" by the townspeople. Another resident lived off the charity of his neighbors although at times he accosted them with insulting speeches and fulsomely addressed the "waving stocks of corn in the fields." Taunton's mad wanderer "sometimes frightened people" by his "wild, insane manner," nevertheless the townspeople responded to his supplications for food and clothing with generosity. New Yorkers were no less generous; the mayor's council periodically lent a local butcher money to help with the expenses of his insane wife and gave shoes, stockings, and other items of clothing to an insane woman everyone called "Mad Sue."[13]

Colonists treated the insane who could not support themselves, even by begging, in the same way as they handled the poor. Paupers, whatever their state of mind, were either boarded out in the community or "warned out" if "strangers." Inherent in the settlement laws of colonies like New York, Massachusetts, Connecticut, or Virginia was the assumption that the community bore responsibility for its own citizens. Townspeople were not willing to bear the cost for natives of other towns, however.

The case of Samuel Coolidge, a native of Watertown, Massachusetts, illustrates the nature of this interaction between the pauper mad and their neighbors. Coolidge graduated from Harvard and was librarian there in the 1730s until his "insolent and outragious manner," his "rude and indecent behavior," and "his hindering the Students from their Business" brought dismissal. The town of Cambridge took no responsibility for Coolidge and, in his distracted and destitute state he wandered back to Watertown. The selectmen of Watertown readily provided Coolidge with clothing and shelter whenever he was "far gone in Despair, sordidness and viciousness." During one period of regained sanity, they found him a teaching position in Westborough. Sinking into "great Horrors and Despair" again, Coolidge lost his job, and the Westborough selectmen sent him back to Watertown. For the townspeople of Cambridge and Westborough, Coolidge's status as a "stranger" had been the problem, not his status as an insane person. They were not concerned with controlling or confining him; they simply did not want to be burdened with the economic dependence of this indigent "stranger." Coolidge's behavior remained erratic for the next twenty years, and the Watertown selectmen frequently retrieved him from nearby towns, sometimes employed him as a teacher, but mostly paid for his board in various families in town. Only in the last few years of his life, when he became violent, was Coolidge confined in a room in the home of a Watertown family.[14]

Confinement, however, was rare in the colonial period, not constant, and it occurred only when the mad person had actually destroyed property or harmed others. The York County court of Virginia, for instance, ordered the sheriff to keep John Stock in a "close room" because he caused "great disturbances," but only until he was able to "govern himself" once again.[15] If colonists were at all anxious about the insane, it was largely with regard to their economic status. Colonists neither feared nor scorned madness; they were neither moved with compassion for the insane nor filled with a need to intervene in their lives.

By late eighteenth century, changes in the colonists' ideas about the insane were evident. First, the Great Awakening had left in its wake that altered sense of religious responsibility, as Enlightenment thought had undermined the supernatural explanation of life. The market changes that had enlarged the sense of opportunity and choice combined with population pressures on land to shatter the old family and community ties. The Revolutionary ideology with its emphasis on citizens as independent and rational beings further weakened the old social order, in which the insane had functioned freely. As a result of these accumulating forces, a new value system emerged that placed responsibility on individuals, giving irrationality a new and threatening meaning.

Second, many Enlightenment writers had singled out medicine as an especially hopeful area for empirical inquiry that would ultimately help to improve human life. One of the early practical results of this quest had been the active intervention in the course of infectious diseases. In the American colonies, however, trained doctors were scarce, and people had often turned to ministers for "doctoring." Cotton Mather was one such "minister-physician" and, in his promotion of inoculation for smallpox in the 1720s, was on the cutting edge of this new type of thought. While ministers occasionally were called in to pray over the "distracted" or treat them with various concoctions, doctors, too, were asked, in these rare cases, to administer remedies out of their pharmacopoeia. As madness became dissociated from the supernatural realm, the clergy less often mixed spiritual and bodily ministrations for the sick or the "distracted," and the mad increasingly came under the purview of the doctor. Madness became another form of disease, and, since optimism and active intervention permeated American medical thought by the end of the eighteenth century, the insane, at least of the middle class, were less likely to live out their lives without interference.[16]

Third, as the medical model of insanity gradually emerged, American doctors applied their explanations for physical illness to madness. While there was hardly agreement among humoralists, solidists, and other medical theorists, some of the explanations for disease offered a way around the dualism of mind and body that the idea of mental illness created for many American doctors. Because their belief in the immortality of the soul precluded any suggestion of a diseased mind, speculations about connections between the brain and other organs allowed them to accept a somatic explanation of insanity. Most doctors agreed that the healthy body maintained a precarious equilibrium within a system of limited energy and that a pathological condition in any body organ upset the balance, affected other organs, drained energy, and caused disease. Excesses of any sort created imbalance. Thus intemperance in food or drink, immoderate physical activities, exposure to the elements, and even emotional reactions or overindulgence in intellectual activities (which could overwork the brain at the expense of other organs) might cause that pathological condition. This emphasis on excesses subtly shifted the responsibility for maintaining health to the individual. With the concept that the body was the sole seat of insanity well in place and with the responsibility for one's actions placed squarely on the individual, God was no longer the actor. The mad person alone was to blame for his or her state.[17]

As a fear of the irresponsibility of the mad emerged and as the mad were perceived not only as diseased but also as having brought on their own madness, they were increasingly isolated from the rest of society. Late in the eighteenth century families who could afford the cost frequently made arrangements for their loved ones in the homes of the few doctors willing to care for the insane. James Otis, for instance, lived with Captain Daniel Souther in Hull, Massachusetts, during his intermittent spells of madness, while the less prominent but equally affluent family of Archelaus Putnam placed him under the care of Dr. Thomas Kittredge in Andover, Massachusetts. Towns able to maintain their homogeneous populations and those least affected by the changing world continued to "put out" their dependent mad, although families more frequently "locked up" their charges.[18]

Other towns with more mixed economies and populations simply no longer wanted their pauper insane in their midst; they happily paid for their support in the almshouses or jails of neighboring communities. The town of Concord, Massachusetts, resisted building an almshouse and by the early nineteenth century regularly ignored the requests of Boston overseers of the poor to remove insane Concordians like Nancy Barrow from that city. Instead, the Concord overseers sent small sums for her support each month. And East Sudbury, Massachusetts, made arrangements for one of its residents afflicted with this "loathsome disease" to be kept in the Ipswich jail.

The most highly stratified commercial communities, like Salem and Boston, New York, Philadelphia, and Charleston, had not only built almshouses by mid-century but, by the end of the century, had created separate quarters within these institutions to confine the mad. The mildly insane worked as farm laborers or at spinning, knitting, and sewing. The more intractable were kept in locked rooms, sometimes in cellars or separate outbuildings.[19] Whatever their social status, by the beginning of the nineteenth century, the mad faced confinement as a way of life.

The Nineteenth-century World

The pressures of a republican order accented the increasingly vulnerable status of the insane in the early nineteenth century because the generation that forged the republican ideology had offered previously powerless groups a voice only because they relied on the capacity of those individuals to act responsibly in their political and social behavior. As Benjamin Rush and others warned, industry, frugality, temperance, and moderation had to become the "national characteristic" and the "regulator[s] of the conduct of each individual."[20] Irrational behavior violated the very essence of these republican virtues, and the inability of the insane to act "virtuously" altered attitudes toward them in the new nation. The republic sustained other pressures, moreover, which not only had led to these changed attiudes about the mad but would force many Americans to reexamine the structures of their society as well.

Especially after 1815 "social change was palpable" as "fundamental institutions as well as the surface of life" underwent dramatic alteration. The sheer force of geographic expansion, whether measured in terms of the numbers of new states or in the push of settlement to the Pacific coast, changed peoples' perspectives about their society and intensified the belief that American republicanism was the "last best hope of earth." Overall population growth was large enough to fill both the demands of urban areas and the agricultural frontiers, and a declining birth rate, at least among white native Americans, indicated that some families had decided to pursue opportunities for social and economic mobility. General economic expansion and improving standards of living, largely fed by the revolutions in steam power and transportation, fostered other opportunities for expanded industrial employment and investment in the production of goods in workshops or factories, while the farmer who moved into commercial agriculture could now cast an eye toward regional, even national markets. And the removal of property qualifications for voting by a number of states in quick succession expanded the electorate, giving most free white men the chance to determine the direction of political life in their own communities and even to have an effect on national issues.[21]

For people of all classes and regions, the focus of life had changed: "Paternity had yielded to fraternity; orthodoxy to heterodoxy; social duties to individual rights." Innovation and achievement became a way of life as personal ambition for oneself and one's children displaced deference, communal stability, and hierarchical obligations. Restlessness and an openness to new experiences marked the lives of many Americans, as Tocqueville so picturesquely captured them in the man who built a house in which to spend his old age and sold it before the roof was on, in the farmer who brought a field into tillage and left it for other men to gather the crops, or in the man "who embraces a profession and gives it up."[22]

While these ambitious Americans congratulated themselves on their prosperity and continued to delight in the liberty and opportunity that the American mission of republicanism had made possible for them, others worried about the disunity they thought endemic in individualism, competitiveness, and material pursuits. For them the expansion of the electorate had undermined the politics of deference and changed the nature of politics. An emerging style of political campaigning that courted the new voters and encouraged partisan organizations more sharply defined factions and left many Americans uneasy, less about political parties and their platforms than about partisan conflict itself. The flourishing of new cities and the growing social stratification in the old sensitized others to the pains and dislocations of this new world. Not only did urban and industrial development undermine the artisans' status and confidence in their ability at least "to get off the bottom"; it also disrupted the lives of shopkeepers, increased the number of dependent poor, and contributed to a decline in morality. Additionally, the immigrant nature of much of the population growth led people to worry about the increasing numbers of poor and "religiously suspect" and to question the spirit of egalitarianism that welcomed them quickly into the political system. Geographic expansion and the revolution in commercial agriculture, moreover, left older rural communities in perilous straits as young people left for the West and cities and as the townspeople struggled to survive economically.[23]

In personal terms, this intensification of change meant that no one escaped its effects. The young men who were to become asylum administrators, for example, experienced the breakdown of community ties, the restless migration of people around the countryside, and the general turbulence of early nineteenth-century American society in their youth. Fifty percent of them were born in rural New England and another 25 percent were natives of other areas of the Northeast, the areas most deeply affected by these changes. While many townspeople fought to retrieve the crumbling traditional social institutions by seeking a new economic base for the town or by participating fervently in moral or temperance societies to restore community control, it was a losing battle. The hometowns of these men retained only a small share of the natural population growth or actually declined in population.[24]

In some cases, their families had contributed to this pattern of impermanence by moving from place to place themselves. Samuel Bell, the father of Luther Bell, was born in Londonderry, New Hampshire, but opened an office in Francestown, where "the people of the town 'were greatly exasperated at his audacity in opening a law office . . . and threatened him with violence.' " George Parker moved from Charleston, South Carolina, to Beach Hill, where his son John Waring was born. Others, such as James Athon's father, who had followed the trail west from eastern Virginia through Tennessee, Kentucky, and Indiana, had made more extensive moves.[25]

Nearly two-thirds of these administrators had experienced some degree of parental or familial instability at an impressionable age, and, for nine, mobility was forced upon them by their fathers' early deaths. While other male family members accepted responsibility for their upbringing, this entailed another move that was seldom their last. Clement Walker's uncle agreed to direct his nephew's future, but only if he studied for the ministry. Walker refused and left Maine for the South, where he spent a half-dozen years tutoring students to earn his tuition for Harvard Medical School. The sons of John Brigham had already seen the futility of farming in their youth in New Marlboro, Massachusetts, and Chatham, New York, when their father's early death left them in the care of their uncle in Scoharie, New York. He died just three years later, and the two boys, now on their own, rejected farming as a livelihood and set off on other careers. The older brother entered the ministry, and Amariah traveled to Albany, New York, back to New Marlboro, Massachusetts, and eventually to Canaan, Connecticut, to earn money for his medical education.[26]

The increasingly subdivided family farmlands, especially in New England, pressured other fathers to send their sons away from home to pursue alternative careers. William Stedman of Lancaster, Massachusetts, sent his first boy off to sea to seek a livelihood. His second son married in Lancaster and received the family farmlands, whereupon William decided that his third and youngest son, Charles, should attend medical school. In another case, Francis Jarvis left his land in Concord, Massachusetts, to his namesake and eldest son and sent his second son to medical school. He apprenticed his youngest, Edward, in a factory in Stow. Unhappy with this, Edward found support from an old friend and entered college, and eventually medical school, on his own. Captain Daniel White of Coventry, Connecticut, left all his farmlands and estate to his eldest son and bequeathed only $1,000 to his other son, Samuel, who, he said, had already received his inheritance through his medical education. The Cutters of Jaffrey, New Hampshire, had enough farmland for their three eldest boys to make a living, but even that stretched only so far. They sent their fourth son, Nehemiah, to college and medical school; the three youngest sons bought their own land.[27]

The very forces that had caused difficulties for many of these doctors in their youth, however, had enlarged the world of their young manhood. The widening opportunities for education opened the doors of academies and colleges for them and enhanced their chances for medical school training. That they perceived neither college nor medical school as part of their entitlement is clear from the need of a number of them to interrupt their studies to earn money for their tuition. The rising tide of democratization that was sweeping away regulation of the professions, moreover, initially made it easier for them to consider medicine as a career and to embark upon their medical practices. And in their personal lives, the moves from place to place to pur-

sue their ambitions enlarged their marital choices; few of these
men married women from their hometowns.[28]

In the world of politics, the rise of political parties had created
opportunities for Samuel Woodward as a local democratic politician, as it had for his father, while the weakening of the power
of the Anglican coastal aristocracy had allowed the Presbyterian,
Whig family of Francis Stribling to gain a political foothold in
western Virginia. And in whatever community William Awl lived
in on his trek through Ohio, he easily entered the political fray
on the local scene. By the time he reached Columbus, he was so
astute about Ohio politics that it was easy for him to pressure the
legislature to open a school for the blind and an asylum for the
insane.[29]

These men, however, were never entirely comfortable with
their changing world. They had grown up in families of the
"middling sort"; none was reared in poverty, nor were any from
"rich and illustrious" families. A few of their fathers were professional men; others were owners of farms, small merchants, or
skilled artisans. Like many people of the early republic, they
were thoughtful about the changing nature of their society. They
believed in, and benefited from, the opportunities offered by
American republicanism, but they had deep roots, too, in the
culture of their ancestors. The traditional values of their upbringing in Congregational New England or the Quaker, Episco-
palian, and Presbyterian middle and southern states had not been
totally swept aside, and so they worried about a society that encouraged democratization, religious diversity, unmitigated ambition, and general freedom.[30]

For many Americans of the period with the same concerns, the
Enlightenment's legacy of optimism about the individual and the
malleability of society meshed with evangelical Protestantism's call
for moral reform. The revivalists of the Second Great Awakening
redirected that optimistic spirit by preaching the perfectibility of
American society and by inspiring many to embark upon moral
crusades to remove impediments to perfection. While shopkeepers,
middle-class families, and mill owners discovered in revivalism
the answer to their anxieties about the loss of authority, deference, and moral force, others identified their particular crusades

as the solutions for the disruptions of widespread social, economic, and political changes. Some worked to alleviate the effects of poverty, improper education, or family disruptions in the lives of individuals; they joined sabbatarian and moral reform societies, taught Sunday school, or campaigned for orphanages or prison reform. Others perceived intemperance, capitalism, or slavery as the fatal sin of American society; for them, "Cold Water" armies, communal living experiments, or abolitionist societies seemed to promise salvation.[31]

While never among the religiously radical and, indeed, suspicious of the more outward effects of revivalism and its emotional excitement, a number of these young men who became psychiatrists responded to the more secular concerns of their generation in their search for authority and recognition. Samuel Woodward as a youth, for instance, wanted to reach out and help all the "wretched and miserable." As a young man he joined a temperance society and became a locally prominent lecturer for total abstinence. Silas Fuller, James Bates, and John Butler also participated in the temperance movement. Some, like Nehemiah Cutter and Isaac Ray, expressed concern about the way in which Americans educated their youth. Others worked on behalf of some of the most vulnerable victims of this rapidly changing society: William Awl and Eli Todd both campaigned for schools for the blind and deaf, while Thomas Kirkbride, Edward Jarvis, Clement Walker, and George Cook offered their services to some of these new institutions.[32]

As they moved through their professional careers, their worries about a society in the process of rejecting traditional values intensified. In 1811 Theodric Romeyn Beck captured the panoply of the concerns of these men as Americans left behind their world of deference, authority, and hierarchy. Beck pointed out the pitfalls of "avarice, domestic fortunes, commercial speculations, political contests, and *enthusiastic patriotism*," but he thought "mistaken ideas about religion" especially dangerous. They inspired exaggerated "enthusiasm or superstition and sudden joy," none of which was easily handled by the ordinary citizen.[33]

Isaac Ray was equally outspoken in finding fault with the ways in which Americans educated their youth. Making a sweeping condemnation of every aspect of society bearing on the methods of child-rearing, Ray declared that "in our anxiety to obtain speedy and tangible results, we manage the education of our children somewhat as we often manage our capital, going upon the plan of quick returns and small profits." Ray argued that families no longer provided the proper moral culture for children and that the watered-down and romanticized juvenile literature held no challenge for them. Moreover, he concluded, the masses set unhealthy examples for youth by caring less for instruction than for excitement, by looking upon the virtue of humility as obsolete, and by refusing to take "opinions on trust, in the belief that others might be better qualified by education and experience to form them." This was a pattern of behavior, he said, "peculiar to the intellectual, moral, political, and social conditions of our times."[34]

Joining in the attack on child-rearing practices, Horace Buttolph felt that the "best safeguard" for a healthy life in this changing world was an "enlightened view of the philosophy of life and living." Edward Jarvis was far more specific. Acknowledging that "most in the United States have some sort of education to fit them for action in the world" in their traditional roles, Jarvis complained that "our people generally not only aim higher than those of most other nations" but are "constantly looking upwards, to see if they may not better themselves." Thus Jarvis felt it necessary "to warn men to prepare themselves, by a better education, for the responsibilities of life." He thought American education, as it stood, did not ready youth for a life of ambitious strivings.[35]

This increased tendency of all sorts of adults to become inordinately ambitious deeply concerned these asylum administrators ironically, not untouched by desire for advancement and prestige themselves. Amariah Brigham argued that the "too constant and too powerful excitement of the mind, which the strife for wealth, office, political distinction, and party success produces in this free country," created problems that few seemed able to handle with aplomb. Edward Jarvis chimed in and took to task every person who was ambitious beyond his natural state. "We find the cultivators of the soil becoming traders," he said. Enumerating further examples of unwise ambition, Jarvis attacked the "patient mechanics becoming manufacturers, the small trader enlarging his business to that of a wholesale merchant, the working man turned speculator" and even the "capitalist going to the stock exchange, and dealing in matters of doubtful value." Those who left the "plough or workshop, and became scholars" or entered the professions, Jarvis believed, found themselves in a "wrong position" and would "stagger beneath their unaccustomed burden."[36]

The churches, which had lost their ability to exercise traditional moral authority, seemed to offer little help. Rising religious diversity and the church affiliations of many reform groups piqued Amariah Brigham to attack churches for opening their buildings in the evening for "what are called Monthly Concerts for prayer meetings to hear accounts of, or to aid, the Bible, Tract, Missionary, Education, Seaman, Colonization, Abolition, and other charitable and religious societies." Totally objecting to revival camp meetings, he urged that "in nothing should we be more careful . . . than in powerfully exciting the minds of the young, and particularly of females." Pliny Earle agreed. Because this country practiced "universal toleration upon religious subjects, and [sheltered] under this broad banner congregations of almost every sect that has ever appeared in Christiandom," Earle concluded that large numbers of people suffered from religious fanaticism.[37]

Another deep concern of these men was the way in which their fellow citizens handled their increased political freedom. One condemned "the quiet workman, or man of business" who "enters the field of politics, and engages in the anxieties and strifes of parties," and another remonstrated that "the Anti-Masonic excitement, the Jackson excitement, and the anti-Jackson excitement, the Bank excitement, the Abolition excitement, and the Speculating excitement" each contributed to the uncertainty of the American social order and to the disruption of individual lives.[38]

As young men, they could not escape reacting to these altered social conditions. They were specific and, at times, vociferous because they lived in a society fraught with changes that had affected, they thought, the quality of the lives of those about them. Perhaps S. Hanbury Smith put their concerns most poignantly when he wondered "what numbers would fly the course they are now following" if they only realized that it would "bring them within the walls of a Lunatic Asylum—some to leave it no more—some to leave it sadder and wiser men—some, in the lapse of time, to exchange its friendly protection for a prison or poorhouse."[39]

The Changing World of the Mad in the Nineteenth Century

The prison or the poorhouse as institutional means for dealing with the criminal or the pauper were as much products of the changing world of the early republic as was the idea of confining the insane. As we have seen, the insane in the late eighteenth and early nineteenth century were increasingly confined in poorhouses and in jails both because of an emerging fear of the irrationality of madness in a world that demanded responsible behavior and because the breakdown of community solidarity had disrupted the traditional means of dealing with dependent people.

Inspired by the benevolent spirit of the Second Great Awakening, some Americans took up the cause of these incarcerated insane because they were especially repulsed by the conditions under which the insane were kept. As early as 1810 the promoters of a general hospital in Boston circulated a letter lamenting that there were no other facilities for the insane poor except in the Charlestown almshouse or in the almshouses and jails of the surrounding towns, where the overseers of the poor usually found the keeping of lunatics "extremely inconvenient." A decade later, a petition of the Connecticut Medical Society was even more acerbic in its description of the insane in almshouses and jails. "The poor maniac," the doctors said, was "doomed to confinement in the lonely dungeon, and often to wear the chains which should be reserved for guilt alone." While these early appeals were loaded with generalizations and played upon sentiment, when the state of Massachusetts made a survey of its insane in 1830, the legislative committee provided hard data. With less than half the towns reporting, they found 289 lunatics, 161 of them confined, mostly in poorhouses, in houses of industry, or in jails where they lived in cells "without light, heat, or air" and were fed gruel through small "orifices" in locked doors, and where their "apartments" appeared fit for nothing more than a "nest of swine." This crusade on behalf of the insane was not an attempt to restore the relatively free condition of the mad of the colonial world but rather a reaction against the contemporary conditions under which the insane lived. These reformers never questioned the concept of confinement itself; they worked only to alter the conditions of that confinement.[40]

Developing simultaneously with the idea of reforming the institutional experience of the insane, and making that move possible, was the impetus to intervene in the course of mental illness. Those Enlightenment writers who had placed their trust in medicine as the "model of the new philosophy and proof of its efficacy" had encouraged an active assault against disease. Making little distinction between physical and mental illnesses, because each was a "mere disorder in the human machine," their influence accelerated the transference of medical intervention to the insane. As insanity entered the realm of the doctors, medical men at first simply applied their traditional pharmacopoeia to the insane. Doctors bled, purged, blistered, and administered large doses of opium to counteract the lack of self-control they thought caused their patients' insanity. If these ordinary measures failed, many recommended a type of "water cure." Dr. Perley Marsh of New Hampshire, for instance, tried to counteract one of his patient's mental derangement by completely immersing him in cold water until he became unconscious. Marsh expected this temporary "stupefaction of the life forces" to break the "chain of unhappy circumstances" of the former life of the patient, allowing him to take up a healthier life style. Other doctors, writing in the *Medical Repository*, suggested the "application of cold water to the head, assiduously persevered in for many days," or the use of a wet handkerchief kept on the head until a "shivering fit" developed.[41]

Intervention in mental illness through this strictly somatic approach, however, was not always successful, and the harsher aspects of it had led some practitioners who would affect American attitudes to seek other methods. The empirical bent of mind of a man like Philippe Pinel of France had led him to deemphasize medical treatment, and a reaction against the conditions of confinement in England and the administering of seemingly useless medicines had provoked William Tuke to look for means beyond the standard medical approach.

Pinel, working at the Bicêtre and Salpêtrière hospitals in Paris in the 1790s, amassed empirical evidence about treatments that worked. Believing that the insane only needed to learn to "master their extravagances" and "habituate" themselves to "self-government," he concluded that a carefully constricted social environment could help bring the emotions under control better than mere medical treatment. Pinel first designed a program of therapy that called for institutionalization to break the patients' associations with a former, inciting environment. Then he insisted on "laborious or amusing occupations" and intellectual and religious activities to distract the patients from their delusions and to prepare them to return to society better able to keep in check their "ungovernable ambition" and other passions encouraged by the disruptions of both the Revolution and Restoration governments. Pinel published his *Traité médico-philosophique sur l'alienation mentale* in 1801, illustrating his success at curing the insane through this program he called "traitement moral."[42]

Tuke and other British Quakers had been appalled by the herding together of patients in public asylums and by the doctors who had administered "secret insane powders, green and grey." In 1792 they opened the York Retreat for the care of Quaker insane. At the retreat Tuke's aim was to provide humane care and to insist upon the moral inculpability of the mad. Like other concerned Britishers, he had come to believe that insanity originated "not in individual passions or feelings, but in the state of society at large." Additionally, his observation that "insane persons generally possess a degree of control over their wayward propensities" led him down a similar path to that of Pinel; he shaped his therapy to include recreational and religious activities and employment on the retreat's farm. William Tuke's grandson Samuel published his *Description of the Retreat* in 1813, spreading the news of the work of the York Retreat to both sides of the Atlantic.[43]

As Pinel and Tuke developed their theories independently of each other, Benjamin Rush, the most eminent physician in late eighteenth-century America, grappled with the problem of the nature of insanity. Coming to a different conclusion about causality, Rush decided that insanity was the result of a chronic inflammation of the blood vessels of the brain and that the doctor had to employ a therapy that transferred the pathological condition from the brain to a less vital organ to restore sanity. Despite the mechanistic thrust of his theory, Rush as an Enlightenment man and a strong believer in American republicanism also decided that disturbances brought on by emotions arising from such activities as political involvement or religious fanaticism could excite physical disturbances in the brain. His combination of physical and social causes led Rush to recommend the use of both medical and social (or moral) means to remove the damages of the emotions. Although for Rush medical treatment was primary and his predilection for bleeding, low diet, and depletion painful for the patient, he campaigned for a more humane program of treatment for the insane. He stressed the importance of the doctor-patient relationship and recommended the use of kindness and honesty with patients. And like Pinel and Tuke, he thought employing patients and involving them in recreational activities would distract them from their delusions.[44]

Despite their differences about the nature of insanity and the efficacy of medical treatment, Pinel, Tuke, and Rush agreed that insanity was reversible. If physical causes could be treated, personal weaknesses strengthened through teaching the exercise of self-control, and social stresses diffused by participation in a program of moral treatment, patients could be directed toward a more stable and healthy life-style. Given the disruptions of a changing American society, this emphasis on personal behavior and social causes struck a special resonance with American doctors. And with the insane already confined in almshouses or jails, it was easy for American doctors to accept the idea of institutionalization and to work toward shaping an asylum into both a humane and therapeutic environment. For them, too, the curability of insanity became an axiom, as did the necessity for treatment in an asylum setting.

The earliest asylums for the treatment of the insane in the United States arose out of the Quaker tradition of benevolence, and, predictably, the founders adopted the ideas of William Tuke. When Friends' Asylum for the Insane opened near Philadelphia in 1817, the Philadelphia Quakers, consulting Tuke's *Description,* had already decided to govern their asylum "by the same liberal and enlightened policy in the construction and management" as that of York. Thomas Eddy, a Quaker and prime mover in the founding of the Bloomingdale Asylum in 1821, similarly proposed a "course of *moral* treatment for the lunatic patients" of the New York Hospital and urged the construction of a separate asylum that would offer treatment like "that pursued at 'The Retreat,' near York, England." Rufus Wyman, the first superintendent in 1818 of the McLean Asylum, not only read Tuke; he also visited Friends' Asylum and later consulted with Thomas Eddy at Bloomingdale. And Eli Todd and Samuel Woodward, who led the campaign in Connecticut to establish an "Asylum for the Relief of Persons Deprived of their Reason," were equally familiar with the work of Pinel and Tuke. They modeled the Hartford asylum on Friends'.[45]

McLean's and the Hartford asylum, although imitating the plan of moral treatment instituted at Friends', were not founded by Quakers. They more nearly reflect the medical profession's emerging authority over the treatment of the insane. The drive to open an asylum for the treatment of the insane in Boston was inseparable from the plan to establish the Massachusetts General Hospital. And in Connecticut, it was the state medical society that initiated the idea, orchestrated the fund-raising, and set up the management of the new asylum. The prominent part that doctors played in the founding of these asylums placed them in a position to leave their mark on this emerging medical specialty. Believing that successful moral treatment encompassed the control of every detail of asylum life, they insisted that a doctor be chief administrator. Whereas at Friends' and Bloomingdale the manager was a lay person, at McLean's and Hartford doctors were in charge.[46]

The founding of McLean's and the Hartford asylum changed ideas about the treatment of the insane in America in another profound way because the organizers of these asylums had shaped their appeals, at least in part, to take advantage of the Second Great Awakening's call for "disinterested benevolence." In Massachusetts the pamphlet writers stressed every person's "obvious Christian duty" to aid the sick and elicited contributions from the clergy and prominent businessmen, as well as from blacksmiths, coopers, sailmakers, tobacconists, and day laborers. And in Connecticut, where revivalists like Lyman Beecher and Timothy Dwight had preached the same message of humanitarianism, citizens "emptied their purses to obey the Gospel's injunctions on charity." Additionally, McLean's and Hartford, although asylums designed to serve middle- and upper-class patients, exercised a wider influence because they succeeded in curing patients and in carrying the message of their success to the public. For a group like the Boston Prison Discipline Society, the message was crucial. They had argued for years that the "sympathetic and compassionate feelings of man toward his fellow" should move the state to intervene on behalf of the mad confined in jails. Horace Mann, deeply imbued with a sense of Christian ethics, took up their crusade in the late 1820s while serving in the Massachusetts legislature. He appealed to his colleagues' humanitarian instincts by asking them to consider their response if the "victims of insanity themselves come up before us, and find a language to reveal their history." He wondered, "who could hear them unmoved?" Buttressing his argument with evidence of curability from European and American asylum reports (he was a close friend of Eli Todd's at Hartford), Mann persuaded the legislators to fund a state asylum for the treatment of the indigent insane.[47]

The opening of the Worcester State Lunatic Hospital in 1833 as a state-supported, therapeutic asylum for all the state's insane assured the acceptance of madness as a disease and procured the new therapeutic approaches even for the poor. Following the lead of Massachusetts, ten more states built asylums for the insane within the next decade or instituted moral treatment. The appeals to state legislatures were remarkably similar in their humanitarian rhetoric and in the assumption that the state should take the responsibility for its citizens. In New Hampshire the governor made "no apology" for calling "attention to a subject which has so much reason and humanity on its side," and in New York the legislature agreed that the "most powerful considerations of humanity address themselves to the State, to provide asylums" for its "insane citizens." In Virginia and in Ohio the results were the same. The Boston Prison Discipline Society praised Virginians for setting up their state asylums in "principles and conduct" as "religious and Christian to an admirable degree," while Ohioans congratulated themselves on their "noble monument" to a "liberal, benevolent, and enlightened State policy." By 1844 three-quarters of the approximately 6,000 hospitalized insane were in state-supported institutions.[48]

Within a century, Americans had moved away from the belief that madness arose from the supernatural world and called for no intervention to an idea that defined madness as sickness and mandated the construction of hospitals at state expense to treat the insane. Belief in God's providence and a mentality of fatalism had given way to disease concepts and optimism about the curability of insanity.

Yet none of the doctors who headed the new asylums and implemented the new therapy had set out to devote their lives to the insane. As young men they had chosen careers in the practice of general medicine not only as a means to earn a respectable livelihood but also as a way to serve humanity. The nineteenth-century world of American medicine, however, was as altered by social and economic change as had been the world of their youth. The emerging constrictions on traditional medical practice would both frustrate their ambitions and expose them to new opportunities as changing ideas about the insane converged with their commitment to medicine.

2 An Uncertain Profession

I suppose it natural with you like others in like places to charge very considerable amounts for which you would in reality receive but a small part. On this point if you could better yourself I should say go [to Worcester]. And further could not the amount due you be collected better if you was gone than if you remained.

Porter to Woodward
5 October 1832

All thirteen men who formed the Association of Medical Superintendents at Kirkbride's in 1844 had started out as general medical practitioners. Yet Samuel White had given up medical practice to open a sanitarium for the insane because "his domestic enjoyment was interrupted" by the "occurance of insanity in his own family." John Galt had planned to practice medicine upon his graduation from the University of Pennsylvania School of Medicine, but his father extracted a deathbed promise from him to take over the running of the Eastern Lunatic Hospital in Williamsburg, Virginia. Others' professional commitment and immediate reasons for switching from the practice of general medicine to institutional psychiatry were as different as those of White and Galt. A stint in the New Hampshire legislature when that state moved to take responsibility for its insane citizens aroused Luther Bell's interest. Samuel Woodward's work on behalf of the insane, at first, was just one aspect of his longstanding sense of benevolence. And William Awl's abortive attempts to establish lucrative practices in medicine in five different communities from eastern Pennsylvania to central Ohio was yet another motivation for him, and others with similar experiences, to convert to the practice of institutional psychiatry.[1]

By 1860 eighty-three doctors had chosen new careers as superintendents of American asylums for the insane. They had shared a deep commitment to medicine, but the professional world they entered as young doctors was as affected by the emerging boisterous capitalist democracy as the communities of their youth. Their personal odysseys leading to careers in asylum administration were marked both by their individual responses to the vagaries of that society in which they lived and by the caprices of the medical profession, in which they chose to work.

Nineteenth-century Medical Education

As young, ambitious men, these eighty-three doctors had grasped the opportunity to follow the well-established routes that had conferred professional status and security upon earlier generations. Generally attending local academies or studying under noted tutors as youths, more than half of them attended college, many earning their own tuition for prestigious schools like Harvard, Yale, Dartmouth, Rutgers, or William and Mary.[2] All but three graduated, and seven went on to attain the Master of Arts degree. Only three men seemed not to have had an early, clear-cut interest in medicine, but they had been ambitious nevertheless. As a young man, William Chipley of Lexington, Kentucky, was interested in politics, but, discouraged by Henry Clay's presidential defeat, he turned to medicine. Pliny Earle, while teaching in Providence, Rhode Island, followed his brother's advice on the best profession to follow for economic success and studied medicine. Edward Jarvis's first inclination was the ministry.[3] Even these three, once they decided upon medicine, pursued their goals with fervor. As a whole these doctors chose their careers early and went to the finest medical schools in the country: ten to the University of Pennsylvania; seven to Harvard; five to the College of Physicians and Surgeons in New York City; four to the Berkshire Medical Institute of Pittsfield, Massachusetts; three to Jefferson

Medical College in Philadelphia; three to Yale; and three to the University of Maryland.[4] Many chose schools with clinical facilities, increasing the quality of their education and raising their career expectations. Moreover, one-quarter of the men studied under medical notables such as David Hosack, John Jeffries, William Parker, William Donaldson, Usher Parsons, Philip Turner, and George Shattuck.[5]

Most matriculated far from home and the communities in which they were to practice, but they had selected the best training at hand. At least a dozen took other steps designed to enhance their possibilities for professional prominence, even at the local level; they sought positions on medical school faculties or as residents in hospitals. Besides strengthening and widening their own medical expertise, they thought that in these positions they could make useful contacts in the professional world and attract a considerable number of patients. A handful studied abroad, pursuing a path that might lead them to the pinnacle of the profession; the others had carefully planned their careers within the confines of their means.[6] These zealous young doctors left little to chance. The extensiveness of their college education, coupled with the quality of the medical schools and renown of their preceptors, clearly indicate that they hoped not only to serve humanity, but also to raise themselves above the run-of-the-mill doctor.

They were ready to take on the profession of medicine, yet that professional world was a troubled one. For these nineteenth-century doctors the rising egalitarianism and anti-intellectualism of the early nineteenth century created not only an atmosphere of suspicion about the quality of (and indeed the necessity for) any formal medical education, but also resulted in an effort to loosen the monopoly of the established profession. Earlier, states had empowered medical societies to regulate their own profession, but even that turned out to be a hollow victory. The state laws generally provided only for the granting of licenses and occasionally for the levying of a miniscule fine if a man practiced without a license. The state medical societies, however, were not given the power either to collect fines or to revoke a license once granted. But even these largely ineffectual regulatory measures ran counter to the powerful egalitarian currents of the day. Beginning late in the 1820s, state after state repealed their earlier legislative actions until by 1852 only New Jersey retained medical licensing laws. Even though two-thirds of the doctors who were to become asylum administrators joined local or state medical societies, in part because they hoped to control the quality and numbers of medical practitioners in their areas, it was a rearguard action.[7] In truth, the disruptive nature of these democratic trends meant that there were no guarantees of success for neophytes. The medical field was wide open to anyone who wanted to hang out a shingle.

As medical students, future psychiatrists already had experienced some of the uncertainties of the medical profession. Men like Rufus Wyman and James Bates, who attended the medical school of Harvard before 1821, for instance, joined the majority of medical students of the day who had no opportunity for clinical learning. Even after that date, when Harvard affiliated with the Massachusetts General Hospital, the ratio of students to patients was so high as to preclude any practical experience, and thus Isaac Ray, Charles Stedman, and Clement Walker (all later graduates of Harvard) were hardly better off. Of all the medical schools, only the University of Pennsylvania School of Medicine and the College of Physicians and Surgeons in New York City gave their students adequate clinical experience on a regular basis.[8]

Even these schools, which also boasted prestigious and stable faculties, did not escape squabbling among their instructors. Both John Butler at Jefferson Medical College in Philadelphia and James MacDonald at the College of Physicians and Surgeons in New York City experienced the disruptions perpetrated by the rivalry within each school's staff. Other schools lowered their admission standards for the sake of attracting students. John Galt, Francis Stribling, Thomas Kirkbride, and Pliny Earle attended the University of Pennsylvania School of Medicine when it was in the midst of such a campaign to enlarge its student body. The fee system, in this case, was the culprit. The fee each professor received from each student for his course, as well as the ones at examination and graduation, constituted his salary. Although many schools professed strict requirements for admission, most gave in to faculty pressures to ignore even minimum standards in order to lure students. Schools regularly overlooked the lack of preliminary education, shortened their terms, lowered their fees, and demanded little but sporadic attendance at two terms of lectures—the second-term lectures being exact duplicates of the first.[9] The drive for mere numbers of students undermined the process of selectivity, of course, and left some dismayed at the disrepute of their fellow students. Pliny Earle, for one, later in life frequently recounted the escapades of his medical school companions of the 1830s, including the son of a governor of a southern state who caned another "gentleman" at the theater and received like treatment in return with "compound interest"; another who stabbed someone with his jackknife; a third "benevolent creature" who shot a fellow scholar in the legs with a charge of buckshot; and one who was bedridden for a month because of wounds received "at the hands of a fellow student." Years later, Earle still regaled his fellow administrators with stories about Philadelphia mothers who governed their "disobedient urchins" with the threat: behave, "or I'll give you to the medical students."[10]

The Exigencies of Nineteenth-century Medical Practice

Philadelphia was a mecca of medical education in the first half of the nineteenth century. And although a fledgling physician might anticipate a practice like that of his mentor, who combined general medicine with highly remunerative teaching and apprentice fees, reality usually varied sharply from expectation. Many doctors gravitated toward thriving cities to establish practices, and by the late 1830s the editors of the *Boston Medical and Surgical Journal* complained about the overcrowding. To them and to other leading medical spokesmen of the day, one doctor for every two hundred people in Chicago and one for every fifty in Cincinnati constituted intolerable ratios. Twelve of the eighty-three future psychiatrists, although rural-born, opened their first offices in cities. They worked hard to attract patients, but starting practice in cities where medical schools abounded meant facing competition from hundreds of apprentice doctors and numbers of well-established medical men.[11] Even a situation that looked promising did not always work out well. In 1835 in Philadelphia, where the doctor-patient ratio (1:822) seemed favorable for young doctors, Thomas Kirkbride opened an office on Arch Street. Even with two prominent doctor friends sending many of their patients to him, Kirkbride had trouble attracting patients and getting them to pay.[12]

Rural doctors did no better. In 1847 a committee of the American Medical Association (AMA) deplored the ratio of one doctor for every five hundred people in the United States. Some regions were even more overcrowded with doctors, as Barnes Riznik's study of doctor-population ratios in New England towns and my study of communities in which psychiatrists lived and practiced confirm.[13] In Litchfield County, Connecticut, Samuel Woodward's home, for example, the ratio dipped as low as one doctor to 379 people in the 1830s. In Cheshire County, New Hampshire, the nadir was reached in the 1810s—1:409—and the ratio rose only to 1:449 in the 1820s. Even when some towns in this county had an apparently favorable ratio, doctors remained vulnerable to the hazards of overcrowding. From 1790 to 1840, Jaffrey (the birthplace of Nehemiah Cutter), a town of fewer than 1,500 people, barely grew. If more than one doctor settled in Jaffrey, or similar communities, the source of the resident doctor's livelihood diminished and the new physician struggled to attract patients. In the psychiatrists' towns, the ratio of doctors to population was lower than 1:600 in two-thirds of the communities in which they had practiced medicine.[14]

Nearly half of the eighty-three doctors who would become psychiatrists by 1860 chose the type of area in which they had been reared and opened their offices in rural communities. Apparently personal preference blinded them to economic reality. Sixteen chose towns that were declining in population or merely holding their own with a natural growth rate; others chose areas already overcrowded with physicians. In Durham, Connecticut, a town of about 1,100 people, for instance, William Rockwell and another neophyte doctor tried to set up practices between 1831 and 1833. They found the competition from the two doctors who had been practicing there for decades too strong. Having studied under Eli Todd of the Hartford Retreat for the Insane while a student at Yale, Rockwell, in the face of his failure in Durham, applied for and received a post as assistant physician at the retreat in 1833.[15]

In the slightly larger New England town of Northfield, Massachusetts (population 1,757), Edward Jarvis tried to wrest patients away from two established physicians. Failing, Jarvis bitterly attacked the townspeople, accusing them of obstructing his determination "to be a better physician and a greater and more useful man" because, he complained, they wanted deference paid to them before they would give him their business. Jarvis was not as fortunate as Rockwell. Leaving Northfield in 1832, he tried to practice for four years in Concord, where he "was still unable to repay any of his debts," and moved on to Louisville, Kentucky, where he met with equal bad luck. In 1842 Jarvis returned to his home state, settled in Dorchester, and wondered, "What is my difficulty? Is it within or is it outward?" The truth was that these young doctors simply could not attract enough patients, especially in rural areas.[16]

Indeed, the overcrowding that the established professionals like the AMA members and the contributors to the *Boston Medical and Surgical Journal* complained about did not even take into account the hordes of "irregular" physicians (as the traditionally trained practitioners dubbed them). Quacks, "Empirical Pretenders," or the legions of those who merely claimed to be healers were not a new problem. The crucial difference in the early nineteenth century was that the growing number of irregulars and the thousands of patients willing to consult them diminished the clientele and challenged the authority of the orthodox medical profession.[17]

The particular bane of the physician in the 1820s and 1830s was Samuel Thomson. Poverty-stricken, unschooled, and embittered against regular medicine for its inability to help his wife when she fell ill, Thomson devised a plan of treatment that substituted vegetable concoctions for the supposedly harsher minerals used by most regular physicians. Roving the hills and valleys of the country during the 1820s, he and his followers sold their "secret" and succeeded as well as regular physicians. They converted thousands of people, not only in New England, New York, and Ohio, but also throughout the South.[18]

Other, longer-lasting movements were equally threatening. Homeopaths prescribed drastically reduced dosages of drugs, operated on the principle of "like cures like," and offered an appealing way of natural physical restoration. Less widespread than homeopathy and more faddish as rivals to the regular medical profession were the eclectics, hydropaths, and Grahamites. Eclectics offered mild vegetable remedies and through their botanic societies and schools preached their opposition to "King-craft, Priest-craft, Lawyer-craft, and Doctor-craft." The diets, baths, and exercises of hydropaths and the grain diet regimen of Sylvester Graham and his followers offered popular alternatives, not only to regular medicine but to any medicine at all.[19]

Orthodox doctors, the future psychiatrists among them, expressed their concerns not only about the harm they thought caused by the prescriptions of the irregulars but also about the propensity of patients to turn to such charlatans. They objected to the commercialism of Samuel Thomson and the therapeutic nihilism of popular health advocates. George Chandler, who as a new doctor had received many "good wishes" but little cash, complained that his sister-in-law was finally recovering from the "prosecutions of Doct. Thompson [*sic*]," and Thomas Kirkbride could do little about his patient who wrote that he intended "to apply to a Homeopathic physician, and lay your medicines aside." Friends' advice and "representations of some wonderful cures recently effected by Homeopathic treatment" had convinced the patient to leave the care of Kirkbride, who had brought about only a "slow and almost imperceptible change." For Francis Stribling there seemed to be no respite from the competition of the "pretenders." While he was practicing in Staunton, Virginia, a doctor whose main remedies were "vapor sulphur baths and a liquid called 'Leroy' " had been one of his major rivals. Later, as an asylum administrator in the same community, he found cause to lash out at the "ignorance and harshness" of such Thomsonian doctors, who could convert a mere "spell of bilious fever" into a case of "positive derangement." Others, like Charles Van Anden, simply competed unsuccessfully with the irregulars. Van Anden was so conscientious, sensitive, and modest that the "self-advertised quack, pushing his own claims, was quite likely to outstrip him in the race for popular favor" in western New York.[20]

These difficulties in getting established as doctors and maintaining professional standards disrupted more than careers; they changed personal lives. In the face of unrealized ambitions and economic hardship, young physicians delayed the gratifications of courtship, marriage, and fatherhood. As several historians have found, whenever it is easy for young men to get started, the average age of marriage goes down; whenever hard, it goes up.[21] Thus it is worth noting that while doctors practicing before 1820 married at the average age of twenty-six, other professional men waited until twenty-eight. Although professional men after 1820 continued to delay marriage, the doctors of these later decades reacted most strongly, postponing their marriages three years longer than their older counterparts. Those who later became psychiatrists delayed a full two years more and were considerably older at marriage than any other professional—31.1 years.[22] They remained bachelors longer than lawyers, ministers, or even general practitioners.[23] Those who were to become psychiatrists spent more time in preparing for their medical careers, and they had experienced increasing difficulties in setting up remunerative practices. Indeed, nearly 40 percent did not marry until they had switched to the alternative career of asylum administration.

Psychiatrists also tended to have relatively small families. Starting around 1800, the national birthrate began declining, and that of most professionals followed this trend closely.[24] The younger psychiatrists, however, outdid everyone. While their fathers had an average of 6.9 children, they had an average of only 3.6 children. Delayed marriages clearly resulted in fewer children, but psychiatrists postponed marriage, at least in part, because of the accumulated frustrations of their early medical careers.[25]

The Convergence of Medical, Benevolent, and Material Concerns

All these doctors were imbued with a sense of their high professional calling and, in many cases, a wider benevolent spirit; none-

theless they still had to make real choices that would affect opportunities for their families, the sources of their livelihoods, and
the direction of their careers. The exigencies of medical practice
in early nineteenth-century America did not necessarily dictate
the reorientation of their careers, but their professional experiences converged with the impulse to treat the insane humanely,
making them receptive to the possibilities for combining benevolence and medicine with new careers for themselves.

Historians have traditionally attributed motivations of altru-
ism to those who turned to asylum administration. Samuel Woodward, for instance, did develop a sense of "social idealism and
warm humanitarian concerns" and accepted the "prevailing faith
in the perfectibility of man."[26] Indeed, if their reflections in later
life about their careers in asylum administration are any indica-
tion, Woodward and the others had felt deep satisfaction at
finally discovering a way to act out their youthful commitment to
disinterested benevolence. By that time William Awl could pay
the highest compliment to Woodward in describing him as
"honorable and useful," and Awl thought there was no other
position in which he himself would have been capable "of doing
so much good and as little evil." Francis Stribling consoled himself in contemplating retirement that he had used his "mental
and physical energies" quite "zealously," although he modestly
hoped someone of even "more enlarged benevolence" might take
his place. S. Hanbury Smith, about to be dismissed by the Ohio
legislature, told Kirkbride, "I love our branch of the profession
beyond description; flatter myself nature intended me to be a
successful cultivator of it, it is my vocation." And Charles Nichols,
at odds with his trustees, lamented his imminent resignation because he had "entertained" all those "hopes that look to a desire
to be useful to my fellow men."[27]

The motivations of these men, however, had not been as
simple as merely wanting to do good. Once again, the situation
of Samuel Woodward is instructive. Woodward wrote to his
brother-in-law, Horace Porter, about his plans to give up his
medical practice in Wethersfield, Connecticut, to take the job of
superintending the Worcester State Lunatic Hospital. Porter reacted with surprise because he had supposed Woodward's income

from private practice to be well above the $2,000 Worcester offered ($1,200 in salary and the rest in room and board for Woodward and his family). On second thought, Porter realized the precarious circumstances of most doctors' livelihoods; he thought Woodward "must charge very considerable amounts for which [he] would in *reality* receive but a small part." He even suggested Woodward take the position at Worcester if for no other reason than to force his patients in Wethersfield to settle their debts to him.[28] Additionally, the consistently declining population of Wethersfield, the increased competition from other doctors in the area, and the struggle to raise his ten children would have rapidly diminished Woodward's income and exerted some influence on his career decisions. In later life, Woodward was not indifferent to the numerous offers he received from other asylums. Although always circumspect about the politics of the situations, he sought advice especially about comparative remuneration.[29]

Amariah Brigham is another case in point. Brigham had been orphaned at the age of eleven, had earned his preceptorial costs by clerking in a bookstore and teaching school, and had tried to set up practice in Enfield, Massachusetts, in 1821 with only "fair" success. Moving on to the larger town of Greenfield, he soon gave up there and in 1831 migrated to Hartford, Connecticut. He regarded that city as a "more prominent and lucrative field," yet his practice in Hartford was not as successful as he had hoped, and in the 1830s he was often in debt. Because he opposed the more extreme manifestations of revivalistic enthusiasm, Brigham gained a reputation in some circles as a man of "scepticism and infidelity," but those who knew him well never doubted his "benevolent interest in his fellow men." Thus, despite his seemingly radical religious convictions, the publication of his *Inquiry Concerning the Diseases and Functions of the Brain, Spinal Cord and Nerves* impressed the board of directors at the Hartford Retreat and won him the post of superintendent in 1840. Two years later, he left Hartford to accept a position at the New York State Lunatic Asylum at an increase in salary of $500. These circumstances do not prove that Brigham was motivated solely by ambition and concerns for financial betterment, but they do indicate that money was of some importance and that his life had not been characterized by economic well-being. He had not married until the age of thirty-five, and he and his wife had five children before his death at the age of fifty.[30]

Others, reflecting on the origins of their interest in asylum administration, pointed to members of their families who had suffered mental illness or to their powerlessness to help insane patients among their general practice clientele. Their motivations were as mixed as those of Woodward and Brigham. Changed attitudes toward the insane and the hope offered by medicine influenced them, but so did their own materialistic and professional ambitions. Pliny Earle, for instance, had a young cousin who died insane when he was at an impressionable age, a younger brother who had "less than his equal share of the mind and capacity of the family," and an older sister who experienced intermittent periods of depression throughout most of her life. Yet as a young man Earle had been concerned about the "comparative profit" of a number of the professions. Only with his brother's remonstrance that a "subsistence" offered "by either of the several professions" was all that he should seek and that "wisdom wants dictate that his choice should be governed by his *taste*," not money, did Earle decide to go to medical school.[31] And for William Awl, his initial inability to deal with a patient suffering from acute mania created an impression that "never left the Doctor's mind." Yet this incident occurred after Awl had left Pennsylvania because he could not get established in medical practice and after he had tried again in three Ohio towns.[32] The specific difficulties, unrealized hopes, or the general feelings of a social conscience of these physicians do not explain satisfactorily why they chose to enter psychiatry. These circumstances simply demonstrate why they were open to the possibility of alternative careers.

Whether they entertained the idea of using their commitment to public service as a means of addressing the problems generated by social change or saw the possibility of taking control of their own lives by carving out new livelihoods, opportunities were rampant in the early nineteenth century. The prosperity of the economy, the revolutions in transportation and print, and a receptive audience made it possible for the first time to earn a living through involvement in reform organizations.[33] As we have seen, young men like Samuel Woodward and James Bates had responded to a solicitude for the downtrodden and for a while had been paid lecturers on the temperance circuit. Others, like Edward Mead, had formed "definite anti-slavery views," and Pliny Earle had enjoyed the company of notable abolitionist orators. These were activities of their youth, however, and had always played a secondary role to their commitment to medical careers.[34]

As young medical men, Clement Walker, William Awl, and Thomas Kirkbride had worked as visiting physicians for houses of refuge or industry, schools for the blind or deaf, and almshouses. As attractive as service in these institutions may have been, two major drawbacks existed. First, the work was part-time. Second, and most important to these young doctors searching for a way to combine their professional expertise, benevolent concerns, and materialistic needs, the superintendents or wardens of these institutions, the people in positions of authority and management, were laymen. Had these doctors been inclined to apply for such administrative posts, they would have had to forego utilizing their considerable medical knowledge and skill in a regular and intricately involved way. Some treatment of the physical problems of the inmates would be called for, of course, but not on a level that would have satisfied their deep commitment to medical practice.

It was at this point that changing attitudes about the insane, the emerging medical model, and the optimism about the plan of moral treatment converged with the needs and aspirations of at least these eighty-three men, making them receptive to the new field. The Americans who had accepted the disease model of insanity, which combined personal excesses and social changes as causes, believed that doctors could, and should, restore sanity. Adopting the pragmatic plans of men like Tuke and Pinel, philanthropists and doctors insisted that the creation of a healthy environment within an institution was the first step necessary for successful intervention. Building asylums for the treatment of the insane and appointing doctors as administrators demonstrated Americans' willingness to apply rationality and optimism even to the mad. In the early years, moreover, the application of medicines to attain bodily equilibrium in the face of the disruptions of mania or melancholia was as important as moral treatment. Thus the insane asylum was the only institution that required full-time medical personnel. If these young doctors felt a particular compassion for the insane or a personal sense of moral stewardship and still wanted to practice medicine, the crusade to build asylums to treat the insane humanely, of all the movements of the era, was the one best designed to meet their needs. For those doctors seeking alternative careers to create "certainty in the place of uncertainty," or for all those with a variety of motives, the management of the asylum met their requirements too.[35]

The Challenge of Asylum Administration

Switching to asylum administration, however, was a big gamble. None of these men had learned about the treatment of the insane in medical school; there was no such curriculum nor any other training facilities.[36] Moreover, moral treatment had emerged from a variety of sources, and much of what they set out to undertake was imperfectly charted. While the earliest read Tuke or Pinel and, in the late 1820s, others observed Friends', Bloomingdale, McLean's, or Hartford, these were not always satisfactory models. Tuke's York Retreat and the imitative American asylums were small, privately endowed institutions serving middle-class patients. As the number of state asylums multiplied, many of these doctor-administrators found themselves facing problems not yet addressed, for example, the complexities of dealing with politicians, the large numbers of working-class patients who increasingly populated asylums, and the pileup of chronic patients.

There was, nevertheless, that attraction of combining an opportunity for service with the escape from the uncertainties of earning a livelihood in general practice. Annual incomes of superintendents were hardly phenomenal, but they were guaranteed, unlike the haphazard collection of fees. Salaries ranged from $1,000 to $3,000; the usual was $1,500, plus room and board for the superintendent and his family.[37] It was far less than the wealth of a physician like George Shattuck of Boston, who reported an income of $9,666 in the year of the Panic of 1837, but it was a good deal more than the incomes of those poor city physicians who experienced "prodigious Ramadans" in their receipts and the struggling rural doctors who averaged less than $500 in fees and kind.[38] William Rockwell agreed to a salary of $1,000 in 1836, but he knew he could count on that as a minimum each year. For the next thirty-six years he enjoyed that kind of certainty.

William Rockwell was not alone in valuing the certainty of an asylum position. Once struggling physicians made the move, they tended to hold their superintendencies well into old age. More than one-third of the asylum administrators clung to their offices until death, and most of the others had long tenures. Of the eighty-three superintendents, sixty served for more than ten years, and of those, thirty-four served more than twenty years. Merrick Bemis, although his assistant and steward had to bring him to the Pennsylvania Hospital for the Insane for psychiatric treatment in 1865, for instance, did not give up his post at Worcester for another seven years. Those who retired did so only with the greatest reluctance. William Awl constantly complained of ill health, of being overtaxed, and of his fear of "going crazy." He retired at the age of fifty-one, exhausted by the rigors of asylum administration and legislative wrangling and because he feared that, with the changing political scene in Ohio, he would lose his job anyway. At only forty-nine Nathan D. Benedict's health broke, and he moved to Florida to recuperate. After noting that he felt cut off from his professional brethren, he lamented to Thomas Kirkbride, "I see no prospect of returning to a specialty to which I have been very much attached."[39]

Only one-quarter ever took another position, and they usually did so only because of intolerable working conditions. Some were victims of the political pressures of the Reconstruction years, like T. R. H. Smith, who was forced to resign his post at the Missouri State Hospital (although he returned in 1873). Richard Patterson had serious disagreements with Indiana legislators (a situation typical of midwestern states), and Charles Nichols and Pliny Earle found it difficult, if not impossible, to work with the board of directors at Bloomingdale because it was never clear who had final authority within the asylum.[40] Others—Henry Buel, James MacDonald, Andrew McFarland, and Edward Mead—grew tired of institutional wrangling and established their own private asylums. And, in old age, men like Horace Buttolph and John Curwen gave to newly established state institutions the benefit of their reputation and experience.[41] Only a few, like Amariah Brigham, aspired to still higher places. As the president of the board of directors at the Hartford Retreat noted in 1842 when Brigham resigned, his "ambition" formed "so prominent a point in his character" that he sought a "more influential position" at the New York State Lunatic Asylum at Utica.[42] Most held only one superintendency during their lifetimes; seventeen of them served for thirty to forty-nine years in the same asylum, and another thirteen remained for more than twenty years. It seems reasonable to argue that, at least in part, the repeated early professional frustrations of so many of these future psychiatrists led them both to risk turning to a new career and later to appreciate the security of institutional jobs.

As hazardous a venture as asylum administration was in the early years, some of these men had sensed its potential for creating "opportunity." However nebulous their thoughts in the beginning, doctors who switched to treating the insane came to realize they gained an enhanced platform from which to address the ills of a society undergoing rapid change. And Americans' increasingly optimistic hopes for restoring the mad to health and their willingness to support the new methods suggested the possibility that this new medical specialty ultimately could provide the chance to reestablish authority, moral force, and status to individual lives even if only in the world of the asylum. Quite consciously, however, men like Thomas Kirkbride thought that it offered a chance for "securing for myself a reputation as desirable as that which I might attain" otherwise.[43]

He and others understood, too, the challenge offered by the opportunity to continue to shape the attitudes of American society toward the mad and to perfect this new system of treating them. While the asylum and its plan of moral treatment had captured the attention of legislators, there was still the need to retain their interest and to encourage others to fund new asylums. The public, too, especially families with insane members, needed to be convinced that the asylum substituted kind treatment and therapeutic results for the sometimes abusive treatment of incarceration in almshouses or jails. Optimism about curability had to be maintained by continual verification of success, and general practitioners had to be convinced of the expertise of asylum administrators so that they would recommend hospitalization to families. All of this would entail tremendous demands on the political astuteness, administrative skill, and public awareness of these doctors. If they were effective, however, asylum administration had the potential for guaranteeing their personal well-being, for allowing them to continue to pursue their goal of serving the public, and for elevating their professional status.

In 1844 the uncertainties of the new profession remained. While hailing the precedent set in Massachusetts for state support of the treatment of the insane, many of these doctors had not envisioned the complexity of issues it portended for them. Relying upon what had become for them the axiomatic nature of hospitalization and moral treatment, they failed to see, in accepting insanity as an illness, that those who proved unresponsive to treatment would remain as part of their patient body. In insisting upon hospitalization in institutions funded by public monies, they were equally blind to issues of control and interference with their exercise of professional prerogatives.

As the number of state hospitals offering therapeutic treatment multiplied, a few of these doctors began to articulate solutions for these new problems. They discussed the definition of "recent" insanity and the need for early commitment because the reporting of high curability rates buttressed their claims of success and justified the continuation of their work. They even more frequently corresponded with one another about the practical problems of implementing moral therapy, comparing notes on the proper hospital size to maintain a therapeutic environment or the amenities essential to the implementation of moral treatment. Informal collaboration, for the most part, brought unsatisfactory results, however, and a realization that the elimination of legislative or other public intervention in the operation of asylums and the vesting of authority in themselves as experts were the real solutions. A growing feeling that formal collaboration could both strengthen their individual positions and enlarge their impact as a group coalesced in the minds of four of these men in early 1844.

3 The Organizers

*I am over head and ears in business, one would think the world
was going crazy. By the by this thing of piloting a lunatic asylum
requires steady nerves. There are dangers both seen and unseen
in every direction and sometimes I think no channel at all,
and the plaguy craft must go somehow for we never can anchor
in any water.*

Awl to Woodward
18 April 1842

When in April 1844 Woodward suggested the meeting to
Stribling, Stribling and Awl in their annual reports had
already proposed a get-together. Woodward was "very anxious
for this measure" because he wanted "to consider the general welfare of institutions in this country." Kirkbride thought "consulting on the subjects in which we are all interested" a useful object.
And Stribling and Awl were concerned about creating an agenda
that determined the "subjects proper to discuss." All of them
were ready, like Awl, to find some "channel" for their "plaguy
craft."[1]

These four were the driving force behind the organizational
move, and each had his own reasons for urging an assembly of
superintendents in 1844. Stribling jockeyed for power and influence with a legislature torn by divided loyalties to two state-supported asylums and through organizational affiliation hoped to
strengthen his political position in Virginia. Awl wrangled so con-

tinually with his legislators over inadequate facilities that he "was very tired of it"; he looked to his colleagues for verification and support of his administrative ideas. And Woodward, fatigued by his struggles to resist hospital expansion, hesitated to face another year that he deemed would be the "hardest of any." He hoped to spread information about the need for maintaining the principles of moral therapy.[2] Kirkbride, whose position at the prestigious Pennsylvania Hospital for the Insane ostensibly distanced him from the political arena, nevertheless had his own special concerns. For him, association offered the opportunity to disseminate his new ideas about the management of the insane.[3] Thus, for individually complex reasons, they came to Philadelphia. But, as we shall see, Stribling, Awl, Woodward, and Kirkbride, despite their varied motives, shared a strong desire for collegial support in their new profession.

Thomas Kirkbride: "Giving a new character to the care of the insane"

Thomas Kirkbride worked with a sympathetic and stable board of managers in a corporate hospital catering to paying patients. Superintendent for four years and only thirty-five years old when he welcomed the other asylum administrators to his city, Kirkbride gained their praise for his dedication to their profession. Visiting the Pennsylvania Hospital for the Insane, they declared it "as complete and well-ordered" as they had ever seen, and "one of which not only Pennsylvania, but our country has reason to be proud."[4]

Delighted with their approval, Kirkbride, for the moment, did not point out what to him were obvious defects in its structure and the implications such flaws had for the success of his regimen of moral treatment. Neither Kirkbride nor anyone else experienced in the care of the insane had been consulted in choosing the site or in planning the building.[5] Although Kirkbride approved of the hospital's location on the outskirts of the city, its physical layout bothered him. The arrangement of the building allowed for only four classifications of illness for each sex (Kirkbride and others suggested room for at least eight of each); it required housing the "noisy, violent and habitually filthy" patients too close to the others; and it provided no completely suitable rooms for wealthy patients. Furthermore, the heating and ventilation systems were inadequate. Judging from the improvements Kirkbride subsequently made and from the plans he drew up for the new Male Department in later years, the parlors, dining rooms, bathrooms, water closets, and patients' rooms were too small; the corridors too narrow; and the ceilings too low. Besides, the hospital lacked certain amenities like walks, flower gardens, reading rooms, and exercise areas. So strong were his misgivings about these deficiencies that he confessed to Amariah Brigham, "I cannot help envying you, who have the building of a hospital to suit yourself—it is one of the things I should like exceedingly to undertake."[6]

Envy was not part of Thomas Kirkbride's nature, but without an asylum planned in every detail to facilitate moral therapy, he believed he could neither persuade families to institutionalize their mentally ill nor guarantee the recovery of their loved ones. His "wondrous patience" and "kindness and skill" in helping the mentally ill would, he feared, be limited by surroundings that failed to provide the architectural amenities to support his ideas of moral treatment.[7]

Kirkbride's deep concern for his patients and his meticulous attention to detail in creating a restorative hospital environment arose quite naturally from the Quaker humanitarianism of his upbringing. His ancestors had been intimately associated with William Penn and had emigrated to Pennsylvania with him. By the time his father, John Kirkbride, settled on the family farmlands in the lower part of Bucks County, the Society of Friends, of course, had long since withdrawn from political life. But in order to maintain the solidarity of the sect and to increase its contribution to American society, Quakers had adopted the social philosophy of humanitarianism and gradually expanded their practice of benevolence within the Society of Friends to general philanthropy.[8] Kirkbride, although he placed "little value on various externals of the society," fondly remembered the example his Quaker father had set for him. He thought "there were many points in his [father's] character you could not but admire," especially "his interest in every matter that was calculated to benefit his fellow men." Thomas Kirkbride learned the lesson well.[9]

His father, moreover, had influenced his career choice. Upon recovering from a long illness, the elder Kirkbride had pondered "what he could do" to relieve the "double burdens" of those suffering from both "sickness and poverty," and he had decided that if his thirteen-year-old son, Thomas, "manifested any taste for the profession" of medicine, he would do all in his power to advance his "education and mental training." Thomas did, and as his father watched over the details of his schooling, selecting academies, tutors, and preceptors, Thomas learned other lessons: the importance of careful planning, the necessity for patience, and the wisdom of waiting for the opportune moment.[10]

For his professional training, Kirkbride planned a preceptorship with a Trenton, New Jersey, doctor, three years at the medical school of the University of Pennsylvania, and then a residency (and later a surgical post) at the Pennsylvania Hospital: all aimed at enhancing his career prospects. The first hitch in his plans came in 1832 when Kirkbride sought the hospital residency. A good friend competed for the same position, and Kirkbride withdrew his application. Deciding to bide his time on his father's farm in Morrisville, Kirkbride received an opportune letter from his uncle, one of the managers of the Friends' Asylum for the Insane at Frankford. The board of managers offered him a one-year appointment as visiting physician at the asylum. With no training and admittedly little desire to care for the insane, Kirkbride, thinking the experience might increase his chances for the prestigious residency, accepted.[11]

Finally, in 1833 he obtained the residency at the Pennsylvania Hospital, and for two years he moved in the best social, educational, and medical circles. The presence of many fine surgeons and the willingness of his roommates to leave to Kirkbride the care of surgical patients, as well as the insane, suited Kirkbride. He had gained experience with the mentally ill at Friends' and, because he planned a career as a surgeon, worked to perfect his surgical skills. Finishing his term at the hospital, Kirkbride rented an office from a fellow Quaker in a Quaker neighborhood, tried to build up his practice, and waited for a vacancy to occur on the surgical staff at the Pennsylvania Hospital. With the help of his former mentors, who recommended patients to him, Kirkbride started out practicing general medicine. He treated a number of walk-in patients and established more regular relationships with others. Additionally, he set up contracts with some for pre-paid family care. While taking on the care of a relatively healthy family meant a less hectic schedule and a guarantee of some income, there were those families among Kirkbride's accounts who took an inordinate amount of his time and care. Like other doctors, Kirkbride received payment from only about four-fifths of his patients and regularly turned over many of his accounts to bill collectors. Yet Kirkbride married in 1839, and he and his wife Ann immediately started a family. From 1835 through 1839, Kirkbride's income remained approximately the same.[12]

During these four years, Kirkbride maintained his contacts at the Pennsylvania Hospital, hoping that his "intimacy with the Board of Managers" would enhance his chances for a surgical post should a vacancy open. Viewing an appointment as clinical lecturer and attending surgeon at the hospital as "one of the most honorable and useful that could be held by any individual," Kirkbride, in 1840, was on the verge of realizing his career ambitions. Dr. John Rhea Barton resigned and recommended Kirkbride as his replacement. Kirkbride's planning, his patience, his waiting had paid off.[13]

At nearly the same moment, according to Kirkbride, "occurred one of those incidents that seem beyond the control of men, and which changed the whole course" of his career. He received from an old Quaker friend, John Paul, an offer to take on the superintendency of the new Pennsylvania Hospital for the Insane in West Philadelphia. Weighing the arduous life of a "successful practitioner of private surgery" and the once-in-a-lifetime opportunity of affiliation with the renowned Philadelphia hospital against the relatively unknown aspects of the asylum appointment, Kirkbride, with little apparent regret, accepted Paul's offer of the post at the new asylum. In later years, he explained:

I saw that from the first I was to have a comfortable residence, a rather liberal salary, the opportunity of starting a new institution, and developing new forms of management, in fact giving a new character to the care of the insane, and possibly securing for myself a reputation as desirable as that which I might obtain by remaining in the city. Besides, my parents favored my accepting this new office as being a certainty in place of uncertainty, and, beyond all else, my young wife approved the plan, knowing as she did, that a successful city practice must necessarily keep me most of my time from home, while the care of the Hospital for the Insane would be sure to keep me somewhere on its premises.[14]

Ann Kirkbride's reluctance to compromise family life and his parents' concern about career stability reflect Kirkbride's own thoughts. Kirkbride's desire for security and comfort were met by a $3,000 annual salary, living quarters, and board. Although he had no idea at the time how immense asylum demands would prove to be and knew that the prestige of institutional psychiatry was yet in doubt, the possibilities for professional innovation and personal satisfaction intrigued Kirkbride. In October 1840 Kirkbride accepted the appointment as superintendent and chief physician and, in December, moved his wife and child into "The Mansion" on the grounds of the asylum.

Setting out to give a "new character to the care of the insane," Kirkbride made improvements in his hospital and its management. In 1841 he persuaded the managers to approve construction of two separate lodges for the more troublesome patients. Realizing that his managers were altruistic and well meaning but more cautious about expenditures then he thought necessary, Kirkbride regularly discussed with them the need for "true economy": the judicious spending of money to maintain the quality of the asylum. He argued, for instance, for improvements in fixtures and furnishings for the "better" wards in order to attract wealthy, paying patients and warned against cutting attendants' salaries and risking loss of quality care for these same patients. He publicized in his annual reports the willingness of the institution to receive "contributions and donations," made clear the procedure for granting "legacies," and solicited gifts and funds from "benevolent old ladies and gentlemen." And in these first four years, Kirkbride pondered solutions for the problems of design and management encountered upon entering this new field of asylum administration at the Pennsylvania Hospital for the Insane.[15]

In 1844 Kirkbride was the only medical superintendent of a Philadelphia asylum. The prestige of his hospital (despite his own misgivings) and the central location of the city attracted his fellow promoters of association to Philadelphia. By making all the arrangements for their accommodations, Kirkbride demonstrated his amiability, thoughtfulness, tact, and efficiency. These first impressions were to be borne out for many decades. For twenty-six years his colleagues honored him with offices in the organization: starting in 1844, he served consecutively as secretary-treasurer for eight years, as treasurer for three, as vice president for seven, and as president for eight.[16]

In his forty-three years at the Pennsylvania Hospital for the Insane, Kirkbride worked so diligently to devise the plans and shape the rationale for ideal asylum architecture that institutions opened in the 1850s and 1860s were built on the specifications of the "Kirkbride plan." Hundreds of requests for his annual reports, for pamphlets on the treatment of the insane, and for information on heating systems, furnishings, and other details of treatment and regimen crossed his desk. Inquiries about particular patients arrived from all over, and frequently patients themselves were sent on to Philadelphia from other institutions. Boards of directors from Indiana, Michigan, Georgia, and Missouri asked for cost estimates of construction and for recommendations of doctors to fill their administrative posts and attendants to staff their wards. And by 1847 ambitious young doctors sought Kirkbride's approval before applying for posts.[17] Once placed, both the men he trained and the ones he recommended retained their superintendencies for decades. He kept the association alive, contributing to every meeting, recording and reporting its activities, and sometimes reminding officers of their duties. He faithfully informed absent members of events and gently prodded a few to attend more frequently.[18]

Kirkbride tactfully responded to complaints of personal dissatisfactions, professional disagreements, and "political disabilities" without alienating anyone. For instance, one superintendent reported that "Drs. Awl and Smith still love each other, about as a cat loves bath soap," yet Kirkbride listened to the complaints of both Awl and Smith and managed to retain the lifelong

friendship of both men. He was so highly respected and so tact-
ful in wielding his influence, that in 1854 he could rebuke Luther
Bell, then president of the association, for his ideas on spiritualism without violating camaraderie.[19]

With all of this, Kirkbride still kept his hospital "ever prosperous" and wrote annual reports that were read "with admiration,
almost with envy" because they showed that Kirkbride was
"mounting still higher and higher in that career of benevolent
enterprise" that had done him "such imperishable honor" and
rendered his hospital *"so useful."* But all of this was in the future, and, in the spring of 1844, discontented with the plan of
his asylum and feeling it would "be a great gratification" to meet
his "fellow laborers," Thomas Kirkbride frequently consulted
with his colleague Francis Stribling about the upcoming "convention."[20]

Francis Stribling: "Appreciating his peculiar fitness for the difficult position"

In 1836 the court of directors of the Western Lunatic Hospital
in Staunton, Virginia, had elected Francis Stribling as asylum
physician. For eight years Stribling struggled to raise the hospital
from what he described as a *"well-kept prison"* to an institution
of which Virginians could be proud.[21] By 1844 he had rid his
hospital of the most hopeless of patients, cajoled funds from the
legislature to maintain a program of moral therapy, claimed high
curability rates, and earned himself a place of respect in this
small circle of institutional psychiatrists. However, this had not
been easy, and Stribling knew his position was not secure.

In fact, Stribling's 1844 call for a meeting of asylum superintendents reflected his growing concern about his professional
position. Virginia maintained two asylums: the Eastern Lunatic
Hospital at Williamsburg and the Western Lunatic Hospital at
Staunton. Both John Galt at Williamsburg and Stribling at
Staunton had instituted programs of moral therapy, but Stribling
had the advantage from the start. He came to office five years
before Galt, was far more personable, and was quite willing to
practice a policy of selective admissions to ensure a high curabil-

ity rate. By 1844, however, Galt and his directors had mounted a campaign to enhance the position of the Eastern Lunatic Hospital.

In order to secure the best care for everyone, the legislature had divided the state into two administrative territories: Williamsburg served the area east of the Blue Ridge Mountains and Staunton that to the west. Presumably each hospital would take its share of chronic patients as well as those more easily cured. But the Staunton directors accepted only the most promising patients from the start, regularly admitting many even from the eastern section (a practice Stribling continued). In 1841 the legislature abolished the Blue Ridge boundary line and required prospective patients first to apply for admission to the hospital nearer their residence. This did not help Galt because by that time three-quarters of the state's population lived closer to Staunton than to Williamsburg. Stribling, with more applicants than he could accept, continued to select those most likely to recover, forcing Galt to take his rejects.

No less taken with curability statistics than Stribling and other asylum administrators, Galt faced the possibility of diminishing funds if the legislature perceived his hospital as merely a "receptacle of worn out cases." To promote Williamsburg as a therapeutic institution he knew he had to produce a high curability rate; he wanted the chance to fill his wards with recent cases of insanity, not with Stribling's nearly hopeless rejects. Galt took action; in late 1843 he petitioned the legislature to reenact the Blue Ridge line, hoping to increase the area his hospital served. In addition, his directors lobbied in Richmond on behalf of the new bill and the Eastern Lunatic Hospital.

Stribling's political friends at the capital notified him about these activities and warned him about the larger numbers of delegates from the east as well as about their bitter determination to rectify the bias in the law. In this unsettling atmosphere, Stribling proposed to Woodward the idea of a meeting of superintendents to "confer together relative to various matters connected with their institutions."[22]

The use of professional, familial, or political contacts to enhance his career prospects was not a new experience for Stribling.

Eight years earlier, as a twenty-one-year-old doctor trying to establish a medical practice in a town already supporting five other physicians, Stribling's chances for a thriving practice or local recognition had been bleak. As a result he had sought the physician's post at the asylum. Even with two of his uncles and another relative as members of the court of directors and a strong letter of recommendation from the renowned Robley Dunglison, Stribling received a majority vote only after six ballots. Nevertheless, the core of votes from his relatives and their friends finally won him the post.[23]

The discord of the contested election, moreover, was short-lived. The directors who had opposed Stribling's candidacy resigned, and Stribling, who previously had shown no interest in the care of the insane, set out to establish new professional contacts. Before taking office, he inspected asylums in Maryland, Pennsylvania, New York, Connecticut, and Massachusetts, meeting the most knowledgeable of his new colleagues. He learned about their therapeutic program and agreed that with more expenditure of funds, provision for better facilities, and early treatment, insanity could be cured. The superintendents of the asylums in the northern and middle states had clearly illustrated this by publishing statistics of curability.[24]

The number of patients cured became his most important criterion for successful management. Just five months after taking over the hospital, he reminded Virginians that it was "a matter of general notoreity" that the number of cures effected in their hospitals "is but trifling" and accused the managers of "a degree of *illiberality* utterly incompatible with, and destructive of, the very objects which they should desire to promote." He persuaded the directors to support his plan for moral treatment by providing funds to purchase land, carriages, books for the library, and other equipment to improve occupational and recreational facilities.[25]

He particularly deplored the long stay of many of the patients in the asylum. In just eighteen months, he discharged as cured as many patients as his predecessor had during eight years. The increase may have been the result of the introduction of moral treatment, but Stribling also worked assiduously to release other patients, especially those whose condition would have meant long-term confinement. Systematically, he presented for discharge those suffering from dementia or idiocy, those who were incurable but harmless, and those whom he claimed "as more fit for the poor house." It is questionable whether these people should have been diagnosed as insane in the first place, and their discharge meant not only more room for new cases, but also fewer hard cases to be considered in determining the rate of cures.[26]

Next Stribling persuaded the directors of the asylum to allow him to reserve cells for recent cases. He then began to recruit private, paying patients to fill these cells. The room and board fees of these patients lessened the pressures of already tight budgets, but more importantly, most superintendents, sharing their charges' middle-class background, thought that they were especially responsive to the amenities of the moral treatment program. In 1838 Stribling expressed his annoyance that Virginians had paid some $5,000 to northern hospitals that, because they were better conducted, attracted patients from the South. A year later he was even more blunt, stating that affluent patients did not enter the state's own asylums because "no means were provided for their accommodation in a style at all suited to their former habits of life." He hoped that "with but few alterations" in the present plan of management, "we may establish a reputation for our Institution, that will secure to it the undivided patronage of the more wealthy class of the insane." Early admission, separate furnished apartments with provisions for the patients' slaves, occupations and amusements suited to personal taste, and daily social contact with the culturally sympathetic doctors would all be conducive to rapid recovery. Stribling's public relations efforts worked. He promptly received letters asking for the admission of a member of "an old and respectable western family," a person "of high respectability of character and family," "a gentleman of fortune," and other patients of similar background. As the number of private patients increased, so did Stribling's rate of cures.[27]

Finally, Stribling pressed for uniformity in reporting statistics. In 1837, for instance, he defined a recent case as one occurring within the previous eighteen months. Others, in an attempt to bolster their curability rates, changed their definition of recent insanity from year to year. Stribling complained that he could report only about 70 percent of his discharged patients as cured, while Silas Fuller of the Hartford Retreat, who used twelve months duration to define recent insanity, boasted 84 percent.[28]

Never quite satisfied with informal agreements to collaborate, like the understanding he had about reporting statistics with Woodward, Awl, Kirkbride, and Brigham, Stribling had very specific "matters" in mind as he planned for the 1844 gathering of his colleagues. In his annual report for 1843, he had strongly urged "greater precision" and "more uniformity" in reporting data so that the "results of treatment in our Asylums" might be presented "with more utility" and "produce something like concert" among asylum superintendents.[29]

The other superintendents agreed about the importance of the statistics issue. The committee on statistics was the first formed and the first to report in 1844. Yet it did not go far enough to suit Stribling. The committee recommended only that records be kept on admissions, discharges, deaths, ages, and mental and civil conditions. Skirting the issue of curability statistics, it did not feel "prepared to urge uniformity in other respects at this time." Stribling may have been annoyed at the inaction, but for whatever reason he skipped several annual meetings, returning only when the pressures of asylum administration in Virginia increased to the point where he once again sought support from his professional colleagues.[30]

After the founding meeting, he did not return until 1852. While Galt continued to assail Stribling's selective admission policies, Stribling collected data on the remuneration of the officers of other asylums to impress his directors. In 1850 the legislature raised the salaries of both Galt and Stribling to $2,500. Even this brought the scorn of Galt, who refused the raise. He termed Stribling's acceptance as "one of the most unpopular proceedings that ever occurred" at the Western Lunatic Hospital. It was one more aspect inherent to the Virginia scene of political and institutional rivalry, but it did seem to Stribling that there was little he could do that did not pit Galt against him.[31]

Even more menacing was the legislative investigation of the

two state asylums in 1850 springing from charges of nepotism, irregularities in staff appointments, and irresponsible use of construction funds. The investigating committee found Stribling blameless, but he was hard put to explain the charges of favoritism in the management of the asylum and the awarding of contracts to relatives and close associates. His remaining friends in this reform-minded legislature managed Stribling's personal exoneration, but they could not control the situation entirely. Changes in the tenure of the members of the court of directors ensued, and the new regulations required that one-third of the directors reside outside Augusta County, the location of the hospital and the base of Stribling's political strength. By 1853 only two of Stribling's former court remained. The changeover was political; the remaining nine directors were Democrats, and Stribling, a Whig, was apprehensive about retaining his office. Once again he turned to the association in 1852 for help in maintaining his professional independence.[32]

In the late 1850s he regained his self-assurance. Galt had not succeeded with his legislative proposals for redistricting the state and had alienated his fellow medical superintendents. Meanwhile Stribling had ingratiated himself and his hospital with the new legislature, surviving and eventually welcoming their investigations. His reputation was enhanced and Galt's so diminished that a newly appointed director for the Eastern Lunatic Hospital at Williamsburg wrote to Stribling for instructions, rather than to Galt.[33]

The association worked for Stribling. He tapped into its strength whenever he needed it to bolster his position in Virginia, and this, as well as his desire for "concert," had been a major part of his motivation in 1844 when he had proposed the idea of a convention to Woodward, Kirkbride, and Awl.

William Awl: "Piloting a lunatic asylum requires steady nerves"

William Awl had previously written "of the propriety of a convention of Superintendents" and in 1842 "still enjoy[ed] a faint hope that such a movement will yet be considered practicable."

Awl had known well the vicissitudes of the medical profession.
He was an old hand at using organizational means to overcome
the "want of harmony and concentration of useful action" to
counteract the competition from practitioners of "irregular"
medicine.[34]

For five years Awl had "made several attempts to get into
medical practice, in various places" in Pennsylvania, "but without success." Then in 1826, with no financial resources but undaunted in spirit, he packed a knapsack and hiked the more than
300 miles from Sunbury, Pennsylvania, to Lancaster, Ohio. From
there he moved to Centreville, on to Somerset, and finally settled
in Columbus in 1833.[35]

Awl had walked into a situation with which Ohio doctors had
struggled since the early 1820s: a wave of egalitarianism that had
culminated in the repeal of all state medical licensing regulations. With competition from the irregulars, especially the Thom-
sonians, who claimed half the population of the state as their
converts, and with highly publicized disputes within their profession, Ohio physicians were generally plunged into "public
disesteem."[36] William Awl, with his usual aplomb, set out to
remedy the situation, and in 1834 the newcomer helped lead the
movement for an annual state medical convention.

As secretary, Awl asked that the convention consider regulation of professional etiquette, reorganization of local medical societies, publication of a journal, promotion of temperance, and
support for the construction of asylums for the blind and the
insane. The Ohio doctors took a strong stand on two of Awl's
proposals. They recommended first that membership in the new
state medical society created by the convention be limited to
those who "shall have been a regular student of medicine under
the direction of a respectable and qualified physician" and that
"all disciples of 'Botanic' or 'Thompsonian' systems of practice"
be excluded. They also accepted Awl's proposal to send a memorial to the General Assembly to establish an institution for the
education of the blind and an asylum for the treatment of the
insane.[37] From 1834 on, the members of the Ohio Medical Society
would reap the benefits of their organizational efforts in the
struggle to elevate their profession in the eyes of the public, but

for Awl the organization's initiative in urging the building of the Ohio Lunatic Asylum overrode his other concerns, determining the direction of his career.

Within two months the legislature authorized the erection of the asylum and appointed a three-man board of directors, Awl among them, to purchase land, supervise construction, and investigate other institutions. The directors toured asylums in Baltimore, Philadelphia, New York, Boston, and Worcester. On their return, they recommended following the plan of Woodward's hospital at Worcester and in 1837 formed a new board to select a medical superintendent. Awl was noticeably absent and actively seeking the post; he had already solicited a letter of recommendation from Samuel Woodward. Awl received the superintendency, resigned from the board for supervising construction, and prepared for his new position by once again visiting the asylums in the East.[38]

In the early years of his administration, Awl tried to explain the comparatively low rate of recoveries despite his establishment of moral therapy. The asylum, he explained, was a state institution and one that had to take in every case, for the "people of Ohio with a noble spirit of enlarged benevolence" had provided that the treatment of all insane persons would be paid for from the common treasury. Praising their generosity, Awl nevertheless pointed out that the measure "entirely precludes the possibility of selection," and, because the public was "quite as anxious to be relieved of their hopeless, as they are of their most favorable" cases, he warned that the asylum would become nothing more than a "receptacle of a large number of unpromising patients."[39] To counteract such liberality, Awl, like his colleagues, reported two sets of statistics: one showing the percentage of all discharged cases cured and one illustrating the recovery rate of only the recent cases he discharged. Awl went one step further and defined a recent case as one having occurred within eight months. In 1842 he recorded 100 percent of recent cases discharged as fully recovered, earning himself the nickname of "Dr. Cure-Awl."[40] But other medical superintendents were manipulating the definition of *recent* also, some interpreting it to mean three to six months, and thus he changed his tactics and began to argue for uniformity in statistical reporting.

By 1843, moreover, Awl faced mounting problems. Not only was the hospital on a "flat and unbroken" site, but the state was ready to double its size, and the number of chronic patients still in the asylum was growing so rapidly that Awl urged that either a new wing be constructed or the county almshouse provide a separate section for them. Although plagued by ill health, he once more inspected the asylums of the East "to discover what improvements had been made in the institutions recently built." Finding "little that will be valuable to him," he nevertheless made an agreement with Kirkbride, Stribling, Brigham, and Woodward to adopt a uniform method of reporting statistics. A year later, still trying to cope with a less than ideal institution and feeling greatly overworked, Awl greeted with delight the letter from Samuel Woodward suggesting the gathering of their professional colleagues.[41]

Harrassed by irregular physicians, Awl had learned the effectiveness of a statewide medical organization, and now, in 1844, beset with difficulties in running his asylum and frustrated with inconsistencies within his specialty, he happily participated in founding and helping to direct the Association of Medical Superintendents of American Institutions for the Insane. Appreciating his role as a principal organizer and realizing the value of his active participation at every meeting, in 1848 the members chose Awl as their new president to succeed the retiring Woodward.

It was a propitious election for him. There was increasing agitation in Ohio for a more democratic state constitution. Awl himself was not involved in party politics (he characterized himself as merely a "republican"), but his tenure at the asylum rested on the political strength of the Whigs. By 1848 Democrats were gaining ascendancy in state politics, and the Whigs were further weakened by the defection of the Free Soilers. Awl foresaw that a constitutional revision would make his position even more tenuous, for holding a superintendency of a state asylum in the West was a precarious job; no man except "one who had the skin of a rhinocerous [sic]" could withstand the pressure. At least in part using the prestige of his presidential office, in 1848 Awl steered through the association a resolution that condemned "any attempt, in any part of this country, to select [medical superintendents] through political bias."[42]

This minor victory offered only brief respite. Over the next two years his position became increasingly precarious. He complained of ill health more frequently, even speculating about where he would like to be sent if he "should ever go crazy." Disagreements with his board of directors and the state legislature occurred more often, and by 1849 he was referring to the representatives as "a beautiful set of blackguards."[43] By now the Whig party was defunct in Ohio, and, at least temporarily, political power had shifted away from the central counties. William Awl, only fifty-one, but a shrewd assessor of practical matters, resigned his superintendency in 1850.[44]

The fact was that despite numerous remarks about being "up to the eyes in business," complaints about the work load being "enough to wear the brains and body both out," or comments about his "unusual lowness of spirit and feebleness of body," William Awl had been reluctant to quit. "I know it will be a hard trial," he told Kirkbride. And it was. Almost immediately a shadow was thrown over his retirement by the first annual report of his successor, S. Hanbury Smith. Smith pointed out all the defects of the asylum. Although his appointment had been politically unpopular and within two years a legislative committee fired him, Smith's comments embroiled Awl in a bitter defense of his own administration. Furthermore, in retirement Awl had returned to medicine but "never acquired a very extensive general practice." A "green old age" escaped him, as he suspected it would.[45]

While he had been "in the halls among [his] patients or in the office giving directions," he had reaped the benefits of professional fellowship and had savored the support of the other asylum administrators. He had "had much to do with originating this periodical assemblage of eminent men," as he noted, and now missed his "co-laborers," such as Kirkbride, Stribling, and Woodward, "in the great enterprise of science & benevolence" to which they had devoted their lives.[46]

Samuel Woodward: Duties "more arduous from year to year"

Among the four organizers, Samuel Woodward had been the first to engage in this work of "science & benevolence" and the one most deeply rooted in the traditions of medicine, public service, and humanitarianism. In the late 1770s Woodward's father had established a medical practice in Torrington, Connecticut, which "soon became extensive, arduous, and lucrative." Acquiring a reputation, based partially on successful treatment and partially on his forthright manner, the elder Woodward not only attracted medical apprentices from all over Litchfield County but also instructed five of his six sons in the art of the profession. More than just a country doctor, Woodward's father took a keen interest in politics, serving in the state legislature for eight terms and eventually allying himself with the Democratic-Republicans. His controversial political views spilled over into his religious activities when he became among the first in town to dissent "from the established society of Torringford." Although he then "was regarded with much doubt by the federal and orthodox Calvinists, and with whisperings of infidelity," his medical reputation did not suffer, nor did the impact his views had on his children.[47]

His father's rejection of the deterministic and elitist elements in Calvinism and Federalism especially influenced his son Samuel. As a young man, Samuel composed essays on the social evils of gambling and drinking, as well as expressing his admiration for those who "assist the wretched and miserable of the human race." Like his father, he was unaffiliated with any specific congregation, but open to the humanitarian spirit of the Second Great Awakening. To the concerns of a society experiencing change, he tried to apply his nonsectarian views of benevolence and was especially popular as a lecturer for total abstinence.[48]

At the same time, Samuel Woodward prepared himself for a career of science and public service in the medical profession. For four years he studied under his father and then stayed on to gain practical "bedside" experience. In 1809 Woodward received his medical license from the Connecticut Medical Society and, at the age of twenty-two, opened an office in Wethersfield.

As the second doctor serving the town's nearly 4,000 people, Woodward looked forward to a substantial practice. Unfortunately, another physician arrived in the same year as Woodward, and within a few years a fourth opened an office. By 1824 three more doctors serviced Wethersfield and the surrounding countryside, where the ordinary charge for a physician's visit was less than twenty cents. Woodward had married in 1815 and by 1824 had five children. To supplement his income and help support his growing family, he kept a store, took in medical apprentices, acted as justice of the peace, and served as visiting physician to the Connecticut State Prison in Wethersfield, for which he received one dollar per prisoner as his remuneration.[49]

Not driven solely by the desire for economic success, Woodward was conscientious in training medical apprentices—frequently taking in two or three students at one time and shepherding them through thirty volumes of medical treatises in a ten-week period.[50] His patients also received his kindly concern and repaid him, if not always in fees, at least with testimonials of high regard.[51] Contact with doctors interested in the care of the deaf and the insane sparked his interest in their plight, and his post of visiting physician to the state prison exposed him to the need for penal reform. Never losing interest in all the "wretched and miserable," Woodward was middle-aged by the time he adopted the cause of the treatment of the insane as his particular work.[52]

Woodward, as did most doctors, treated a few insane patients, and he had been concerned about housing the insane together with criminals at the Connecticut State Prison. His regular conversations with Eli Todd, a Hartford doctor whose father and sister had died insane, deepened his interest in the plight of these unfortunates. In 1821 Woodward, Todd, and others conducted a survey of the insane in Connecticut and proposed that the state medical association establish a "Society for the Relief of the Insane." Acquiescing, the medical society launched a highly organized crusade to raise funds for an asylum, centering their appeal on what they saw as the major cause of increasing insanity: the unusual social and economic mobility of American life. Campaigning throughout the state, Woodward and his colleagues received such an immediate response that within three years the

Hartford Retreat for the Insane opened its doors. Eli Todd agreed to be its superintendent, and Woodward maintained his ties with the asylum, serving as a director, member of the prudential committee, and visiting physician.[53]

This association with Todd and the retreat paved the way for Woodward's appointment to the superintendency of the Worcester State Lunatic Hospital in 1832. The trustees of the Massachusetts hospital first offered the post to Todd, who declined but recommended Woodward. As he would many times in the future, Woodward hesitated before he uprooted his wife and, now ten, children. Salary seemed uppermost in his mind, as it was the only matter about which he sought advice. His brother-in-law, Horace Porter, with whom he consulted, did not even know of Woodward's interest in the insane and asked him, "How wants the care of the Insane suit yr. feelings [?]" Discussing pure finances first, Porter suggested that if, in comparison to his income in Wethersfield, Woodward "could better" himself, then he should go to Worcester. On Porter's more general advice that "if the situation pleases you and circumstances settling yr. affairs at W[ethersfield], will permit, I should advise yr. going," Woodward decided to accept the job.[54]

Having pursued his interest in the insane in the congenial atmosphere of a well-run corporate hospital, Woodward now faced a different situation. In his first year as superintendent of a state asylum he not only had to oversee the completion of an unfinished and inadequate physical plant, but he also had to face the problems created by the admission of a large number of patients suffering from long-term insanity. Initially undaunted, Woodward organized the hospital to his own satisfaction and in the early years reported 82–92 percent of his discharged patients cured.[55] Over the course of the next decade, Samuel Woodward became the mentor, and his asylum the training ground, for men interested in the care of the insane. Pliny Earle and John Butler had visited him often as young medical men, and Woodward groomed George Chandler to take over the new state asylum in Concord, New Hampshire, in 1842. More importantly, Woodward and his asylum influenced the treatment of the indigent insane in states throughout the nation in those early years.

The publicity garnered by the 1830 survey of the insane in Massachusetts (which had been launched to justify the building of the state-supported asylum) set off a series of similar censuses in New York, New Hampshire, Vermont, and Maine. Within a decade, each of these states built publicly funded asylums.[56] As newer states built asylums and as more men moved into the role of asylum superintendent, Worcester became the place to imitate and Woodward the expert to consult. In 1835 William Awl and his colleagues who were in charge of planning Ohio's new asylum in Columbus visited a number of institutions in the East, but they settled on Worcester as their model. Francis Stribling of Staunton, Virginia, on being appointed the new superintendent of that state's Western Lunatic Hospital, wanted to institute moral treatment but found no precedent in the administration of his predecessor or at the Eastern Lunatic Hospital in Williamsburg. Stribling traveled to Worcester and settled upon its plan. In turn, Awl and Stribling were consulted about plans for state asylums in other western and southern states. And Thomas Kirkbride, selected in 1841 to head the new Pennsylvania Hospital for the Insane, was sent by one of the managers of that hospital to consult with Woodward about the best system of management and treatment.[57]

Although Woodward's personal fame outshone the many difficulties he faced in administering a state-supported asylum, the problems were formidable. Growing industrialization flooded his hospital with debilitated workers, increasingly of Irish birth. While Woodward deeply believed that easy access to therapeutic care must be maintained, he worried that the urban living conditions that made insanity more visible and less tolerable would continue to increase the number of patients in his hospital and undermine the efficacy of his efforts. Twice in Woodward's thirteen-year tenure at Worcester, the asylum was enlarged, and by 1844 it accommodated 379 patients—a far cry from his original ideal of 120. As a result, his long-standing practice of offering preferential treatment to paying patients became even more pronounced. Finding it impossible to visit all the patients daily, Woodward withdrew more and more from intimate contact with them. Increasingly, he discharged patients as merely improved or nondangerous and expended a great deal of energy arguing with town officials over patient support and resisting legislators' attempts to make Worcester an exclusively pauper asylum.[58]

In the spring of 1844, when the Massachusetts legislature approved still another addition, making it plain that his asylum was in danger of becoming a mere custodial institution, Woodward turned to his colleagues. His trip south and conversations with Francis Stribling gave birth to the idea of establishing a national professional association. Home again, by August Woodward, in collaboration with Kirkbride, had written to Bell, Butler, Stedman, Rockwell, Ray, Brigham, Chandler, Earle, and Awl about the time and place for the meeting and other organizational matters.[59] Respecting his reputation, the medical superintendents elected him as their first president. Woodward presided over the first two meetings, in 1844 and 1846, and guided discussion on moral and medical treatment, hospital construction, prevention of suicide, statistics on insanity, support for the pauper insane, proper provision for insane prisoners, treatment of incurables, proper size of institutions, and effects of alcohol and tobacco on the insane.[60]

But Woodward by 1846 was worn out and, although he would be remembered as the patriarch of American psychiatry, in his last years of active practice some colleagues complained impatiently about his unwillingness to adopt new ideas and techniques. Thomas Kirkbride, for one, thought Woodward relied too heavily on drugs and, after visiting Worcester in 1845, remarked that Woodward possessed that "happy temperament, which believed whatever he has, is the best that can be had, and of course never seems very anxious for improvement." Isaac Ray thought certain aspects of the Worcester State Lunatic Hospital outmoded and was unhappy with Woodward's acceptance of "verandahs as Dr. Woodward styles them," but mere "cages" as far as Ray was concerned. Woodward himself seemed to have realized his growing complacency for, in rejecting an offer to travel to Europe with Kirkbride and Awl, he said, "I should not expect to be so much wiser for it as some suppose, my views of insanity and hospitals will not probably be changed at my time of life." A few months later, in 1846, Woodward resigned his superintendency and retired to Northhampton, Massachusetts.[61]

Many times during his career at Worcester, he had thought about giving up his post. In 1838 he had submitted a letter of resignation and in 1844 had told Horace Mann he wanted to retire. Twice, in 1834 and 1840, he seriously considered taking the superintendency at the Hartford Retreat, and that at the New York State Lunatic Asylum in 1842. He always asked friends for financial advice and worried about his reputation and the local political situation.[62] On every occasion he refused the offers, but in retirement he had one last plan to promote his cause. With his son Rufus, whom he had trained at the Worcester State Lunatic Hospital, Woodward planned to open a small, private retreat for the insane in Northampton. Unhampered by the parsimony of legislators and free to select his patients, he could overcome even the veiled criticisms of his work that his colleagues had expressed. He could once again practice moral therapy, prove the curability of insanity, and continue to illustrate how the insane should be treated.[63] That was what he had wanted when he had approached Francis Stribling in April 1844 and what he still planned for in July of that year when he wrote Pliny Earle about the way in which the British association had exerted "new zeal for improvements." Woodward hoped that his American colleagues would remain equally zealous as he returned home from that first meeting in Philadelphia in 1844.[64]

Woodward, Awl, Stribling, and Kirkbride had suggested the meeting because of their individual needs to respond to the particular problems of their careers and situations. But, in discussing Kirkbride's concern about asylum design, Stribling's and Awl's about political positioning, or Woodward's about hospital size, they had evoked a strong response from the others. Much as the exigencies of a changing American society and medical world had shaped the lives and determined the direction of the individual careers of these four men, those same forces had impinged upon the lives of their colleagues. As a result, whatever doubts they may have entertained about the wisdom of creating a permanent organization disappeared as they joined together to elect officers, form standing committees, and establish agendas for future meetings.

Within four years the intensification of the difficulties presented by state asylums especially drove them to a deeper commitment to the path upon which they had embarked. They quickly recognized the potential of an organizational framework for identifying their competence and conferring authority upon themselves as experts. As we shall see in the next three chapters, increasingly they controlled the structure of their organization, using it to define the best policy for the treatment of the insane and placing themselves as medical superintendents at the very core of that treatment. Conferring authority upon themselves, however, would be an empty gesture, as they realized in choosing to wage a campaign to convince the public of their special expertise.

4 The Organization

*The time spent in Philadelphia was one of the most profitable
and agreeable sessions that I have ever enjoyed. I trust much
good will come from the convention and hope the ardor manifested at the meeting will not be suffered to cool.*

Woodward to Kirkbride
21 November 1844

Kirkbride, Woodward, Stribling, Awl, and the others came
away from the Philadelphia meeting delighted with what
they had done and looking forward to the next meetings. Woodward's apprehension that the "ardor manifested at the meeting"
might "cool" proved unfounded. From 1844 to 1860 additional
asylum administrators joined the organization, strengthening its
political influence and extending its geographic base. New institutions accounted for much of the growth of the association in
the 1850s, but the superintendents of the older asylums in the
United States and Canada demonstrated their commitment to
the new course of action by seldom missing a meeting.[1]

The members worked hard to create a network of like-minded
professional men who could present a united front to the public
about the treatment of the insane. From the beginning, they
were aware that careful attention to organizational structure
could establish a community of practitioners who both participated in and recognized the authority of the association. Their
use of organizational techniques was blatant, and the ardor with

which they pursued organizational unity was unusual in the early nineteenth century.[2] They wasted no time in implementing the principles of limited membership, fashioning organizational control through the policing of decision making and dissent, and defining competency through the establishment of professional credentials.

Membership Control

In 1844 the founders had taken the one deliberate action they knew was essential to assure success: they insisted upon exclusivity of membership. After hours of discussion about the nature of their organization, they chose to call themselves the Association of Medical Superintendents of American Institutions for the Insane and admitted only institutional psychiatrists.[3] Exclusivity was more than an organizational ploy for them; they wanted, first, to avoid that disrepute associated with general medicine that had interfered with their commitment to career and public service and, then, to delineate their particular competence as medical specialists treating the mentally ill.

So deliberately had they chosen to distance themselves from the broader medical profession that even when the American Medical Association organized in 1846 few psychiatrists joined, although the planners of the AMA had passed a special resolution "to invite the Superintendents of Lunatic asylums." At least in the beginning, their reluctance to be identified with the AMA proved a wise move. Early AMA meetings had "sometimes become rancorous" and tumultuous, and sessions were little more than social gatherings with little content. Some critics accused the AMA of heading toward "downward progress to disgraceful imbecility."[4] For the next three decades there was little the AMA had to offer that convinced individual psychiatrists or the Association of Medical Superintendents as a body that their initial decision to avoid affiliation with it had been in error.

This feeling that contact with the AMA as a professional body left much to be desired and a reluctance to be absorbed by the larger organization persisted. When Francis Stribling (one of the few psychiatrists who had joined the AMA) suggested in 1853 that the Association of Medical Superintendents plan to meet at the same time and place as the AMA "to diffuse information on the specialty," Kirkbride rejected the idea as "utterly impracticable." Not only did the Association of Medical Superintendents have more than enough business of its own, but Kirkbride "considered it most important that they should keep themselves entirely distinct from all other bodies whatever."[5] Regular invitations from the AMA to meet together to discuss "matters of important business" continued to come, but the psychiatrists rejected them. It was not until 1867 that the first official AMA delegate was invited to attend the medical superintendents' meetings and another three years before the asylum administrators bothered to send a representative to an AMA meeting. And even this belated association with the AMA began merely as an attempt to protect psychiatry as a specialty from the incursions of the organized medical men. Charles Nichols warned Kirkbride that the AMA members were discussing "questions relating to insanity and putting forth strong views." Judging their ideas as coming from "theoretical and uninformed sources" and thus frequently "erroneous," Nichols suggested that prevention was a better tactic than ineffective refutation once the speculations were "parading around the country."[6] But the exchange of delegates occurred in the late 1860s, and the psychiatrists had no official relationship with the AMA before that although they remained curious about its activities.

The psychiatrists' narrow definition of membership barred many who were interested in the fate of the insane. Among those denied associational affiliation was Theodric Romeyn Beck, one of the managers of the New York State Lunatic Asylum at Utica. He had taken on the burden of editing and publishing the *American Journal of Insanity* for five years after the death of Brigham and kept it alive when all others thought "its continuance quite doubtful." Another was George Parkman, a Pinel student, who had conducted an 1813 survey of the insane in Massachusetts, worked for the establishment of the McLean Asylum, served as advisor there, wrote one of the earliest American treatises on managing the mentally ill, and regularly appeared as a psychiatric witness in court trials.[7] Others, like Edward Jarvis, who by 1844 had gained widespread recognition for the pressure he had put on the Kentucky legislators to improve their facility, and Edward Mead, who had written over seven hundred letters to drum up support for the Illinois hospital, where he acted as its medical trustee, had also been frustrated in their attempts to attain institutional appointments and thus membership in the association. They could not gain admission to the association until they opened their own private hospitals.[8] Even lay heads of asylums and members of boards of trustees were not admitted. And not even the work of Dorothea Dix moved the superintendents to create a special device, such as honorary membership, to acknowledge her crusading efforts.

The association was not so closed that it totally ignored these sympathetic people; the members learned to encourage any base of support. Throughout Dix's struggle to gain federal funds for the benefit of the treatment of the insane, for example, the association sent annual resolutions of support to her.[9] They acknowledged others in a more formal, but limited, manner beginning in 1849, when they allowed "Boards of Trustees, managers, or official visitors of each Insane Asylum on this continent," and "such gentlemen" whom members "deemed proper" to sit in on meetings. The privilege of attendance was by invitation only, and the right of membership did not follow.[10] Indeed, the only widening of participation occurred at the second meeting, when the association specifically included Canadian superintendents and extended lifetime membership to "all those who have heretofore been Medical Superintendents."[11] Change in the membership rules would not come until 1885, when the superintendents finally admitted their assistant physicians.

Organizational Control: Officers, Committees, and National Representation

Not only did the association immediately and deliberately limit membership, but it also used other strategies for building an effective organization. The offices remained in the hands of the founders; Woodward, White, and Kirkbride were the first elected in 1844, probably in recognition of Woodward's early leadership,

White's position as the oldest member, and Kirkbride's efficient handling of arrangements. In the years following Woodward's retirement, Awl, Bell, Ray, Kirkbride, and Butler moved into the presidency. Each principal office holder served as vice president first, assuring and regulating the line of official succession. Once installed in the highest office, each of these founders served until he retired or died; in this way one of the "Originals," with one exception, filled the top office until 1873. The office of secretary did descend upon later joiners, but the men who held the post, Buttolph, Nichols, and Curwen, were protégés of "Old Originals."

Even among themselves the founders exercised selectivity; four never held office, and one did only in old age. Pliny Earle was unemployed from 1849 to 1864 but would become president in 1884, twenty years after he had returned to active practice in the profession and just before his retirement. Both Charles Stedman and Nehemiah Cutter retired in the early 1850s before they had a chance to be rotated into office, although it is likely that the association dragged its feet in acknowledging Cutter because of his outspoken manner and seemingly irreverent views. Neither John Galt nor Francis Stribling, the two remaining founders, came to meetings on a regular basis. Galt, who alienated his colleagues with his unpopular views, did not join them after 1850, and Stribling did not attend between 1854 and 1867.[12] Their devotion to therapeutic psychiatric practice was not questioned, but their commitment to the professional association was.

The leaders of the association were a clique within a clique and reinforced their position by coordinating the makeup of committees. They dominated every important committee and thus managed the business of the meetings and the official positions of the profession. In this way they assured the dominance of right-minded men and mollified prominent, but sometimes dissatisfied, members. When John Fonerden of Maryland, not in line for ascent to office, suggested a change in this policy in 1852, Charles Nichols warned Kirkbride that if "Bell or Ray should hear of such a proposition, I fear they would resign and then we would be in a pretty fix."[13] Both Bell and Ray tended to be mavericks and immune to attempts to make them conform to the official line of the association, but both were nationally and internationally known, and the association could not afford to lose their support. Nichols need not have worried: the system prevailed. Bell remained as president until Ray took over in 1854 for a four-year tenure.

To assure widespread support for their work and further recognition of their expertise, asylum administrators also took pains to attain interregional representation in the organization and geographic balance on committees. They worked diligently to bring all medical superintendents under their aegis and to assure each man's satisfaction with his role within the association. The four original organizers, of course, had represented major geographical areas: Woodward was from New England, Kirkbride from the middle states, Stribling from the South, and Awl from the West. Whether this was deliberately planned by Stribling and Woodward when they first discussed the idea of organizing in the spring of 1844 is a matter of conjecture. It is more likely that, already well acquainted, they naturally cooperated in such an endeavor. But obviously it would benefit an association to have a broad base and, whether by chance or by plan, the national idea grew. Within two months of first hearing Stribling's idea, Woodward expressed hope that "those from the South will not keep back."[14] Stribling did not, nor did his fellow Virginian, John Galt. The other four southern superintendents did not attend the founding meeting for personal and business reasons, but three came to the second meeting. In 1844 the Southwest had only two asylums, in Kentucky and Tennessee, and their superintendents joined in the third and fourth meetings, while William Awl faithfully represented the West.[15]

Because there were more asylums in their area, northeasterners dominated the active membership of the association but the members selected individuals for committee service in such a way as to give the organization a national image. From 1848 on, there were six regular committees. With the exception of the thirteen founders, new members from the Northeast attended three or four meetings before they sat on any of the committees, while a superintendent from the South, Southwest, West, or Canada generally served on some committee upon attending his first or second meeting.[16] The exception to this pattern, at least for the first decade, was the business committee. Its function was to select the papers to be read, and therefore the issues raised and points of view heard; the "Old Originals" were unwilling to place such power in the hands of newcomers. Nevertheless, about half of the members served on the remaining committees at some time or other, with northeasterners most often ignored.[17]

Despite these efforts to make the organization a national one, full participation from each section of the country was never achieved. Before 1860 only one southern superintendent attended more than half of the meetings.[18] The other nine southern asylums fell far below this mark. From the Southwest, only Missouri was well represented, while the superintendents of the Tennessee and two Kentucky asylums attended intermittently. The western states had better than half of their asylums represented, with the exception of those in the relatively new states of Iowa and Wisconsin, but the northeasterns stood out. They dominated each convention, except those in 1856 and 1859, which, significantly, met in midwestern cities.[19]

The practice of holding meetings in east coast cities or communities with limited transportation facilities contributed to the ineffectiveness of efforts to maintain balance. The difficulties of both time and cost involved in travel in the early nineteenth century clearly precluded the journey for many a superintendent. Distances were long, conveyances uncomfortable, and connections uncertain. Few were as tenacious as William Awl of Ohio, who would delight in a journey by steamship, rail, and stagecoach, and even suffer the annoyance of a wound from the flying sparks of a steam locomotive with aplomb as long as he could attend professional gatherings.[20] The attendance at the 1849 meeting, held in Utica, New York, illustrated the importance of holding sessions in cities of easier access or great attraction. Only seventeen superintendents participated, the lowest figure for the entire antebellum period. The following year, when Boston was the site, twenty-seven psychiatrists were present, as were a number of interested visitors from out of town. Not until the 1856 meeting in Cincinnati, though, did the association pay some homage to the greater travel difficulties of their western brethren.

When it came to preparing papers and leading discussions, northeasterns also stood out.[21] Men like Kirkbride, Ray, Jarvis, and Bell (all northeasterners) presented from eight to sixteen papers apiece. Others—Joshua Worthington, John Curwen, Pliny Earle, John Gray and Amariah Brigham (northeasterners too)— presented five each.[22] Only John Galt of Williamsburg, Virginia (who did not attend but sent papers to be read), and J. J. McIlhenny of Dayton, Ohio, came close to such active participation. The only other southerners or westerners who presented more than one paper were John Fonerden of Maryland, Andrew McFarland of Illinois, and William Awl of Ohio, and most of those were at the request of the president. At only three meetings, 1850, 1852, and 1859, did non-northeasterners present as many as one-third of the papers. Particularly significant was the Cincinnati convention of 1856. Westerners, especially Ohioans, dominated the ranks that year. Sixteen of the twenty-eight members present headed asylums in the West, yet only one westerner read a paper. Northeastern men, by contrast, delivered the remaining seven.

Man for man, northeasterners did not dominate the discussion. The most individually talkative delegates, when they attended, were the southwesterners. Accounting for more than their share in the commentary, they led all others in the number of times they spoke out. Especially loquacious were T. R. H. Smith of Fulton, Missouri, and William Chipley of Lexington, Kentucky, but they were no radicals. Smith concurred with men like Kirkbride, Bell, Stribling, and Curwen on a number of issues while studiously avoiding comment on the most controversial questions. He did manage to pique the ire of Bell at one point, however. Smith demanded the creation of a standing committee on uniform statistics and provoked a condescending reply from Bell that perhaps some of the "junior members" might wish to redo the work of their "elders." Smith also stood alone in approving of private asylums at the 1860 meeting. And largely through his yearly efforts, the association finally met in a western city, Cincinnati, in 1856—and then in Lexington, Kentucky, in 1859.[23] William Chipley, on the other hand, rarely deviated from the consensus. His paper on force-feeding was merely descriptive in nature, provoking no controversy, and his plans for a book on the "vice" of masturbation received the wholehearted approval of the members.[24]

In comparison, southerners seldom spoke, while northeasterners had such an edge in numbers that they had to dominate unless they self-consciously chose not to do so—which they did not. Thus, overall, northeasterners dominated the association's activities.[25] With the exception of the founder William Awl, elected president in 1848, all offices were filled by men from the Northeast. Even the presidency of Andrew McFarland in 1859 did not really alter the pattern. He was a New Englander who had entered the profession in New Hampshire and then moved on to Illinois.

Unwilling to relinquish this image of national participation when sectionalism reared its head in the early 1850s, some members tried to offset its divisive effects within the association. The effort largely turned on Francis Stribling. Not only was Stribling a good friend of many of the other founders, but he also administered his asylum efficiently and handled his state legislature in a way admired by all.[26]

Stribling had attended the founding session, but not the next five meetings. Realizing that his absence might become permanent, in 1849 William Awl fondly prodded him, writing that "we all regretted your absence both at N.Y. and at Utica and I am pleased with the expectation of seeing you with us." John Butler "was right glad . . . to see even your signed name!" and assured Stribling he would "be most cordially welcomed by all his brother Superintendents." Luther Bell also wanted to see him, and Charles Stedman hoped that "nothing will prevent your being present at the next meeting of our Association." Stribling did not come to that meeting in 1850, and Butler and Kirkbride both wrote to say that all had missed him.[27] Finally, in 1852, Stribling began to attend meetings again. But during the late 1850s he was absent, although he received numerous and pressing invitations from his friends in the North.

As the nation moved closer to civil war, a valiant effort was made to preserve some modicum of the association's solidarity. In November 1860 Charles Nichols spearheaded a plan for himself,

Kirkbride, Brown, and Buttolph to visit Stribling. Maintaining contact with someone in the South was the purpose. Nichols felt that the trip "really *needs* to be done," and he had "written Brown and urged him to join us in our proposed descent upon Stribling" and told him that he would "have none of the immortal credit of saving the Union" if he did not come. The proposed visitors were among the most active members of the association. This particular mission was abortive, and, after polling the members, the association decided not to convene in 1861.[28] For the next four meetings they struggled on without their "rebel" brethren until superintendents from the South began once more to attend.

Organizational Control: Setting the Limits of Dissent

With all their attempts to attain unity, asylum administrators nevertheless tolerated some nonconformist behavior. For example, because of his age, they generally ignored or indulged Nehemiah Cutter's irreverent description of the profession as the "crazy business."[29] They allowed a similar leeway to men like Luther Bell and Isaac Ray, although on other issues and for different reasons. Both Bell and Ray came in for a good deal of criticism in private for their stand on the proper nature of annual reports, especially for their remarks against the inclusion of long statistical tables. It was a sensitive issue with most psychiatrists because they had illustrated their initial success through the use of such statistics; the entire institutional movement had expanded because of the optimism the statistics of curability had generated; and one of the major motivations for the founders had been to gain uniformity in the reporting of these numbers. But even before the first meeting of the association, Bell had acquired a reputation as an "anti-statistician" for his vocal insistence that statistical reporting was subject to manipulation and misinterpretation. Many disagreed with him, particularly Awl and Brigham, but Ray became Bell's ally on the subject as early as 1849.[30]

Ray sharply criticized the "minuteness of detail" in most reports. He conceded that the printing of curability rates allowed supporters of asylums to take delight in the charitable services they provided and even helped superintendents to broadcast their success. Nevertheless, the inordinate amount of time necessary to accomplish the work irritated Ray. He was even more incensed at the propensity of everyone to believe the numbers simply because they seemed to have emerged from a "strictly inductive method of inquiry" and carried with them the weight of scientific "facts." It was this "very appearance" of certainty that misled people and caused them to go on "hugging" these "treasures of knowledge," never realizing they were nothing more than "empty show."[31]

Amariah Brigham, true to his open policy with the *Journal* of printing all views, published Ray's remarks, but in private he ranted in disagreement with him. He thought Ray "wrong—very wrong." Brigham reacted irritably to both Bell's and Ray's attitude even more than to their statements. He felt obliged to "couple [Ray] and Bell together and show them up as 'doggedly crabbish and snarlish' and no more wise, learned, *accurate* or *scientific* than their neighbors." He disliked their boasting of the superiority of their asylums over others and thought them "quite uncourteous and too dictatorial."[32] As editor of the one journal dedicated to the work of the profession, Brigham had been generous in accepting criticism of statistical reporting, even publishing an article just the year before in which a French psychiatrist had observed that "statistical researches" had become monotonous, disconnected, and lacking in a uniformity that would allow useful comparisons.[33] But Brigham was equally committed to establishing the credibility of American psychiatry. Suggestion for reform in reporting techniques was one thing, but Ray's attack on the validity of the figures and his implications of credulity on the part of his fellow administrators was too much for Brigham; he planned to take Ray to task in the next issue. Brigham died before he could carry this out, but Beck, who replaced him, published a rebuttal, albeit a less heated one than Brigham's.[34]

Most of the association members continued to include statistical tables in their annual reports, but they still had to contend with the dissatisfaction of Ray and Bell. In 1855, when T. R. H. Smith, the outspoken superintendent of the Missouri State Hospital, had made that suggestion about the association appointing a committee to devise a uniform system of statistical reporting, both Ray and Bell had been exasperated. Ray reminded the gathering that after much debate in the earlier years, Pliny Earle had worked out a method for recording numbers in a way that would allow comparisons, but few had adopted it. But Bell was most adamant, making point after point in reiterating his long opposition to statistics. He acknowledged that he had made himself "somewhat notorious" with his "annual diatribe," but he continued, noting, among other things, that the nature of patient populations differed from institution to institution and gave rise to unfavorable comparisons. Tabulations could easily be manipulated—those of death rates, for example—simply by urging patients nearing death to spend their last months with their families, thus removing them from the hospital's rolls and mortality statistics. Acknowledging that some improvements had been made in the "style" of the annual reports, Bell, nevertheless warned that further undue concentration on statistics might reawaken the "race of self-glorification" of the old days and interrupt the association's present "harmony and fraternal feeling." Smith, "with all due deference to Dr. Bell," was not convinced and still believed a uniform system necessary and possible. The sentiment of the majority of members was with Smith. The "Cult of Curability" had waned, but most members still felt the need for statistical reporting to illustrate their continuing work and to provide the public with some familiar means by which to evaluate it.[35]

Ray, with the backing of Bell, took an unpopular stand on another issue—the holding of annual meetings. Ray thought them unnecessary and virtually useless and was so piqued that he proposed to offer a resolution in 1853 that those who voted for yearly meetings "shall pledge themselves to attend." He informed Kirkbride that "we [are] meeting too often," arguing that "our reunions would become more profitable if the intervals were longer."[36] To Kirkbride and most others, this sentiment was anathema. Annual meetings provided some respite from the toil of asylum routine and, more importantly, created opportunities for the fruitful dissemination of ideas within the profession. Aware of this strong feeling, Ray nevertheless amended the recommendation of the committee to select a place for the next meeting. Not only did he prefer Providence, Rhode Island, to Washington,

D.C., but he persisted in moving that the next meeting be held "two years from that date" and doubted that the association exerted any influence whatever upon the community in which it met. In disagreement with Ray, Kirkbride worried that the "influence of the Association would be much impaired were its meetings to be held less frequently." Bell, reversing his earlier position supporting Ray, thought the local community "would reap the benefit of what experience the Association" had. Recognizing that annual meetings both enhanced their image in the community and encouraged compliance with association policies, the members "severally rejected" Ray's proposals. Ray continued to attend the annual meetings and never again raised the issue—nor did anyone else.[37]

Although the challenges on the specific questions of statistics and meetings had to be answered, the members of the association distinguished between the commitment of Ray and Bell to the profession and their personal dissatisfactions with some of the profession's record-keeping and organizational idiosyncracies. In the long run these were not real issues because the other members understood that Ray's ramblings about too frequent meetings arose from his momentary pique at the unwillingness of some to present papers and that, with Bell, he simply questioned the form of the data kept on patients and the amount presented to the public. More important to their colleagues was the firm commitment of Ray and Bell to the asylum system and their plan of management for it.

Establishing Professional Credentials and Networks

The problems of assuring the appointment of men committed to their plan of management increased as state after state built new asylums. As boards of trustees of these new institutions consulted the members of the association about the best doctors to manage their hospitals, psychiatrists responded at first on a case-by-case basis. In the early years they were rather unfocused and thought the kind but firm doctor would serve well enough. They had recommended doctors who, besides being benevolent of spirit, manifested "equanimity of temper, self control, firmness of purpose and gentleness of manners." As they clarified their ideas about their roles as medical superintendents, however, they shifted their emphasis. They recommended doctors who met the "intellectual qualifications" rooted in a general education, but especially those who had a capacity for business. Additionally, they looked for men with the political and social skills necessary for dealing effectively with trustees, legislators, and assorted other persons interested in the care of the insane or likely to interfere in the running of the asylum.[38] From their own experience they had learned that, while being of good heart alone sufficed for doctor-patient relations, in the struggle to build support for well-run asylums mere good intentions were easily lost on politicians. A man also had to be able to command the respect and obedience of his entire staff in order to keep the rather complex operation of an asylum running efficiently. Thus a candidate who "appeared intelligent" and desirous of a post did not necessarily meet with their approval if he also seemed "rather unpolished,"[39] because they knew one man's failure to manage the treatment of the insane reflected on the entire profession.

Members of the association also shifted their strategy; they increasingly took an active role in finding positions for those who did meet these standards and who shared their ideas about asylum management. Thomas Kirkbride, for instance, recommended his assistant physician, John Curwen, for the superintendency of the new Pennsylvania State Lunatic Hospital at Harrisburg. Curwen was so much Kirkbride's protégé that after receiving his appointment he importuned Kirkbride with inquiries and pleas for advice on every minute detail of running an asylum from the management of attendants to the use of charcoal as a deodorizer. George Chandler benefited similarly from his work as Woodward's assistant; Woodward recommended him for superintendencies at the Maine Insane Asylum, the New Hampshire Asylum for the Insane, and the New York State Lunatic Asylum and assured that his former assistant replaced him at Worcester. And Francis Stribling, while he suffered some criticism for using Virginia facilities for the benefit of a neighboring state, nevertheless trained Edward Fisher for the post at the State Hospital in Raleigh, North Carolina.[40]

Others, like Richard Patterson, an assistant to William Awl for five years, while following more circuitous routes, still benefited from their mentors' commitment to establishing professional networks. When Patterson resigned from the Ohio Lunatic Asylum in Columbus, Awl sent him to Philadelphia to see Kirkbride, whose help the "commissioners of Indiana" had already asked in finding a superintendent. Patterson received the appointment at the Indiana Hospital for the Insane but found the legislature "impossible" and returned to Columbus in 1853 to practice general medicine. The Asylum for the Feeble-minded in Columbus, one of Awl's pet projects, opened in 1857, and Patterson was named superintendent. He stayed for three years and then once more traveled west to superintend the Iowa Asylum for the Insane. The Iowa position had been offered first to David McGugin, an old friend of Awl's in Ohio in the late 1830s; McGugin refused the offer and recommended Patterson at Awl's behest. Coincidentally, the president of the board of directors, Maturin Fisher, had been a member of the board of directors of Awl's close friend Woodward in 1842. Patterson's connections with Awl, and Awl's with Kirkbride and Woodward, paid off.[41]

The situation was less complicated for the protégés of John Gray. While acting superintendent at the New York State Lunatic Asylum at Utica, Gray was hired to direct the construction of the Michigan Asylum for the Insane, and the midwestern board members sought his recommendation for a superintendent. Gray selected his assistant physician, Edwin Van Deusen. Gray played a role in Andrew McFarland's life as well. Along with Butler, he recommended McFarland to the board of trustees of the Illinois State Hospital for the Insane when they visited the East in 1852. And so well had Nathan Benedict performed during the outbreak of cholera at the Blockley Almshouse in Philadelphia in 1849 that he garnered the support of Kirkbride, Awl, and Stedman in obtaining the Utica post. Grateful, and obviously aware of the influence of his colleagues, Benedict thanked Kirkbride because "the 'Meeting' set me up finely and I have been doing well since."[42]

Horace Buttolph, on the other hand, unabashedly used the network to develop his own connections. When he heard in 1842 that Samuel Woodward had been offered the superintendency at Utica, Buttolph, "strongly desirous" of an appointment as his assistant, wrote to Woodward immediately. Woodward did not accept the job, but Buttolph was hired as assistant physician. In 1847, anxious to gain a superintendency, Buttolph petitioned Thomas Kirkbride, "frankly" admitting his "wishes" that Kirkbride promote his cause in New Jersey. Buttolph's listing of his credentials of six years in general practice, four years as an assistant physician at Utica, and his trip abroad to study European asylums is illustrative of what the members of the association had come to expect. Medical experience was necessary because medical treatment remained an important part of their therapeutic plan. Four years spent under the watchful eye of Amariah Brigham presumably taught Buttolph the principles of moral treatment and the necessity of political astuteness and administrative skill. His willingness to observe the broader professional picture indicated his seriousness of purpose and commitment to the care of the insane. Indeed, Buttolphs' acknowledgment that he was "aware of the high esteem" in which Kirkbride's "opinion of the requisite qualifications for such a station would be held" and his supposition that his work would never compare with that at Kirkbride's "noble hospital" illustrates that he had learned well the lesson of political shrewdness. He obtained the position he sought.[43]

When men were lacking the full array of credentials, the members of the association did not try to push the candidacies even of those they knew well and respected personally. Chauncey Booth, for instance, had served as an assistant physician in three different asylums over a period of nineteen years. The association members did not question the sincerity of his benevolence nor the depth of his commitment to the task of caring for insane charges. Their depictions of his unusual modesty and uncommon naïveté as a result of never having been "in the world," however, indicated that they had recognized his shortcomings. He was a fine workhorse in the asylum but deficient in worldly experience and in the skills of management.[44]

Failures in Organizational Control

Association members selected good men for administrative posts, but they could not always guarantee an appointment, as a number of men discovered. For Charles Nichols in 1852, the moment simply was not right. Tired of squabbling with the Bloomingdale directors, he searched for another position. Told that Luther Bell's retirement from the McLean Asylum was imminent, Nichols sought the endorsement of Kirkbride and Dix, but Bell did not leave for another four years, and Nichols looked elsewhere.[45] Sometimes, despite the members' efforts on behalf of one of their own, the moment was propitious for a newcomer. George Choate, an unknown twenty-eight-year-old doctor from Salem, Massachusetts, received the Taunton State Hospital post even though Bell had recommended Andrew McFarland, with seven years' experience at the New Hampshire Asylum.[46] But Edward Mead ran afoul of partisan politics in Ohio and could not even recover his credentials because they were "mysteriously displaced of" by one of the board members "to accommodate his partisan" candidate. Politicians in the western states, especially Ohio and Indiana, were notorious for appointing relatives, friends, and political allies to superintendencies and other posts in the asylums, and if a man had no stomach for a "scramble" or were "unskilled in log-rolling and subsoiling with legislators," he failed to hold his position.[47] There was little even the most powerful association member could do except warn about the dangers of such practices to the smooth running of the hospital and the health of the patients.

They were equally unsuccessful at times in convincing every asylum superintendent of his equal status within the association. In reality, of course, some men exercised more power than others; the men from the northeastern asylums still dominated, and hints of dissatisfaction from those of other regions occasionally emerged. One western superintendent, J. J. McIlhenny, complained to Pliny Earle that he was "well aware that you Eastern men regard us Western men as inferior in point of education and capacity to manage" asylums. McIlhenny had been active in the association for the six years that he had run the Southern Ohio Lunatic Asylum at Dayton, but he felt some condescension from those men, "particularly from New England."[48] And Andrew McFarland resented the eastern men's practice of "giving written testimonials" to any attendant who left for the West. McFarland had found these migrating attendants filled with "a spirit of insubordination and mischief," as well as guilty of "notorious abuses" in his asylum. He upbraided his eastern colleagues for their thoughtlessness and insensitivity in sending him people with letters in hand that were nothing more than "almost a fatal license in the work of evil."[49]

Their lack of total control was, in part, a result of the nature of the professionalism of these mid-nineteenth-century psychiatrists. For all their seriousness of purpose about personal and professional status, the prestige of their organization, and the well-being of their patients, there was a marked informality about their relationship. They were good friends and judged themselves and others by nineteenth-century standards of character and good fellowship.

They visited one another's homes, sent gifts to one another's children, brought their wives along on trips to the association meetings, and planned excursions together. William Awl even named his son after Samuel Woodward.[50] They passed on friendly gossip and especially ribbed colleagues like Pliny Earle and Charles Nichols, both bachelors in the 1850s. Isaac Ray told Kirkbride about "poor Earle," who had been "unsuccessful in his wooing" because he was "eclipsed" by a "mustachioed fellow in regimentals." Earle, in turn, remarked to Kirkbride about Nichols's apparent success at courting. He described Nichols as "a gone goose," while John Curwen reported that Dorothea Dix, visiting Nichols shortly after his marriage, found him "in Elysium."[51]

They cared about one another's personal and professional problems as well. Whether it was the death of the Nichols's first child, the mental collapse of Merrick Bemis, the injury of Thomas Kirkbride by a patient, the harassment of Nichols by his managers, or the absence of Pliny Earle from their circle of camaraderie, they kept track of one another and offered their concern and support.[52]

This spirit of good fellowship sometimes spilled over into the conduct of their meetings. As Nichols wrote to Kirkbride, he felt that the *"mads* had some *pension* for gentility" and wanted "to indulge it" when they "get off for a little caper."[53] They readily interrupted their sessions to call out the carriages to take them off to a particularly interesting museum, library, or botanical display. At many of their evening sessions they enjoyed the relaxed atmosphere of the parlors and fine collations of museum curators, city officials, or fellow superintendents.

The members' inability to enforce their every policy and suggestion, however, was much more a result of the institutional nature of their profession. Budget decisions ultimately rested with state legislatures or boards of managers, as did their appointments as asylum administrators. Their tenure and the success of their program depended more on their ability to lobby and argue persuasively than on any real authority vested in their policies.

They chose, however, to cast the best possible light on their rather tenuous position. Their attitudes toward the various types of institutions they visited and passed judgment upon during their annual meetings is revealing on this point. They toured asylums like the Pennsylvania Hospital for the Insane, McLean's, the Boston Lunatic Hospital, the New York State Lunatic Asylum at Utica, and St. Elizabeths in Washington, D.C., and routinely expressed "great interest and satisfaction."[54] That they had no official criticism of their own major asylums reflects both a bias on the part of the regular association members and a willingness to trust each man to carry out the principles of moral treatment as best he could. With other institutions they were less tolerant. They condemned the Blockley Almshouse in Philadelphia for its lack of occupational therapy and the Blackwell's Island Almshouse in New York and the Baltimore Almshouse for their neglect of the pauper insane. At their meetings they talked about these institutions as "miserable apologies for insane hospitals" and as "unworthy of the age," but they had little impact on these asylums, and they knew it.[55] These asylums lacked a medical superintendent and thus had no connection with their association. The best they could hope for was that the moral force of their disapproval could effect change. They remained unaware that these institutions, for all intents and purposes, were the harbingers of the future and optimistically presumed that even almshouses and city asylums would soon capitulate to their new plan of treatment.

Their progress, after all, in persuading states to support the treatment of the insane and to adopt their plan of moral therapy characterized the age. Less concerned about what they could not control, they chose to perfect their plan of treatment, their system of asylum management, and the structure of their professional organization so that the very moral force of the association would bring the treatment of the insane fully under their control, garnering them real authority. Their success in shaping that professional organization had met a variety of social, personal, and professional needs for them. And because they had established authority within the association, their organizational control would give them a vehicle to work out the details of their expertise and a platform to promote their profession. American society's acceptance of institutionalization, moreover, impelled these psychiatrists to tie their organization, and therefore their careers, to the asylum. Their plan to elevate their profession became inextricably bound to the institution and to their roles as managers within it.

5 Asylum Management

I particularly like to see all the movements of the internal and somewhat complicated machinery of an asylum, made as if they were timed and directed by the swinging of a pendulum. These, to me, are the permanent beauties of an institution provided, nevertheless, that the system of moral treatment is elaborate.

Earle to Stribling
16 August 1847

Samuel Woodward had described the first meeting as "without definite object" except to consider the "general welfare of institutions in this country," but, as we have seen, it was not long before he and other superintendents shaped the association so that it resulted both in "exalting the condition of the insane" and in empowering the profession.[1] The association had appealed to most superintendents because they appreciated the forum it provided for the exchange of ideas and the opportunity for drawing upon the support of their colleagues, but to a marked degree they understood the contribution it made to the development of their own influence.

As the public exhibited an acceptance of the plan of moral treatment by bringing their mentally ill to hospitals, these asylum doctors used the power of their association to perfect their plans for the asylum. They especially directed their energies toward guaranteeing its smooth functioning. No detail escaped them because they believed that the location of the hospital, the layout of the building, the amenities of the rooms and the corridors, and the obedience of the staff were as integral to moral treatment as manual labor or recreational and religious activities. Convinced that any imperfection in the system jeopardized their ability to implement their therapeutic plan and cure patients, in the early 1850s they hammered out a series of policy decisions on asylum design and personnel organization. The capstone of their plan to assure the "permanent beauties" of the asylum and to coordinate its "internal and somewhat complicated machinery," however, rested on their role as medical superintendents.[2]

Asylum Design

The laymen who had been the first asylum planners had lacked a coherent rationale for the design of buildings. Many early asylums had become an amalgam of the low-cost, seemingly advantageous, aspects of a series of other types of social institutions. Not involved in the building stages, the first moral therapists who became medical superintendents readily found fault with their hospitals. They felt that buildings that looked like prisons projected an undesirable image. They worried, too, about poor heating and ventilation, insufficient facilities for the separation of quiet and violent patients, and imperfect safeguards against self-injury. All would undermine the potential curative effects of their therapy program.

As a result, one of the first tasks the association undertook was the formulation of a model plan for the asylum. Perhaps the most energetic, and certainly the most noted, of the superintendents who contributed to this campaign was Thomas Kirkbride. He had been deeply concerned since 1840, when he had taken over the administration of the Pennsylvania Hospital for the Insane, a building about whose construction he had not been consulted. Dissatisfied with its floor plan because of the difficulties it imposed on his working out of therapy and organization, Kirkbride pondered solutions. Eventually he devised a scheme for construction of the ideal hospital for the insane. His conceptualization of the asylum as a place that should engender "a generous confidence" so strongly appealed to the others that the association mounted a zealous campaign to promote what quickly became known as the Kirkbride plan.

Leaving nothing to conjecture, Kirkbride addressed the issues of location, acreage, hospital size, water supply, building materials, room layout, heating and ventilation, and sanitation. He wanted to convince the public that the institution was safe and the patients free from physical harm and comfortable. Fire, for instance, was a real hazard for nineteenth-century institutions. Thus Kirkbride demanded buildings constructed of brick or stone, stairways with easy access made of similar materials, and gas used for lighting (because it was convenient, clean and economical, but especially because it was safe). He insisted that the steam boilers for heating be housed in separate structures. In other words, if his admonitions were heeded, the security of the institutional plant was guaranteed.[3]

He did not overlook the safeguarding of the individual patient either. Inmates would not be at the mercy of one another's eccentricities or psychotic actions. In an institution of 250 patients (the maximum size Kirkbride recommended), the staff could accommodate easily tractable patients apart from the dangerous, noisy, and violent ones if there were enough room for eight classifications of the mentally ill of each sex. A separate wing or floor off the central building housed each group. To secure the surveillance of individuals, he planned the rooms of the attendants (at least two nurses for each dormitory) as part of the ward. If isolation of a patient became necessary, Kirkbride wanted all solitary rooms built above ground and constant communication throughout the asylum maintained by a system of "speaking tubes."

Even more important to many families of patients were his assurances that he and the other superintendents cared as much about the patients' comfort and contentment as they did. He described the model asylum as located away from the hustle and bustle of a large metropolis and enclosed by a wall, unseen by inmates but secure enough to keep out curiosity seekers. A lot of at least one hundred acres, cultivated both for the pleasure of the patients and for their useful activity, created an image formulated to ease the guilt and fears of families contemplating hospitalization for their loved ones. He sketched the internal arrangements to allay worries about neglect and dirt. He wanted the parlors, dining rooms, and sitting areas flooded with sunlight and fresh air from many large windows. Similarly, he paid careful attention to the problems of general ventilation and sanitation, both serious problems with patients who were frequently incontinent and prone to unpredictable behavior.

Kirkbride was not alone in his dissatifactions with early asylum design; he did, however, lead the Association of Medical Superintendents to action. By 1849 he and others were ready to test some of these proposals in the association. Accepting recommendations about an "abundance of pure air" and sufficient warmth without debate, the members passed on to the committee on construction of hospitals (which Kirkbride chaired) a mandate to make a full report. Convinced that proper asylum design was crucial to their success and could be effected by the association's endorsement, Kirkbride and the committee presented twenty-six resolutions to the assembled body of psychiatrists in 1851. They embodied every principle Kirkbride and others had described over the previous decade. So convinced were the members of the association of the necessity of each detail of architectural planning that there was little discussion of the proposed resolutions. The association "maturely considered" the plan and in adopting it as official policy thereafter considered the Kirkbride plan sacrosanct. While the members would continue to debate the relative merits of steam or hot water heating or the building of separate asylums for each sex, generally they delighted in the plans of new hospitals that complied with the new association standards, viewing each new asylum built on its tenets as a sign of their increasing influence.[4]

Organization of Asylum Personnel

The group next addressed the crucial issue of the organization of hospital administration. There had been little consistency among hospitals as to who hired staff, who set policy, or who was ultimately responsible for the overall operation of the asylum. In

1853 the association set out to define the duties of each asylum officer. First, they commented on role of the trustees.[5] William Awl, usually on good terms with his trustees, still found that on some issues they were reluctant to recognize his authority and expertise. At one point, he depicted them as so obdurate that they thought there was "peculiar merit" in holding to their position even when they were wrong. He compared them to the "juror who told his friends that he had to stay out all night, because he found *eleven* of the most stupid and stubborn men he ever came across." D. T. Brown simply hoped that others could exert some beneficial influence on his governors. He was disappointed when one of his board members missed seeing Thomas Kirkbride because Brown felt "it does all our men good to have good impressions *burnt* into them by a few words from the Fathers in our department."[6]

Acknowledging that the "general controlling power should be vested in a board of trustees or managers," the psychiatrists quickly pointed out the danger of allowing partisan politics to intrude on the work of the boards. The board members, they decided, should be "individuals possessing the public confidence," and men who were "distinguished for liberality, intelligence, and active benevolence," but free from political influence.[7] Even these paragons of virtue were not to have a free hand within the asylum walls; they could appoint the superintendent, but no other officer without his consent. Board members also inspected the asylum and supervised its expenditures and general operation, but they were to keep in mind that the superintendent was the chief executive officer. All others on the staff—assistant physicians, steward, matron, chaplain, supervisors, and attendants—went about their duties "under the direction of the superintending physician."[8] So widespread was the dissatisfaction with boards of trustees and so strongly did the association feel on the subject of the superintendent's complete sway over his asylum that it ordered the propositions of 1853, with their blunt statement of policy about the limited role of the directors, "to be published as the unanimous sentiments of the association." Each superintendent included them as part of his annual report, which was submitted to his board and distributed to the general public, and lobbied his trustees for their acceptance of this definition of the superintendent's authority.[9]

The psychiatrists had equally high standards for their assistant physicians. The issue was different since assistant physicians were clearly in subordinate positions. The superintendents did not worry about authority as much as they worked to gain the willing cooperation of their assistants in maintaining the deepest commitment to the profession and the highest standards for the asylum because assistant physicians were in daily contact with the patients as they administered medicines or directed recreational activities. They expected these assistants to be doctors "of such character and qualifications as to be able to represent and perform the ordinary duties of the [superintendent] during his absence."[10]

Thirty-three of these superintendents had started out as assistant physicians, so they understood the rigor of the job. The annual salary for an assistant was generally only $500, but the security of the job and hopes for promotion had been major motives for many in accepting this poorly paid post.[11] A few had manifested interest in the care of the insane, and for them any chance to practice psychiatry had been worth the temporary financial sacrifice. Pliny Earle accepted a secondary post at Friends' after writing his graduating thesis on "The Causes, Duration, Termination, and Moral Treatment of Insanity" and spending two years visiting asylums in England and on the Continent. Both John Gray, who had served a residency at the Blockley Almshouse, and Horace Buttolph, who "for a number of years" had been interested in "'mental science' and in the proper treatment of insane patients," became assistant physicians for similar reasons. Others, like George Chandler, simply had been struggling along in private general practices, receiving "that kind of patronage that usually falls into the hands of young physicians," nothing more than "emoluments" of "gratitude and good wishes." Becoming an assistant physician in the asylum brightened their professional prospects, but their sometimes mixed motives led superintendents to insist upon a careful monitoring of them as apprentices.[12]

Assistants received the attention of the more experienced men

through daily exposure to asylums managed on the patterns established by the association. And as the members grew to know one
another better, they reinforced the lessons of asylum practice by
encouraging their assistants to visit their colleagues, even occasionally taking these young men to association meetings.[13] As
assistants responded to this informal training process, they gained
more responsible duties. Medical superintendents delegated much
of the daily patient care to the best of them. The varied tasks of
administration—writing annual reports, preparing papers for the
association, corresponding with colleagues, planning strategy for
dealing with state legislators, attending meetings of the board of
directors, maintaining public relations, keeping in touch with
relatives of patients and with former inmates, overseeing the general operation of the asylum, ordering supplies, and organizing
occupational and recreational therapy—left them less time to
spend with individual patients than they would have liked.

On the occasions that demanded their absence from the asylum,
superintendents were relieved to have trustworthy assistants to
take up their administrative duties temporarily. Few heads of
asylums kept as close to their hospitals as Rufus Wyman, who
in fourteen years was absent only five nights.[14] Most other superintendents traveled on professional and personal business on a
regular basis. At the least, they were away five or six days at the
association meetings. At other times they spent weeks touring
other American asylums, traveling abroad, or journeying to restore health.

This professional confidence that superintendents developed in
the assistant physicians they trained sometimes took the form of
refusals of salary increases for themselves as they pointed out the
low pay scale of the subordinate officers in the asylums.[15] The
time spent with their assistants also meant that superintendents
could recommend them for promotion to administrative posts.
Despite its informality, this system of selection and training
worked remarkably well. On the average, assistants who moved
into superintendencies received their promotion within five to
six years and meanwhile the superintendents gained well-trained
assistants to help their asylums function smoothly.

More than any other staff member, the attendants, or nurses, were in the constant company of the patients, more so than even the overburdened assistant physicians and certainly to a greater extent than the superintendent. Thus their conduct engendered deep concern and strict attention from the asylum administrators. Held responsible for anything out of order in their wards, attendants had no authority and little remuneration. Understandably, superintendents complained of the difficulties of keeping reliable people and sought recommendations from one another. In an era before the existence of formal nursing education, psychiatrists preferred to train their own and looked for a certain naïveté in the candidates. Andrew McFarland, for one, wanted untrained, raw recruits, and Isaac Ray refused to recommend a former attendant of his because, since his time of employment by Ray, he had traveled to "California, Minnesota, and Lord knows where else," and "he would be likely to know too much for an attendant."[16] Inexperience was not a virtue in itself, although properly supervised training and a compliant attitude were. Attendants were to be moral, disciplined, long-suffering, responsible, subservient, and meticulous.

Rising at dawn to greet, wash, and dress patients, and to have time to clean and ventilate the corridors and rooms before the physician's visit at eight o'clock, they faced a similarly rigid and grueling schedule for the rest of the day and evening. Yet they were to be cheerful, realize that the hospital claimed "their whole time," take no "offense when their defects [were] pointed out," and validate their knowledge of and compliance with the rules by having their copies of the regulations signed by the superintendent every week.[17] The superintendents believed so strongly that all these restrictions were essential for a successful asylum regime that in 1852, when John Curwen presented to the association meeting his model *Manual for Attendants* encompassing all of these principles, the members wholeheartedly approved and recommended it "for general adoption in American Institutions for the Insane."[18] The behavior of the attendants, especially on the wards, was crucial to the superintendents' image of their asylum because, except for accusations of illegal and coercive commitments, the major complaint against asylums was that of abusive treatment or neglect on the part of attendants. If attendants

could be convinced of the important role they played in the curative benefits of the asylum, the psychiatrists' work would be more
effective, and another level of their organizational plan secured.

Asylum Control and the Medical Superintendent: The Justification

The superintendents agreed, when discussing their own role,
that the entire staff should "implicitly and promptly comply with
the wishes of the head of the institution." They demanded such
obedience, they said, because society had committed to them "a
stricken fellow-being" whom they were responsible to protect and
to cure. The success of therapy rested with the doctors and their
ability to implement and control every detail of moral treatment.[19]
Thus they argued that they needed the authority to hire the most
qualified people and to dismiss unsatisfactory ones, to purchase
the best supplies, to integrate the many activities of the day, and
to enforce their directives.

This perception of the superintendent as the all-powerful central authority in the asylum emerged only gradually. At first, as
we have seen, American psychiatrists simply had stressed the character and personality of the physician, depicting him as fatherly
and promoting the image of the asylum as a family environment.
William Rockwell, for example, advertised that he welcomed patients into his "immediate family" at the Vermont Asylum for
the Insane, where his "kind, assiduous and skillful treatment"
promised to bring about a "restoration of reason."[20]

As long as psychiatrists were treating a relatively small number
of patients, this image of the fatherly, but firm, physician who
watched over his charges in a family atmosphere served well.
Samuel Woodward, in the early years of the Worcester State
Lunatic Hospital, depicted his patients as "children and kin-
dred" and himself as the "loving father of a large family." He
visited his patients daily, listening to their problems, carefully
noted their symptoms and behavior, and generally believed in the
efficacy of "kindness and indulgence."[21] William Rockwell promised the families of his patients that all in the asylum profited
from the "truly parental" atmosphere of the hospital by joining

in "family worship" and by sharing the "enjoyments of [the] social life" of the doctor and his family. Rockwell, at first, had ample time to carry out these intimate encounters with his patients. Through "constant care and watchfulness," he tried to connect the patients' daily experiences in the asylum with their changing mental state and spent enough time with them to be able to discern if a patient was depressed, jealous, or suspicious. When patients seemed on the road to recovery, he invited them to take meals "with the family." He even interpreted the poetry of patients in his casebook records.[22]

But, within a few years, as both men were confronted with increasing numbers of patients, their ability to spend this time with their charges diminished and all pretenses of family care, and even the rhetoric, disappeared. As Rockwell's patient numbers reached over two hundred, his remarks on patients became less frequent and less discriminating; he slipped into noting the behavior of most patients as merely "excited," for instance. By the time Woodward left Worcester, his average patient population had risen to well over 300, and he frequently felt put off by the "vulgar" and "abusive" behavior of many of them. For both of these men, and for most of their colleagues, that careful attention to the individual patient, the model of family care, and the exercise of "personal influence" was no longer possible. They found themselves increasingly involved in the administrative affairs of their growing hospitals.[23]

Since moral treatment was essentially a system of management of the total life of the patient, it worked best with small patient populations. Its success, however, brought increasing numbers of patients, and the moral therapists continued to try to apply their principles of moral treatment to all their new patients. The intricacies of scheduling the day's activities, finding space, providing funds, and overseeing implementation of the program for hundreds of patients promised to be a herculean task, but one they were willing to tackle.

Adhering to their ideals, moral therapists shaped every detail of the plan while trying to keep the patient's benefit in mind. A "wholesome and nutritious diet" was crucial, for instance, because the superintendents wanted to supplant the "long category of medicines which have sometimes been employed" with the patients before they reached the asylum.[24] These superintendents had regularly received patients who had been subjected to "bleeding and powerful cathartics," a multitude of remedies ranging from emetics to "antispasmodics, ether, castor, assafetida, oil of amber," or a "varied round of stimulants, tonics, [and] narcotics."[25] From the superintendents' point of view, a good diet both helped the patients to be satisfied with the institution and contributed to their therapy because it induced "sleep at night and quiet by day."[26] Besides the concerns about overseeing the purchase of food supplies from local merchants, providing some produce from the asylum grounds, and watching economies of scale, the superintendents had to be concerned on a daily basis with the balancing of the nutritional needs of the general patient population with individual needs for special diets and medications.

Scheduling recreational activities and occupational therapy was equally complicated. Superintendents obtained ministers willing to conduct religious services and guests to read poetry or to discourse on suitable subjects. They scheduled the day to provide opportunities for carriage or sleigh rides, excursions outside the grounds, and gatherings of patients for billiards, chess, checkers, ball playing, or singing, dancing, and reading. Providing both the space for the activities and the money for the purchase of billiard tables or books for the library meant negotiating with boards of trustees, legislators, or private donors. Crucial to the therapeutic value of these activities were the superintendents' decisions about which patients would benefit from them. Similar issues of scheduling, space, money, and judgments about the therapeutic value of patients' labor consumed their time and energies. Occupational therapy, like the other activities, "promote[d] health, induce[d] sleep, favour[ed] self-control, satisfie[d] the individual of the confidence reposed in him by the officers of the institution, and produce[d] quiet and contentment."[27] A careful balancing and smooth functioning of all these components of moral treatment, the psychiatrists believed, contributed to the mental health of all their hundreds of patients.

Almost imperceptibly, moral therapists moved from being the

confidantes of individual patients to being managers of the institutional life of the entire patient body. At first, they tried to balance the two roles. William Awl was most "at home" in the "halls amongst" his patients, but enjoyed "giving directions" from his office. Thomas Kirkbride ritually attended the weekly tea parties of his patients long after he stopped his daily visits to the wards. The truth of the matter was that because "a large portion" of his time was "unavoidably taken up by consultations in reference to the hospital and patients," Kirkbride had to admit that administration was the "most profitable mode" in which he could be "employed for the hospital."[28] Like Kirkbride, most moral therapists became managers of their asylums.

It was no less essential a function. A steward who wanted to save money by purchasing inferior food supplies was as much of a problem in their scheme of things as the legislator who begrudged the inmates carriages for excursions, books for the library, or billiard tables for afternoon diversions. A matron who bought shoddy material for clothing meant the asylum and its superintendent risked the complaints of patients' families about neglect. The asylum farmer who was overly concerned about production easily missed the point of the therapeutic value of labor. Attendants who left patients on their own, even for a moment, created situations in which patients might injure themselves, "elope," or commit suicide. And a sympathetic trustee who refused to enforce the superintendent's prescriptions of labor for a patient undermined the doctor's ability to cure.

Unable to see every patient themselves, the superintendents realized that they had to manage every employee who came into contact with the patients so that their plan of moral therapy would still benefit each patient. To accomplish this, they needed the authority to manage the total environment of the asylum. Given the expansion of hospital administration, in 1853 the association insisted that only with a medical superintendent who had "entire control of the medical, moral and dietetic treatment of the patients" and the "general supervision and direction of every department of the institution" could the asylum continue to promise curative treatment.[29] The office of the medical superintendent emerged as the keystone of their plan; the medical superintendent would hold together all the complexity of administering moral treatment for hundreds of patients within the asylum walls.

Through these official actions on architecture in 1851 and on organization in 1853, the association set up the ideals for the asylum and its internal order. These were policy decisions and provoked little or no debate at the meetings. The consensus over the propositions, however, hid many of the real difficulties of implementing policy.

Asylum Control and the Medical Superintendent: The Reality

Thomas Kirkbride represented the ideal. His ideas had helped forge the models, and he had precisely the level of authority in his hospital for which the association had called. Adamant about his possession of complete authority, Kirkbride nevertheless believed that, once having that authority, he would be unlikely to have to exercise it. The mere "knowledge of its existence" by the staff would prevent their "wrangling" and "secure regularity, good order, and an efficient discipline" in the asylum. But in reality, Kirkbride did not leave it at that. As Nancy Tomes has found, he not only created "supporting roles for the various necessary personnel" in the therapeutic process; he also subtly manipulated patients' attitudes and behavior.[30]

He turned over the routine treatment of the patients to his assistant physicians, frequently consulted with them, and gave them advice on the handling of difficult cases. And for most, he encouraged their professional aspirations and sometimes actively helped them to move on to their own superintendencies. Giving his assistants an increased sense of their importance in the hospital enhanced their commitment to the higher aims of the asylum and secured their close attention to the details of moral treatment.

Because ward attendants were in the hourly presence of the patients, their job was demanding, and Kirkbride knew they were the members of the staff who were most likely to have difficulties with the patients. Kirkbride paid special attention to these attendants. He carefully selected the candidates for the position himself, personally instructed them in their duties, and supervised their work. He understood the tension inherent in the job and showed sympathy when some patients, with their "lying representations," wrongfully accused attendants of misdeeds. He also understood that, no matter how faithful to their duties attendants were, accidents occurred. He always investigated the circumstances and never summarily dismissed a good and faithful attendant. His attendants generally responded to Kirkbride's sense of fairness with cooperation in the smooth running of the asylum.

With the patients, Kirkbride was even more ingenuous because he believed that they had to participate in their own recovery. Kirkbride used a method that all superintendents employed; he moved patients between wards. Those who reached the first or second wards knew that their status within the hospital and their mental health had improved. Kirkbride and his assistants also noted the amount of time patients spent in the ward parlors as a sign of their greater efforts to change their behavior. Those who spent too much time in the halls promenading or alone in their rooms were rewarded less. Kirkbride rewarded those patients who exercised a good influence on others, encouraged friendships among patients, and invited some to the social occasions attended by the officers and their families. While a bare recital of these methods conveys an atmosphere of manipulation and repression, Kirkbride believed this reward system hastened his patients' progress.

In the first years of his superintendency of the Pennsylvania Hospital for the Insane, Kirkbride personally worked hard with his individual patients to help them regain mental health. He spent considerable time in conversation with patients, first to convince them that the hospital was the best place for them and that their families had acted wisely in committing them. Then Kirkbride persuaded the patients to trust him; he talked to them about their thoughts and feelings and brought them to the point of admitting their delusions. He insisted that only the patients could resist their own insane impulses, gave them advice about the joys of a regular life, and rewarded their efforts to reform their behavior by granting them privileges like access to the grounds or excursions into town.

Clearly, Kirkbride's was an all-encompassing plan. But he could carry it off because he did have the ideal amount of authority vested in him as superintendent. He could, and did, discharge unsatisfactory stewards, matrons, or attendants and dismissed (or pressured to resign) assistant physicians who did not live up to his expectations. His directives were law within the asylum, and, whether he had to exercise power explicitly or not, he did not have to worry about having it.

Without that kind of authority, the successful implementation of moral treatment was less certain. The tenuous position of the resident physician at the Bloomingdale Asylum, for instance, was well known throughout the profession. At Bloomingdale, the steward exercised the powers of a superintendent, the board of managers regularly interfered in the governance of the institution, and the resident physician only prescribed moral and medical treatment.[31]

Pliny Earle served as resident physician at Bloomingdale from 1844 to 1849. Fresh from four years' experience as an assistant physician at Friends', Earle was anxious to implement his ideas about moral therapy. With the cooperation of the board of managers, he eliminated the use of most mechanical restraints, introduced the keeping of case records, increased the number of attendants and raised their salaries, established a school for the patients, built a bowling alley and improved the conservatory for them, and wrote a guide for attendants that remained unchanged for fifty years. But the managers had no sympathy for one of Earle's crucial plans; they refused to allow him to force their middle-class patients to participate in the manual labor program.[32]

In his graduating thesis, Earle had stressed the necessity of labor in the curative process. He remained wedded to the principle that manual labor was the "most potent curative means" and bemoaned that it was not required of a patient "without his cheerful volition." Earle complained that "drugs and medicine may be forced upon a patient" until the patient became a "perfect apothecary's shop," but "an attempt to force him to the

genial, wholesome, and curative exercise of manual labor" was
seen by some as an "outrage upon humanity." Despite his arguments, the managers refused to enforce his directives, and Earle,
finding the situation intolerable, resigned his post at Bloomingdale in 1849.[33]

Few men before Earle stayed more than a year or two, and
Charles Nichols, Earle's successor, remained only three. Nichols
did not think that enough changes could be made even in another five years "to warrant one in staking the value of a farthing
upon it" and told Kirkbride, "You have no idea how queerly
things are managed here." He thought "it would be cruel to advise" a colleague to go to Bloomingdale. Isaac Ray told Dorothea
Dix that Nichols "should unite with Earle & Wilson [Earle's
predecessor] in a manifesto to the public, setting forth the state
of things at that institution."[34]

Meanwhile Earle went off to Europe, visiting thirteen asylums
and making careful notes on the use of manual labor. Returning
to the States, he settled in at his family home in Leicester, Massachusetts. Earle was certain that his devotion to moral therapy
and his reputation as an efficient administrator would bring him
new offers. But for fifteen years, none came. Earle's professional
arrogance prevented him from actively seeking the help of his
colleagues. He created such an image of lack of interest that
many referred to him as the "monk of Leicester" and presumed
that he "did not consider [himself] as at all open to any calls to
re-engage in the superintendence of any insane hospital."[35] His
friends were wrong. In the early 1860s Earle finally overcame his
self-defeating pride and agreed to take the superintendency of
the Northampton State Lunatic Hospital in Massachusetts, although he refused to be "a *candidate,* for the place, in competition with others."[36] Earle became medical superintendent and
treasurer of the hospital in 1864. At last he had obtained a post
that "delegated the sole administrative power, both within-doors
and without, to the superintendent." Still smarting from his long
hiatus, Earle doggedly implemented every aspect of moral therapy. He systematically managed the hospital from the mowing
of the lawns to gaining the "confidence, respect, and affection"
of the patients, but he paid special attention to occupational

therapy. The laundry, kitchen, sewing room, bakery, and boiler room buzzed with the activity of the patients. Inmates kept the roads and walks in good order and cultivated the extensive farmlands. Within four years, the asylum was out of debt and recorded an annual surplus for the remainder of Earle's administration.[37]

It was not long before other superintendents praised Northampton as the *"Model Hospital* of American State Institutions." They hailed Earle's annual reports as "out of sight, the ablest and most satisfactory," and sought his opinions because "in all the Union there [was] no man on whose utterances" others dwelt "with so great confidence." But the greatest triumph for Earle was symbolized by Isaac Ray's hope that Earle would "neglect no opportunity to let Superintendents" who visited him "see what can be done" if the occupation of patients formed a "prominent part" of the management of an asylum. Earle proved, finally, that as a medical superintendent with full authority, he could exercise his "many gifts" and use his "wonderful faculty of knowing how to do it and *doing* it."[38]

The Consequences of a Weak Superintendent

Sometimes the issue of the superintendent's authority was settled when the man in the position had a strong and forceful personality. Francis Stribling of the Western Lunatic Hospital in Virginia did; John Galt of the Eastern Lunatic Hospital in the same state did not. John Galt, as Norman Dain has described him, was "a gentle, scholarly person with little administrative ability and not much self-confidence." As a young man, Galt had shown great promise as a physician, but his sister had worried that he would fail because of his "want of *proper confidence."* Galt understood this about himself and remarked upon his propensity for "reserve and solitariness."[39]

Galt assumed the superintendency of the Eastern Lunatic Hospital at Williamsburg on his father's death and inherited a board of directors accustomed to admitting and discharging patients, hiring and firing staff, and generally conducting a good part of the routine administration of the asylum. For the next twenty years, this introspective and mild-mannered superintendent suffered the situation.

Like others new to the specialty, Galt had traveled to the North to learn from his more experienced colleagues. He adopted their ideas about a good staff, the classification of patients, and recreational and occupational therapy. But Galt remained hampered by his situation at Williamsburg. His board of directors regularly granted him increased authority and then withdrew it. For instance, in 1847 they gave him the power to appoint the subordinate officers of the institution but rescinded it in 1850. And in 1859 they allowed him to appoint the gatekeeper, changing their minds a year later. Galt finally gave up and even refused to exercise authority when the board granted it to him in emergency situations.

For all intents and purposes, in the 1850s Galt withdrew from the hospital. He lived off the premises and worried that he ought "to busy [himself] about the Asylum & Asylum matters." His asylum functioned less than ideally. The staff and their families lived in rooms meant for patients and used the asylum's cook to serve them; staff members had bitter disputes with one another; and some developed problems with alcoholism. As Dain has noted, Galt's inability to manage the asylum in an effective manner resulted in "lowered staff morale," and the patients suffered because of "deficiencies in food, clothing, and upkeep of buildings and grounds."[40]

The boards of directors at both the Eastern and Western asylums had the same kind of authority, but by sheer force of personality Francis Stribling exercised much more control over his asylum than Galt ever managed. Stribling was outgoing, self-assured, and well-versed in political realities. For instance, in the dispute over the 1841 law that threatened to redistrict the state to force Stribling to take more of the less desirable, chronically ill patients, Stribling did everything right. He invited legislators to his asylum so that they could see firsthand his plan of operation and sent them his annual reports to verify his success at curative treatment. He wrote letters to them, performed services for them, and made friends with many. Stribling was not only a better administrator than Galt; he was also a better politician.

Stribling later extended his network of support by turning to the Association of Medical Superintendents. Both Stribling and Galt had participated in the founding of the association, but Galt's behavior, even with his colleagues, was true to form. He frequently felt inferior, sometimes acted in a rude manner, and was so concerned with his health that, even when attending meetings, he often absented himself from the sessions. Generally, he felt "social companionship tends to break in upon habitual observance requisite for health."[41] Furthermore, although he practiced moral treatment at Williamsburg, he was developing ideas about its implementation that would eventually diverge from those of the association as a body.[42]

While he attended, all went well, but by 1853 Galt had fallen from grace with his colleagues. He had often leaned toward positions unpopular with them, and the association members thought they had exhibited a long-suffering patience with him from the early years. A prolific writer, Galt, in an overview of Continental psychiatric practices in 1846, glorified the advances of his transatlantic colleagues in their repudiation of patient restraints.[43] Given the association's 1844 stand that the "attempt to abandon entirely the use of all means of personal restraint is not sanctioned by the true interests of the insane," Galt's promotion of nonrestraint was impolitic.[44] He tapped an issue of increasing sensitivity with his American associates, who, although always maintaining their sense of obligation especially to their British predecessors, were growing weary of the frequent, and sometimes odious, comparisons made with them.

And then, in 1850, in an essay, "On the Organization of Asylums for the Insane," Galt advocated that each asylum have a consulting or visiting physician. Although he answered all arguments about an apparent division of authority within the institution and the possibility of the "growth of cabals and intrigues against the superintendent," he did not convince the association members that their positions of control would remain untouched.[45] Having given up attending meetings, he sent two papers in 1853 containing suggestions based on the English practices of allowing the public to tour asylums and of placing faith in patients' promises of good behavior. The members condemned

Galt's promotion of open visitation as "retrogressive," adding that everything else he recommended had been "adopted and practiced in every institution making any pretensions to respectability in this country." They then summarily dismissed pledges of the insane on the ground that the revered Woodward had once placed great trust in these promises but later found them useless.[46] So much for Galt's adulation of the British.

But Galt persisted. In an 1855 article in their journal, he once again cited European examples—the farm of St. Anne at Bicêtre and the village at Gheel in Belgium. The telling blow this time was not the European reference but the very nature of treatment at these places. Galt praised both asylums because they were decentralized, with patients living with individual families and working in the communities.[47] To buttress his argument, he described New England institutions as "mere prison houses" and claimed that some of the association members were mere "tinkers of gas-pipes," contributing "absolutely nothing" in the way of even "one new principle in the government of those laboring under mental alienation."[48]

Galt's depictions offended the association members, and they spent an entire morning at their meeting that year defending themselves and condemning Galt. D. T. Brown wondered why Galt had not been restrained "either by *esprit du corps* or by literary comity" and delivered an eloquent tribute to his older colleagues under attack. He spoke of them as "men who have labored long and earnestly in their holy mission" and hailed them as the "authorities of psychological medicine in America." Passionately, he proclaimed, "They are our boast, as they are our guides." Nichols reviewed the work of Kirkbride, Ray, Bell, Earle, and Jarvis and remarked that even at that he "did not pretend to have recited a tithe" of their accomplishments.[49]

Member after member spoke out against the article and its author. And already, in private, Galt had suffered both denunciation as "a 'windmill'—well enough to let alone" and blame for bringing disrepute on the entire American profession if his remarks were "picked up" by the "London and Paris psychological journals."[50] Never again did Galt participate, even in absentia, in the activities of the association. The condemnatory sentiment dominated the association, and Galt's alienation was complete.

Only Edward Fisher of North Carolina and Joseph Workman of Toronto expressed surprise at the outburst. Fisher wondered if it was not a bit ungentlemanly to attack Galt in his absence, and Workman thought the New Englanders "rather thin-skinned," since even they acknowledged that their asylums were "very far short of perfection."[51] Fisher and Workman were newcomers and had missed the point. Beneath the condemnatory sentiment expressed against Galt lay the members' discomfort with Galt's advocacy of decentralization. Without a centralized and tightly controlled organization commanded by the medical superintendent, as Galt's own experience vividly illustrated, patients suffered, the asylum fell into the hands of incompetents, and the entire profession's reputation was at risk. For these psychiatrists, the authoritarian medical superintendent was the very heart of American asylum administration.

Elevating their positions as asylum administrators served their personal needs; many of these men had found their niche in the medical world by taking care of the insane. It was the answer as well for acting out their deep commitment to benevolent interests; as asylum doctors, only they fully understood the intricacies of moral therapy, the promise of health for their patients, and the ultimate benefits to American society that a carefully coordinated plan of treatment for the insane held. And the exalting of the role of medical superintendent, of course, served their associational goals; it was precisely this recognition of their expertise that they had sought in choosing to organize as the medical superintendents of institutions for the insane.

Individual doctors had exercised the authority vested in them as medical superintendents with ingenuity and sensitivity, but as a group they had strengthened their positions by working out the rationale for the necessity of that broad authority. It remained for them to use the platform of their association and the model of their asylums to publicize their competence and gain public sanction for their role.

6 Selling the Profession

Our principal object in this report will be to enable the people of this State, and especially all those who have friends at this Asylum, or are proposing to commit insane relatives to our care, to know in what manner such unfortunate persons are treated. We fear that many have erroneous views respecting the management of lunatic asylums.

Amariah Brigham
1845

In 1844 the "Original Thirteen" had only speculated about the "good" that would come to their "cause," but by 1861 their efforts had given such "character to the Association," that its "usefulness" to them was "steadily on the increase."[1] This rising sense of power had been the result of the members' own handiwork. As we have seen, they paid close attention to the mechanics of organization to bring about consensus, and at the same time they kept control in the hands of right-thinking men. Using their association to create policy about the best way to treat the insane, they stamped that policy with a particularly American characteristic by vesting autonomy in themselves as medical superintendents.

While juggling organizational concerns and policy decisions, they never lost sight of the need to maintain the good reputation of their organization, to achieve broad acknowledgment of their expertise as medical specialists, and to minimize the effects of negative images of their asylums and their profession. In 1845, Amariah Brigham was still using his annual report to assuage fears about asylum life and to disseminate optimism about the fate of the insane, but he and the others quickly came to realize the potential of their association as a vehicle for those very public relations purposes. Especially through its annual meetings, the association grasped every opportunity to correct "erroneous views" and to enlighten the public about the "management of lunatic asylums."[2] Their construction of a positive public image regarding complex issues from what to call asylums to monitoring suspect practices within some of their asylums and censoring maverick colleagues consumed much of their energy.

Public Relations: From Individual Efforts to Organizational Channels

As individual administrators, they had been accustomed to reaching out to the public through their annual reports in order to promote the good work done in their institutions, stress the necessity of funds, and warn of the consequences of delay and medical quackery. The consistency of their comments is remarkable, as is their recognition of the importance of their message to the public. Amariah Brigham, for instance, fearing those "many" who held "erroneous views," meticulously enumerated the visits of the overseeing managers, explained the care taken to supervise legal confinement procedures, and assured his readers that the resident officers not only lived on the premises with their families but had "no other business" nor "any interest in the pay of patients." Isaac Ray conveyed his deep concern for the "personal feelings" of his patients and their families and assured them that even chronic cases "generally obtained the benefits of these institutions." Even governing boards, whose comments were part of every annual report, sometimes expressed strong sentiments. In 1841 the trustees of the Maine Insane Asylum bemoaned the propensity of some to seek help outside that offered by the asylum and attacked the misguided treatment of "vegetable doctors" and "homeopathists." These remedies produced nothing but "mischievous consequences" and a "higher grade of mental hallucinations," and the trustees predicted the dire result of a "more tardy recovery," or none at all, if hospitalization were delayed.[3] From the beginning, then, each man had been his own public relations agent. These early appeals made the transferring of the principles of public relations to the purposes of a national organization an easy and natural move for the psychiatrists.

Having once established that national organization, the psychiatrists adopted a number of techniques to shape public reactions. Amariah Brigham's *American Journal of Insanity,* although only months old, became their first vehicle for publicity. Brigham published the journal at "heavy pecuniary expense" to himself but opened its pages to his colleagues, soliciting their scholarly contributions and reciprocally making available to them the ideas of British and European practitioners through reprints, abstracts, and translations.[4] In 1844, Brigham's journal announced the news of the founding of the Association of Medical Superintendents of American Institutions for the Insane. And the superintendents wasted no time in proclaiming the birth of their organization, their goals, and their intent to manage the specialty to the rest of the medical world through the pages of other journals. Thomas Kirkbride, for one, was delighted at all this activity because he felt it gave "character" to the association.[5]

Because they now had an organizational base, they received increased press coverage, and, to assure accurate and detailed reporting, the association hired a phonographer to record the proceedings of their conventions. They welcomed, as well, the reporters sent to observe their meetings because newspapers published accounts of those meetings, reported judgments about local asylums, and reprinted excerpts of articles psychiatrists wrote for their own journal and for other medical journals. And as state institutions became the norm, editors followed more closely the legislative debates and the opening of new asylums. In a number of cases, newspapers even printed the full text of the annual reports of the local asylum.[6]

While delighted with this kind of publicity and their own emergence as public figures, the psychiatrists became increasingly self-conscious about shaping their public image, and discussions about the power of words to shape impressions of their work became regular subjects of debate at annual meetings. At various times they voiced their objections to such terms as *moonstruck, madhouse, keeper, cell, asylum,* and *retreat* because they wanted their image to reflect none of the "most painful associations" of the past, which were "unworthy of the profession and the progress of the age." Nor did they want any mistaken connection with such unpopular institutions as the "poor house, prison, or small pox hospital." But it was hard to get agreement. On the one hand, Francis Stribling of Staunton objected to *hospital* because in his state a hospital was a "resort for paupers, the outcast, friendless, and those unable to take care of themselves from any cause." He argued that "nothing would be more revolting to the feelings of a Virginian than to be taken to an institution with such a name." On the other hand, James Athon countered that *asylum* meant "poor house" in Indiana and that the people preferred "hospital for the insane." Unable to reconcile their differences after protracted discussion, they realized finally that the real issue was one of overcoming local prejudices and stipulated that the name of every institution should conform to the "tastes of the community" in which it was located.[7] Ordinarily a group striving for national recognition could not afford to give in to local, and potentially divisive, biases. But for each psychiatrist, the larger good of provoking a sympathetic response from his audience and the need to project the best possible image of his asylum outweighed, in this case, mere principled conformity.

Moving toward the idea of banishing the most objectionable terms from the "nomenclature of the profession," they vowed to work toward a uniformity of language to squelch the possibility of misinformation reaching the public. They were not entirely successful because disease classification and causation were matters of conjecture throughout most of the nineteenth century. Psychiatrists lacked a systematic explanation for mental illness and consequently failed to reach accord, but they recognized the need to develop a professional language aimed at clarifying their role, and they never ceased to try.[8]

This increasing concern with disease nomenclature and dis-

cussions about institutional designations spilled over into a growing uneasiness with the ways in which they had earlier described
themselves and their profession. The more seriously they took
themselves, the more careful they became about descriptions. As
long as someone like Nehemiah Cutter, an elderly founder, was
considered "curious" and "great 'on Saturday nights,'" other
medical superintendents cited, with tongue in cheek, his depic-
tion of asylum administration as the "crazy business."[9] No one
else took credit for any similarly pithy and slightly outlandish
statements. At that, Cutter's phrase was one reserved for private
correspondence between close friends; it was not quoted in public. Even the term "mad doctors" or "mads" was used sparingly
and usually in an attempt at lightheartedness. Rather, psychiatrists settled on "medical superintendents," "members of the Association," or "brethren" to describe themselves and, aware of
their increasing professional uniqueness and importance, on
"branch of the profession" or "specialty" to designate their realm
of work.[10] As they emerged from near oblivion as isolated practitioners to a realization of their professional worth as a group,
their preciosity of language became one of their many means to
alert the public to their growing significance and status.

They were especially wary of the possibility that misdiagnosis
or unintentional maltreatment of the insane by general practitioners might reflect unfavorably upon their profession. When
D. T. Brown, as early as 1854, suggested setting up a committee
to act as a clearinghouse for texts on the treatment of the mentally ill, the association members endorsed the idea enthusiasti-
cally. Fully appreciating the necessity of disseminating accurate
information to the public, they urged doctors to consult their
own psychiatric journal for the best guidance and were generous
with praise for those like Andrew McFarland who had made arrangements to reproduce the Illinois State Hospital reports in
large numbers and distribute them throughout the state. Pliny
Earle, whose extensive analyses of all annual reports appeared
in the prestigious *American Journal of Medical Science* and the
influential and widely read British psychiatric journal of Forbes
Winslow, also received their commendation.[11]

By 1857 the association was ready to take full charge of its own publicity by sending copies of "all their past and future reports" to libraries for "permanent preservation." An association committee, headed by Edward Jarvis, enlisted the aid of the Smithsonian Institution to compile a list of depositories. The association then sent dozens of volumes of asylum annual reports to state historical societies and state, university, college, and city libraries; in short they willingly reached out to anyone needing information. "Managers, legislators, and all interested in 'human suffering'" received copies, as did atheneums, mercantile and mechanics' libraries, the "German Library" in places like Belleville, Illinois, and the "Young Men's Associations" in states as far-flung as Wisconsin and Michigan.[12] Clearly, no matter what social class or stage of life one experienced, insanity could strike, and the members of the Association of Medical Superintendents had news of the best help at hand. While the reports served as vehicles for publicity about treatment, this directed effort to make information available to the contemporary reading public was in truth the capstone of a long campaign to elevate the recognition of the association itself as well.

Annual Meetings and the Subtleties of Shaping Public Images

Many of the association members' convention presentations or discussions were indirectly linked to the issue of shaping public reaction. Construction plans and descriptions of administrative organization intended for the information of members served to edify the public as well. Papers promoting the perfection of moral treatment, while crucial for the continuing effectiveness of their work, also increased the esteem of the psychiatrists and their association in the eyes of their public.[13]

Papers presented on the relationship between psychiatry and law, for instance, were frequent subjects for discussion both because insanity raised a variety of legal issues not yet addressed and because legal decisions not only took place in the public forum of the courts but received newspaper coverage as well. As psychiatrists developed a distinct field, questions about admission procedures became increasingly important. Confinement, if man-

dated by the courts, relieved asylum superintendents of the legal
responsibility of institutionalization because most magistrates and
judges (even before compelled by statute) acted only after receiving affidavits from at least two physicians of a person's incom-
petency or potential danger to self or community. But the class
of patients committed by relatives, friends, or guardians (the most
common type of admitting agents in this era) raised different
questions, and the practice often resulted in accusations of slip-
shod and malevolent commitment practices. In neither case,
moreover, was there any recognition, administratively or judi-
cially, of the suspension of the legal and civil rights of the incarcerated patients. A crucial and knotty problem in medical
jurisprudence and one puzzled over most notably by the best and
most informed legal mind of the profession, Isaac Ray, it was
nevertheless also a potentially explosive issue in terms of professional image and public relations.[14]

Realizing their vulnerability to charges of "kidnapping" and
forcibly administering "poisonous medicines," the association
created an *ad hoc* committee to address the problem at the first
meeting in 1844. Other men, like John Galt, William Stokes, and
Luther Bell, joined Ray in struggling with the issue through the
1850s.[15] It was not until 1868, however, when the number of attacks had increased and the publicity had intensified to intolerable levels, that the association itself managed to agree on a
policy and tried to exert organized pressure on each state to adopt
uniform regulations to set principles of confinement, clarify
standards for guardianship, and establish procedures for review-
ing cases.[16] Their campaign to persuade state legislatures to implement their policy moved at a snail's pace; nevertheless, for
three decades they had worked at it because they believed a uniform code would remove misunderstandings on the part of the
public about institutional practices of commitment.

Involvement in assessing responsibility in criminal cases and
in resolving validity in will and contract cases stemmed from
psychiatrists' initial interests in the legalities of commitment as
well as from the public's increasing recognition of their specialty.
Catapulted into public view through their increasing appear-
ances in court, men like Ray, Bell, and Stokes worked to educate

their colleagues about the intricacies of the courts and psychiatric experts. Speaking from considerable experience, Ray conceded that the testimony of the expert was necessary but often handled unsatisfactorily by the judicial system. Thus he cautioned his associates to "be on guard" against lawyers' propensities for "supposing causes" to draw out the witness in support of their clients and their lack of precise language in questioning, which often led to "wrong impressions." Also, lawyers' attempts to create an atmosphere of "cordiality and fellow-feeling" might endanger the independence of the witness and, consequently, the credibility not only of the expert himself, but of the entire profession. A last "favorite maneuver of counsel," Ray warned, was to ask for a definition of insanity, and the witness should be well prepared, because the lawyer's object was not to throw any light on the case but merely "to perplex and embarrass" the psychiatric expert.[17] Although deeply concerned about the relationship between the law and the determination of insanity, Ray hoped above all that his colleagues would preserve a dignified and professional image whenever called upon to testify.

Ray often emerged as the spokesman for the association members in their concern about their public image. One of the few intellectuals of the group, he lost no time in getting to the heart of the matter of how asylum administrators could maintain "their place in the popular estimation." Admitting that "no class of charities" had obtained "so strong a hold on the public sympathies" as the profession's system of therapeutics, Ray reminded his colleagues that because some people did not know much about the inner workings of asylums they were ready to believe that cruel and harsh treatment, abusive therapy, neglect, enforced isolation, and questionable commitment procedures were the lot of the institutionalized insane. Worried about this "strong undercurrent" of public "bad feelings" and even "fierce hostility," he found no difficulty in identifying sources. The tales of patients, especially those discharged only "partially restored," and complaints of friends of inmates who never would be satisfied that enough had been done accounted for some charges. But Ray urged his fellow administrators to look to themselves; real abuses existed in some of their hospitals. He railed against the debilitating effects of political appointees on boards of trustees, amateurs consulted about the location and construction of institutions, and limited budgets. These were, unfortunately, beyond the control of the individual psychiatrist, Ray admitted. The superintendent, however, did have the upper hand within the asylum. He should manage the entire staff, control policy regarding visitation and public purview, and work out his own commitment to his vocation. If he did not, Ray warned, he may have "mistaken his calling" and thus would weaken the profession itself by his failure to gain that "public confidence which ought to be as the very breath of his nostrils."[18]

The other members generally shared Ray's views about counteracting "scandalous gossip" and gaining public confidence. Yet frequently they sought to strike a balance between concern over their patients' welfare and the seemliness of discussing some issues in public. S. Hanbury Smith's administration at the Ohio Lunatic Asylum is a case in point. Immediately following Ray's presentation, the members asked Smith, the successor to William Awl, to explain his part in arousing public indignation in Ohio. Although his appointment had been unpopular in Ohio, a state beleaguered by partisan politics, Smith quickly became the darling of the association meeting in 1851. He served on five committees, read a paper for the absent Galt, and at every session offered suggestions and resolutions. From praising Kirkbride as outgoing secretary to initiating a move to publish the transactions of the association with a history of its "rise and progress" to commending Curwen's manual for attendants, Smith in his eagerness and commitment seemed the consummate professional.[19]

Even in his first annual report, Smith carefully cited all the most prominent members of the association to support his own views on moral treatment and institutional administration. He spoke of Awl's regime as the institution's "genesis" and of his own as a "new epoch," a time for further development. Much less successful at manipulating the legislature than Awl had been, in the following year he moved from descriptions of needed improvements to diatribes about "wants and deficiencies." A subtle shift in language became a major tactical error for Smith. Since his earlier suggestions had been ignored by the legislature, he graphically described the consequences of allowing structural defects to continue uncorrected. His account of water freezing in pipes only ten feet from hot air flues led many to believe that the health of patients had been impaired severely, as Smith himself stated, and some to surmise that patients might have frozen to death. Smith made it clear that these conditions had existed since the opening of the asylum, and his accusations, which he intended as a condemnation of the niggardliness of Ohioans and their legislators, were also an attack on the Awl administration.[20] Smith was calling into question the reputation of one of the most prestigious psychiatrists of the day; William Awl was one of the founders and their most recent president. The association found this hard to take. But their dismay went even deeper. In keeping with their own idea about the power of annual reports for informing the public, Smith's explicit description of grievances, no matter how well intentioned, was uncalled for and out of place. The members had little sympathy for him.

Later, Smith wrote a long, complaining defense of himself to Kirkbride, blaming his troubles on the "secret, but increasing efforts" of his predecessors to damage his reputation, a legislative reorganization of all state charity institutions, and a board that was so "savage" at their own "sorry" treatment that they would not "move one peg" to vindicate him. He hoped Kirkbride would help him to "look for a place."[21] Apparently unaware of the view his colleagues took of his methods, Smith, after he was fired from the Ohio Lunatic Asylum position, found no other post. Although the members had abhorred the conditions Smith portrayed, they had felt he simply had been too accusatory, and especially too explicit. They feared the potential for harm of such a public airing of deficiencies; it contradicted the image they strove so hard to fashion.

For different reasons, owners of private hospitals also felt the sting of the association's attempts to exercise control over its image. Samuel White and Nehemiah Cutter, private asylum managers, were among the founders, and they, and others like them, were still welcomed in 1848 when George White delivered a paper for his recently deceased father extolling the unique advantages of private institutional practice, but hints of uneasiness

existed. Eleven men, representing seven different private establishments, participated at some time in the meetings, but none
ever served as an officer, and only one served on a committee.
Given the ways in which the leadership of the association used
committee assignments to guarantee the loyalties of the members
to the organization, this slighting of the owners of the private
asylums took on even greater import. Moreover, besides George
White's proxy role for his father, only Samuel White, Nehemiah
Cutter, and Edward Jarvis delivered papers.

Jarvis remained on the fringes of the profession, however, because he never received an asylum position. He simply could not
obtain the endorsement of these men whom many already recognized as experts when they sought opinions about the best men
for openings in new hospitals. Nine times Jarvis unsuccessfully
sought a superintendency. In some cases the other candidate was
well known and experienced; in others, he was not. Once Jarvis
opened his little private asylum (largely run by his wife), the
association granted him membership, but, as with other operators
of private asylums, they did not accept him as a full partner.
Meanwhile Jarvis worked out a career for himself as a wide-
ranging theoretician on issues related to the treatment of the
insane. At association meetings he presented his theories about
separate provisions for the criminal insane, the incidence of disease among the "colored population," the apparent increase of
insanity, and the perfection of statistical analysis. The association members listened with "marked attention" to his many
presentations throughout the 1850s, expressed their "entire con-
currence" with his ideas, and praised him for his "extraordinary
care and accuracy."[22] His concerns were theirs, yet Jarvis was
never granted any other participatory role in the organization
beyond a platform for exposing his views. The *Journal* published
his papers, but that was all. Indeed, it was Jarvis's own paper on
"The Proper Functions of Private Institutions or Homes for the
Insane," delivered in 1860, that brought out the real feelings of
the members about small, privately run asylums.

D. T. Brown, who had served in four different large asylums,
initiated the discussion by admitting "that there was a very great
prejudice, on the part of the gentlemen connected with large

institutions, against those of a private character." He thought, though, that private care served the needs of a growing American class consciousness. Brown had little support. A few members hesitantly endorsed private asylums if they met association standards or if they were as good as Jarvis's, but Kirkbride, Rockwell, Butler, Worthington, Buttolph, and Chipley were decidedly opposed to the concept of private institutions. They were as aware, and accepting, of class distinctions as Brown, but they knew they risked running afoul of "popular feeling" if they openly and officially supported such elitist principles. Professionally they feared that private asylums were outside their control. Most, because of their handful of patients, could not offer proper classification of patients, nor could they provide a complete program of moral treatment. Another serious potential problem for the association members was the lack of surveillance that was endemic to such institutions. Any recognition of the legitimacy of such asylums might lead "any unprincipled man or vicious woman" to open houses that would be exploitive of the helpless victims of insanity and their families. There was just too much potential for abuse; not only were private houses exempt from the surveillance of any statutory policing agency, but they were also beyond the reaches of the association sanctions. Not only would patients suffer, but also the odium of the institutional deficiencies would reflect on the reputation of the entire profession. The public made no fine distinctions between hospital types.[23]

Annual Meetings as Vehicles for Correcting "Erroneous Views"

With all their concern about public opinion, it was not simply individual egos that were at stake but rather the effects of adverse publicity on the willingness of patients' families to hospitalize them. Consequently the members of the association remained vigilant about practices or theories that bordered on the heretical or seemed to provoke untoward public attention. The discussion of Thomas Kirkbride's 1853 paper, "On the night care of the insane," is especially illustrative. When Kirkbride called for regular indoor and outdoor night watchmen to guard against fire, the majority agreed; Luther Bell alone objected. Arguing that hiring night watchmen was but a "debt paid to public sentiment" (which was precisely the intent of Kirkbride and others), Bell contended that regular attendants could be taught to sleep lightly enough to be on guard and further pointed out that the presence of such a night employee at his asylum had succeeded only in keeping the "whole house in an uproar" because some patients saw the night watchman's visit as an opportunity to gain attention. But Kirkbride remained unsympathetic to Bell's argument and pointed out that the destruction of the Maine Insane Asylum by fire in the preceding year (in which twenty-seven patients perished) had aroused widespread public outcry about the safety of the insane, a reaction they could ill afford to ignore. Furthermore, he added, the "constant vigilance of attentive persons" hired for night service could, and did, prevent suicides as well. The other association members, recalling the bad publicity resulting from such disasters in their own asylums, ignored Bell's objections and agreed to adopt Kirkbride's policy.[24]

Bell, however, supported Kirkbride and the others on another potentially volatile issue of publicity arising from the same discussion. A few had buttressed the need for night watchmen by citing their presence as useful in discouraging the "filthy habits" of some patients, and the discussion quickly turned to the best method of handling such behavior. Elijah Kendrick of Ohio stunned the group by suggesting the use of "injections of icewater into the rectum" to prevent incontinence and smearing. Immediately, Kirkbride was on his feet objecting to the use of "any means of torture," and Nathan Benedict, Edward Jarvis, and Bell joined him in condemning the barbaric measure. Bell further wished to have it "widely and distinctly known that the views and sentiments of the Association" were "directly and emphatically adverse to any penal or coercionary means being used or permitted" in hospitals for the insane.[25] Disagreement over the means used to prevent fire was one thing, but when it became a question of retrogressive and cruel treatment, Bell, like his colleagues, wanted the public to know precisely where the profession stood.

Controlling the potentially harmful actions of mentally ill patients remained a problem for these doctors. Their plan of moral treatment could not eliminate every occasion that necessitated restraint. And their reassurances about their commitment to benevolent therapy, they realized, did not always satisfy those quick to criticize. Thus, to dissipate as much bad publicity as they could, they endeavored to monitor the use of any device that might be construed as coercive. In 1855 the issue was the unsightliness of the crib-bedstead. Similar in structure to an ordinary baby's crib, it had the addition of a latticework top piece that could be locked over the patient. Designed to prevent their getting out of bed, the contraptions meant that patients could do little but turn over, and even that with considerable strain and difficulty; they could not even sit up. Horace Buttolph, nevertheless, recommended the crib-bedstead as the best form of mechanical restraint. Significantly, Buttolph's suggestion was generally criticized on the ground that such a device would have an adverse effect on visitors, not that restraint itself might be unnecessary or undesirable. The essence of the comments ranged from Charles Nichols's observation that the "crib-bedstead was an ungracious-looking machine" to that of Joseph Workman of Canada who noted that both visitors and fellow patients would feel a "general repugnance toward this means of restraint." Bell thought that the device had such "an ungracious look" that "it would require considerable argument to reconcile friends on a visit to a patient confined in it." Thomas Kirkbride was adamant about the effect of the crib's appearance and raised "great objection to its use." The "moral effect," he felt, was "undoubtedly bad." To illustrate, he recounted his experience when "some distinguished men, members of the medical profession," visited the Pennsylvania Hospital for the Insane. They asked to see "patients in chains" and were told "there were none." When they persisted and asked to see "those in cages, or crib-bedsteds" and received the same negative answer, Kirkbride stated, making his point quite clearly, "they said they had seen them in Utica" and "expected to find them everywhere." "That is the impression," he concluded, "which the cribs make on the friends of the patients, on the patients themselves, and on medical men."26

In 1857 the use of "lodges" or "strong rooms" to isolate trouble-some patients provoked a similar debate. John Tyler of the New Hampshire Asylum for the Insane went to great lengths to defend his use of seclusion. Believing that the appearance of the room was the important issue, he said at Concord they had built rooms for the violent insane: "light commodious, comfortable, elegant, and very strong" ones. George Choate, new head of the Taunton State Hospital in Massachusetts previously notorious for its use of such methods, contended that in New England "strong room" was synonymous with "prison-cell" and he, for one, was convinced that the "moral effect" of seclusion was always bad. James Athon of Indiana agreed and praised Choate for closing down the rooms at the outset of his administration. Edward Jarvis, though, best summed up the underlying objection of unfavorable public reaction, which would be detrimental to the image of humanitarian care they worked so hard to create. While serving on the Massachusetts Commission on Lunacy in 1854, he and others had visited the Taunton State Hospital. One of the commissioners, on leaving the asylum, remarked "I have learnt one thing, that is, what should not be built." The association could not risk flying in the face of such public condemnation, and once again Thomas Kirkbride termed the "lodges" as "obnoxious" and wanted it on record that members should guard against any endorsement of this method of restraint out of respect for both the sensitivities of the patients and the reactions of their friends and relatives.[27]

In keeping with its ideas about appropriate practices and their impact on the public, the association exerted equal vigilance over some of the speculative inquiries of its members. When some members continued to express faith in the use of bleeding or the administration of large and vigorous doses of emetics, the association quickly rebuked them. The venerable Nehemiah Cutter said at one meeting that he liked to administer large doses of medicine "to produce a good shaking up of the system" and thought "that not enough medicine was given at the present day." Kirkbride objected strongly, but the secretary of the association, Charles Nichols, in a parenthetical note to the minutes of the convention, explained that Cutter began his career when "insanity was not exactly the same thing that it is now."[28] Cutter did not need to be rebuked harshly; he was sixty-eight years old, no longer heading even his own little private asylum (which had been burned out years before), and out of the mainstream of professional activity.

Others who dabbled in questionable fads or theories that the association thought smacked of quackery were handled differently. Especially sensitive because of their own earlier encounters with Thomsonianism and other medical practices they deemed quackery and their present efforts to elevate the reputation of institutional psychiatry, the association members tolerated nothing that bordered on charlatanism. When Horace Buttolph presented his paper on phrenology, the members generally rejected his conclusion that the discipline had any connection with psychiatry or could be useful in diagnosis or treatment.[29] Although some of his colleagues had earlier endorsed phrenology, unfortunately for Buttolph, by 1849 they no longer did so. The scientific theories of Franz Joseph Gall and Johann Spurzheim about localized and separate brain functions had been exaggerated and distorted by popular enthusiasts into a pseudoscience of character analysis and behavioral predictability. Gall and Spurzheim were serious scientists; but more ordinary practitioners, frequently in a sideshowlike atmosphere, claimed, for example, that if a particular protrusion of a subject's head aligned with the phrenologists' location of the faculty of "Destructiveness," criminality or manic behavior might be not only explained but predicted.[30] Consequently, the whole subject quickly fell out of grace with the medical and psychiatric professions. The president, William Awl, in his own inimitable fashion, closed the discussion of Buttolph's paper by reciting anecdotes typifying the attitude of the association. He spoke of a man whose head had been examined and who expressed his opinion of the procedure by saying, "it is hard to tell what meat is in the smoke house by putting your hand on the roof." Awl then related his own experience with a "noted blind Phrenologist" who visited the Ohio Lunatic Asylum. At first, Awl had presented himself as a violent patient and, after feeling the contours of his head, the phrenologist "pronounced him deficient in mental development." Later, revealing nothing about their earlier encounter, Awl introduced himself as the hospital superintendent and was examined; "the verdict was essentially different." In 1849, Awl used ridicule; others heatedly disagreed with Buttolph's ideas. Four years later phrenology had fallen into such disrepute with the psychiatrists that only three members, Buttolph, Bell, and T. R. H. Smith, dared support it, and they "appeared to be, however, largely in the minority," according to the secretary—Horace Buttolph himself.[31]

Spiritualism was another professionally suspect subject by the mid-1850s, and the leaders of the association combined tactical leadership, group pressure, and effective censorship to dissociate themselves from the issue. In 1854, Luther Bell, superintendent of Boston's prestigious McLean Asylum and current president of the association, read a paper on "Spiritual Manifestations." There was virtually no response.[32] Many in the association clearly wanted to avoid a subject "so much connected in the public mind with the ridiculous," and after the meeting Kirkbride tried to get Ray and Stribling to intercede with Bell. Fearing the destruction of the "character and usefulness of the Association," he urged Stribling "to be sure to be at Boston next May, as we may want all our strength to keep the Association straight." Imagine his dismay when Nathan Benedict, retired from the New York State Lunatic Asylum and living in Florida, wrote that he had news of the paper and that it was "a great pitty [sic] that Dr. Bell should be engaged in the spirit rapping business!"[33]

Bell persisted and, still irritated by the rebuff, in 1855 expressed his surprise that at "so large a meeting of persons whose lives were spent in investigating the reciprocal influences of mind and body" that "scarcely a single member had given a moment's notice to a topic directly in their paths." Acknowledging that there were many who might inquire, "Quis custodiet ipsos custodes?" if hospital directors discussed spiritual phenomena, he claimed nevertheless that it was their unique duty to do so. There was considerable curiosity about Bell's descriptions of levitating tables, conversations with the dead (even his own brother), alphabetical rappings, and other clairvoyant manifestations but open relief at his emphasis on mental phenomena and his dismissal of any endorsement of spiritual communications. The few who joined the discussion hoped that the phenomenon would be deprived of "much of its power for evil" by divesting it of its "terror" and "mystery," and then, perhaps, they, as professionals, could counteract the "broad-spread epidemic." Only Isaac Ray supported Bell's "courage" in raising "inquiries which other men, from one motive or another," were "careful to avoid." For the most part, skepticism prevailed. Joshua Worthington summed up the opinion of the majority in his terse remark that "he would sooner disbelieve the evidence of his own senses than believe that tables were moved without contact." Half those present were silent, although for men like Kirkbride, Curwen, Rockwell, Athon, T. R. H. Smith, Harlow, and Ranney, this was out of character. They could afford to be silent; their silence was tacit disapproval, and the association had decided beforehand not to publish either of Bell's papers.[34]

As psychiatrists sought explanations for aberrations in mental processes, so early phrenologists devised a way to demonstrate how the mind functioned, and spiritualists (many of them followers of Swedenborg) produced connections between body, mind, soul, and the beyond. In the light of twentieth-century knowledge, one was as unscientific as the other, but for asylum superintendents who took their professionalism quite seriously, popularized phrenology veered too close to fortune-telling and spiritualism to magic.[35] Faculty psychology would contribute to the development of biological determinism and Swedenborgianism to secularism, but these were not the worry of the psychiatrists. Each trend had become for much of the public merely a form of entertainment, and frequently a fraudulent one at that. As psychiatrists saw it, they could not afford to have their specialty connected with such chicanery in the public mind. Promotion of such dubious theories could easily engender ridicule, endangering their role as the acknowledged masters of the psychiatric profession and bringing into question the efficacy of their system of asylum management.

Measures of Success

The superintendents' campaign to create a positive image of
themselves and their asylums worked. There were still a few areas
they could not control, like the occasional exposés, which in-
variably led to investigations. But in these cases the superintendents themselves were usually exonerated as the victims of
unregulated commitment procedures. William Rockwell, for instance, suffered from the attacks of Jackson Vail, an upstate rum-
runner, who wrote a tract about his incarceration at the Vermont
Asylum for the Insane at the hands of his political enemies. Despite Vail's accusation that Rockwell should have seen through
the ruse of his enemies, the legislative investigating committee
chose to dismiss the complainant as a deluded malcontent and to
praise Rockwell's administration and laud the asylum as "highly
honorable and useful to the State and well entitled to the pa-
tronage of the public."[36] There was little the asylum doctors
could do either about the mixing of politics and asylum appointments except to publicize their dissatisfaction. And in the face
of legislators' propensities to build larger and larger hospitals,
the best they usually could manage was to hold the line against
expansion by lobbying. Indeed, a number of them, like William
Awl, Charles Stedman, and Francis Stribling, were quite successful at political arm-twisting and admired by all as "consummate"
politicians.[37]

With these exceptions, their public image was a remarkably
positive one. Regional newspapers like the *Springfield Republican* in Massachusetts and the *Ohio State Journal,* and more local
papers as far-flung as the *Vermont Phoenix,* the *Northampton
Gazette* in Massachusetts, or the *Kalamazoo Gazette* in Michigan
regularly reported news of the asylums, printed articles on insanity written by the states' asylum superintendents, and were
generally sympathetic to the superintendents' appeals for funds.
The editors of the *North American Review,* in their comments
about the annual reports of dozens of asylums in the 1850s,
agreed so completely with the asylum administrators that their
editorials could have passed for the annual reports themselves.
And the *Boston Medical and Surgical Journal* supported the

psychiatrists' ideas about asylums and the role of the superintendent. The journal praised men like John Butler as a "veteran
in the management of lunatics" and one "who is never happier
than when promoting the happiness of others." Similarly, the
journal venerated Bell, Ray, Chandler, Stedman, and others and
frequently carried articles excerpted from the *American Journal
of Insanity*.[38]

Other indicators of their success at promoting their plan of
treatment of the insane abounded. Within their profession, no
man became a medical superintendent without joining the association, and most attended annual meetings with a remarkable
degree of regularity. In whatever city they met, they listened to
city fathers and various other local luminaries praise their work,
and their meetings became so notable that they received more
invitations to visit hospitals and libraries or to meet with civic
groups than they could accept. And while no medical school offered regular courses in the treatment of the insane before 1860,
a number of association members began to receive engagements
to offer short courses on "psychological medicine" at schools like
the Berkshire Medical Institute in Pittsfield, Massachusetts, the
Woodstock Clinical School of Medicine in Vermont, the College
of Physicians and Surgeons in New York, and the College of
Physicians and Surgeons in Baltimore.[39]

There remained always, of course, the problem of maintaining
the fine line between pandering to "public sentiment" and exercising some mastery over their profession when much of their
environment was determined by public policy. Yet they had persisted and succeeded in persuading legislators and others to look
to them as experts. By 1860 no one questioned either the concept
of institutionalization, the legitimacy of moral treatment, or the
state's responsibility to care for the insane. The details of their
plan of asylum design and management were widely adopted,
and the association members passed up no opportunity to high-
light their growing influence. For example, they were delighted
when the planners of the Missouri State Hospital wrote their by-
laws to "correspond with the opinions" of the association "as expressed in their proceedings" of 1851. At other times they joined
in efforts to pressure legislatures to accept their expertise about

the proper plan for asylums. In 1852 the construction committee for the Alabama Insane Hospital appealed to Kirkbride for help and included his reply in their annual report, as did the South Carolina Lunatic Asylum trustees in 1853. And as late as 1860 the *Boston Medical and Surgical Journal* had high praise for the new superintendent of the Northampton State Lunatic Hospital, William Prince. Prince's remarks about the social causes of insanity and the necessity for moral therapy, the journal thought, should "be widely known in the community," if they were not already, and his "important warnings" should be "duly heeded." The Northampton State Lunatic Hospital followed the Kirkbride plan in its architecture and in its internal organization, and Massachusetts was only one of twenty-six states supporting asylums that adhered to the guidelines set by the association.[40]

In the years between 1844 and 1860, American psychiatrists had managed to reach an equilibrium between their professional self-interest and their benevolent concern for patients. As young men, striving for service-oriented careers that would provide them a livelihood and standing in the community, they had been disappointed. There had been little they could do to counteract the competition of irregular practitioners in a vast medical field with no enforceable professional standards or regulations. They had had no special monopoly on cures for the myriad of physical illnesses that afflicted their patients.

Once they switched to psychiatry, it had been a different story. There were few who wanted to take on the arduous and frequently unpleasant duty of dealing with seemingly obstinate cases of insanity. They had moved into a limited and controlable field with attractive prospects for rewards. The asylum correctly managed and the regime of treatment properly implemented could, and did, bring professional good fortune for them. With the asylum at hand and a plan of treatment that they shaped to accent the role of the medical superintendent, his discretionary powers, and his total sway within the asylum walls, they had carved out an area of specialty for themselves.

To procure, to guarantee, and to perpetuate this position of benevolent sovereignty and material well-being, individual asylum administrators had sought collegial support through formal professional association. As their image of each of these institutions—the asylum, the therapeutic plan, the superintendency, and the professional body—took shape, their professional organization, at first a mere umbrella agency, gradually emerged as the underpinning of their careers, their service, and their status. These institutional forms became so intertwined that it was impossible to extricate one from the other, and this first generation of institutional psychiatrists had no desire to weaken any of them. Their profession, the one they themselves had framed, had done well by them—finally.

7 The Demise of the Asylum

I do not see how any reasonably objective view of our mental hospitals today can fail to conclude that they are bankrupt beyond remedy. . . . [They] should be liquidated as rapidly as can be done in an orderly and progressive manner.

Harry C. Solomon
President, American Psychiatric Association
May 1958

Our public facilities are deteriorating physically, clinically, and economically; our chronically ill are either "transinstitutionalized" to nursing homes or deinstitutionalized to our cities' streets.

John A. Talbott
President, American Psychiatric Association
May 1984

From meager beginnings in 1844, the members of the Association of Medical Superintendents of American Institutions for the Insane established and shaped the profession of psychiatry in the United States. These ambitious and well-intentioned men grasped the opportunities offered by the creation of the asylum system and its regime of curative therapy. They reoriented their goals to take advantage of the career opportunity and to exercise their considerable medical skill in serving humanity.

Their drive to gain professional recognition had led them to take responsibility for the care of those whom others found difficult, while their therapeutic institution had offered the public a practical, systematic method of dealing with the mentally ill. Binding their professional identity with their institutional role, the association members regulated the practice of asylum management by formulating policy and urging adherence to it. They passed on their sense of professionalism by preserving the nature of their organization as an exclusive association of expert healers and managers. In the antebellum years their policy statements were virtually the law for the planners of new asylums. As medical superintendents of institutions for the insane, they emerged as the "masters of madness" and their association as a power in asylum medicine and politics.

Their system worked as long as they maintained a united front and as long as the public was willing to accept their policies and hierarchical asylum. Their authority, however, had never been real; it had rested on the deference of states allowing them the autonomy they sought, on the dearth of alternative plans, and on the whims of public support. In the last third of the nineteenth century, as the country struggled with the problems created by massive immigration that seemed to threaten American values, recurrent business cycles that produced sporadic unemployment and labor unrest, and a growing urban population, increased crime rates, and a surplus of dependent peoples, medical superintendents faced a decline in public confidence that undermined both their authority and their autonomy.

While it is not the purpose of this study to examine closely the century after the medical superintendents had created the professional world of American psychiatry, a few highlights of that period after 1860 illustrate why the next major change in attitudes toward the insane consisted of a total rejection of their asylum. The antebellum asylum and the medical superintendent's role survived the century, but the nature of that asylum changed, and economic, social, and professional developments vitiated the authority of the superintendents. As the public redefined insanity to include a whole range of "inconvenient" people, Americans began to view asylums more as custodial than as therapeutic institutions. Attempts to deal with the more unfortunate victims of an industrializing nation, moreover, led some to look to the state (and ultimately the federal government) rather than the medical superintendents for solutions that were efficient and, especially, economical. Meanwhile, developments in psychiatry outside the asylums raised questions about the competency of asylum doctors and, eventually, led a later generation of association members to challenge the concept of moral treatment and the nature of their professional organization.

The Changing Nature of Asylums

From the beginning, asylums had served a dual purpose. Superintendents had encouraged families of those deemed incurable to bring them to the institution because they believed that these patients would at least receive better care than in almshouses and that "in almost every instance" they would be "improved in their habits." Besides, sometimes they "recovered, contrary to the anticipations of every one." The reality of the situation, however, even in the antebellum years, was that chronic patients created problems no one had anticipated. Those who had been confined in almshouses or jails for long periods before coming to the asylum were more likely to spend their lives within its walls, as were the idiots, imbeciles, and epileptics who had been candidates for the asylum in a medical world that had made little distinction between those conditions and insanity. Additionally, there were always some patients, even if not originally diagnosed as incurable, who failed to recover and spent years in the asylum.[1]

As institutional treatment carried the day—seventy-seven new state asylums were built between 1860 and 1890—families and public officials increasingly used the facilities to care for a variety of other dependent peoples. Older persons suffering from senile dementia, those afflicted with a variety of organic diseases (especially general paresis, the tertiary stage of syphilis), alcoholics with delirium tremens, opium addicts, and impoverished immigrants (particularly in Massachusetts and New York) populated the asylums.[2]

Superintendents were aware that the pileup of these chronic patients endangered the image of their asylum and interfered with their ability to administer moral treatment, but they were willing neither to enlarge their institutions nor to support the idea of building separate asylums to isolate the chronically insane. As we have seen, the asylum superintendents organized in 1844 in part to resist the move to increase the size of asylums, and in their 1851 propositions they had set the ideal asylum size at 250 patients. By 1865, however, half of the state hospitals maintained a much larger population. Men like Pliny Earle, John Gray, and Charles Nichols, all superintendents of hospitals well over the ideal size, reluctantly sought some realistic cap for their already bulging institutions. Late in the convention of 1866, when only fourteen of the original twenty-six members in attendance remained, they reaffirmed the association's 1850s policies on construction design and internal management but altered its statement on hospital size. Deeply committed to the association's leadership role in establishing humane practices (even for the chronically insane) and concerned about meeting the needs of their patients, they had experienced quite personally, nevertheless, the reluctance of state legislators to spend large sums on patients not likely to benefit from the expensive moral treatment program. By a close vote they changed the size of the ideal asylum from 250 to 600 patients. It was in many respects a rearguard action as well.[3]

In 1865 the state of New York had authorized a separate asylum for the indigent chronically insane built on the premise of providing merely decent surroundings at a minimum expense for 1,500 patients, and the superintendents feared others would follow. The matter had come to a head in New York because over the course of the previous decade state funding for the New York State Lunatic Asylum at Utica had doubled while the asylum's recovery rate had dropped. Furthermore, the Association of County Commissioners of the Poor had complained that insane paupers could not be sent to Utica because of overcrowding at that institution, and a state investigation revealed that the insane in the county almshouses were maltreated and without medical care. Disillusioned about declining recovery rates and unwilling to invest any more tax money in the expensive type of asylum, the New York legislature ignored the Association of Medical Superintendents' policies on hospital size and on keeping the chronic and acute patients housed together. While the opening of the Willard Asylum for the Chronic Insane in Willard, New York, in 1869 was not immediately imitated, the legislature's disregard for the medical superintendents' policies and failure to consult them was the first sign of challenge to the superintendents' authority.[4]

For another decade most superintendents continued to offer their traditional objections to isolating the incurables from the others because they feared that, in an institution where none would recover and leave its walls, the patients would "soon become objects of but little interest to anyone" and the asylum one in which "neglect, abuse, and all kinds of misrule would exist, and exist without detection." It was a real enough fear; their knowledge of the condition of the insane before their own moral therapy regime and the constant reminders of Dorothea Dix, as she continued to "memorialize" state after state, haunted them and moved them to oppose every suggestion that they thought might result in nothing more than care "identical with the insane section of poorhouses we now so justly deplore."[5]

State after state enlarged asylums with the growing number of chronic patients in mind, however, and their counterarguments about efficiency and economy increasingly carried the day. As Frederick Wines, the secretary of the Illinois Board of State Commissioners of Public Charities, put it in 1879, "the pressing problem with regard to the future of the insane in this country is: how can the chronic insane pauper be most cheaply cared for, consistently with a proper regard to humanity?" The medical superintendents were less convinced about the states' commitment to humane care, and the association continued to use its time-honored technique of passing resolutions that condemned the attitude on the grounds that "neither humanity, economy or expediency" justified the "care of the recent and chronic insane" in "separate institutions," but to little avail. John Chapin, the superintendent of the Willard Asylum for the Chronic Insane, perhaps best expressed the reality of the changing world of the asylum and of the medical superintendents. He defended the Willard Asylum by pointing out that it was simply no longer possible to persuade the states to support the incurable insane in the same costly facilities as the acute cases. Refusing to accept the states' decision on this matter, he thought, would only condemn the chronic cases to those almshouses once more. In the 1880s the typical state hospital housed 500 patients; within a few decades many patient populations reached the 1,000 mark; and by the 1920s, when the patient body increasingly consisted of the aged senile and others with somatically based illnesses, men like William Alanson White saw nothing unusual about state hospitals that cared for 4,000 to 5,000 patients.[6]

The changing nature of the asylum and the tendency of the states to emphasize economy had been only the beginning of the diminishing professional impact of the medical superintendents. In the 1870s and 1880s other events would empower the states' relationship to the insane with an authority unimagined in the antebellum years.

State Control

The asylum superintendents, of course, had sought the states' involvement to fund their asylums and their program of moral treatment from the beginning. But in those early years state legislatures had acted only as a result of prodding to finance new hospitals, expand existing ones, or vote annual appropriations for facilities largely in keeping with the medical superintendents' policies. Moreover, most superintendents, while complaining about legislative niggardliness or interference in the running of their asylums, had lobbied these politicians successfully enough to negotiate compliance with the Kirkbride plan and the association's statements on asylum management.

With the impact of immigration, urbanization, and the expansion of welfare in the postbellum years, however, most states faced both spiraling costs and unstructured arrangements for providing for their dependent peoples. In the case of the insane, the situation was only exacerbated by the changed nature of the asylums. As the gap between the promises of cures and the realities of custodialism widened, asylums came under attack as "palaces" where people were wrongfully confined and where the record of accidents "sounds like the list of casualties of a Bulgarian campaign," while some calumniated the superintendents as "unparalleled" in their "despotism." Some of these attacks were fueled by the nationwide newspaper coverage of Elizabeth Packard's activities. Committed to an Illinois asylum by her husband, upon her release she sued him and won a jury declaration of her sanity. In 1866 she launched a multistate campaign to expose the asylum abuses she had experienced and persuade states to enact legislation for the protection of people, especially married women, from wrongful confinement. In the 1860s and 1870s, as investigations of asylums multiplied, superintendents spent more of their time defending themselves against journalistic gibes and their asylums against vilification.[7]

Both this rising distrust of the medical superintendents and a trend toward more rational and efficient administrative techniques led a number of states to create boards of public charities to coordinate and centralize their welfare responsibilities. Massachusetts, with its three state insane asylums, three almshouses, a reform school for boys, an industrial home for girls, a hospital for sick and disabled aliens, and four other institutions receiving state funds (and in part influenced by anti-immigrant sentiments), was the first in 1864. Other states quickly followed, and by 1875 there were boards of charity in all the northern and middle western states.[8]

For the first decade the powers of these boards were largely limited to gathering data and some efforts at coordinating public programs. The new boards of public charities, however, differed from asylum boards of trustees in that the former had a full-time staff and an executive officer who functioned on a daily basis. Over the course of the 1870s the members of these boards, having a vested interest in their emerging positions and a strategic place within the state government, expanded their powers by gradually participating in both investigatory and policy planning decisions. In the mid-1870s a number of charity boards launched investigations of their state asylum systems. While some were seemingly motivated by personal or professional rancor, even the more objective investigators not only recommended major changes in attitudes toward the treatment of the insane but also openly sought to limit the authority and autonomy of the medical superintendents.[9]

The state of New York, for instance, hired Hervey B. Wilbur, the medical officer of the New York State Idiot Asylum at Syracuse, in 1874 to visit British and European asylums to discover any administrative techniques that might be useful for New York institutions. Comparing the American to the British system, Wilbur found American administration deficient and placed the blame on American superintendents, who demanded "extravagant, ornamental and palatial" asylums, refused to consider any but their own system of management, and allowed patients to remain idle. Wilbur especially attacked John Gray, who, he said, let abuses of patients go undetected because of his dictatorial power and "secretive policy." Wilbur resented Gray's ability to obtain larger appropriations for the New York State Lunatic Asylum at Utica than he could ever manage for his institution at Syracuse and blamed Gray for the rejection of his application for membership in the Association of Medical Superintendents, yet his criticisms of the asylum administrators and suggestions for change differed little from those of more sympathetic charity board members of other states. Wilbur, like Frederick Wines of Illinois or Franklin B. Sanborn of Massachusetts (who regularly attended association meetings and refrained from personal attacks on the medical superintendents), all believed that the state insane asylums should be part of a centralized system. Assuming that the superintendents did not understand the complexities of statewide welfare administration and that, with their vested interest in the "continuation of the system already established," they would be major impediments to reform, these critics suggested that each state create a lunacy commission to which the superintendents would be held accountable. Such a commission, in their eyes, would bring the judgment of objective observers to the coordination and efficiency of state asylum administration and act as a buffer against abuse or wrongful confinement.[10]

As the superintendents saw it, of course, lunacy commissions would destroy the relative autonomy they enjoyed under their

individual boards of trustees and weaken their authority by inter-
jecting lay decision making into their medical world. They continued to pass resolutions that depicted lunacy commissions as
"not only wholly unnecessary, but injurious and subversive" and
increasingly viewed them and other suggestions for change as
threats to their integrity and competency. In 1883 John Callender, the association's new president, best expressed the growing mentality of the superintendents that they were under seige
from state officials and others when he complained about the
"carping current in certain quarters" from those who accused his
colleagues of triviality in their concerns about asylum management and denigrated their endeavors as "but meagerly scientific
in direction." On and on Callender flailed, defending the medical
superintendents against the charge of "illiberal exclusiveness";
denying that their association was a "mere self-protecting guild";
rejecting the charge that it was "perfunctory in character," that
it offered valueless suggestions, that it ignored the "behests of ad-
vancing society" and remained "wedded to obsolete ideas and
methods."[11]

Although equally "carping" in their defensiveness, and indeed
resistant to change, Callender and his colleagues were wise to be
suspicious about the impact of lunacy commissions on their professional autonomy. In Pennsylvania, for example, the lunacy
commission, established in 1883, gained the power to license and
inspect all asylums and substantially changed the superintendent's position within his institution. No longer did he control
admission or discharge procedures; his prescriptions of drugs, restraint, and seclusion were subject to the regulation of the commission; and even the format of his case records on patients was
dictated by that external agency. States like New York, Massachusetts, and Ohio quickly followed suit, some even enacting legislation that required civil service examinations for appointments to
asylum positions. Through its lunacy commissions and public
charity boards, the state had embarked on a path of active intervention in asylum management and had removed many of the
decisions about the fate of the insane from the hands of the medical superintendents.[12]

The Challenge of a New Medical Speciality

The truth of the matter was that the medical superintendents had remained "wedded to obsolete ideas and methods" at least as far as they resisted professional developments outside their asylum walls and opposed other rising professional groups intent upon defining some aspect of mental illness as their bailiwick. Especially indicative of the changing attitudes about the control of the care of the insane was the emergence of a new group of medical specialists, the neurologists, and their loose coalition with a number of other groups in the 1870s and 1880s.

Neurology had originated in Europe in the mid-nineteenth century, and a number of urban American doctors had become interested in the specialty through their work on Civil War soldiers' wounds involving nerve tissue. Within a short time, they had achieved the critical mass necessary to form the New York Neurological Society (1872) and the American Neurological Association (1875). The neurologists' concern with the brain and central nervous system led them to the conclusion that insanity was rooted in anatomy, not society, and that the asylum superintendent's attempt to reform behavior was merely treating symptoms, not causes. Believing that superintendents paid little attention to the new scientific principles of neurology, and rejecting the psychiatrists' methods and theories, neurologists depicted institutionalization as unnecessary, if not harmful, and attacked the superintendents as "autocrats" or "monarch[s]" reigning over the "great palace" of "pills," "muffs," and "handcuffs" and their association as a "national confederation" of "isolated despotisms."[13]

Neurologists, however, were hardly altruistic or scientifically pure-minded in their attack upon the superintendents. Ironically, they were driven by the same force that had spurred the asylum administrators in 1844. Convinced of the accuracy of their theories and the scientific soundness of their ideas about the physiological causes of mental illness, neurologists, in truth, had little to offer in the way of substantial substitutes for the superintendents' program; to a great extent, they merely wanted a "space in the basement" to carry on their experiments.[14]

With their professional rivalry with the superintendents and despite the personal rancor of much of their rhetoric, neurologists tapped into the growing dissatisfaction with the inflexibility of asylum administrators. As we have seen, changing attitudes about welfare administration at the state level had given rise to a group of "social administrators," many of whom created the National Conference on Charities and Corrections in 1874. They viewed the care of the insane as merely one of their many concerns and perceived the asylum doctors as an obstacle to their goals. Additionally, a number of general physicians, lay reformers, lawyers concerned with patients' rights, and even some asylum physicians "in rebellion against the official policy of the Association of Medical Superintendents" joined the fray with the social administrators and neurologists, forming the National Association for the Protection of the Insane and the Prevention of Insanity in 1880.[15]

This association was short-lived, but its formation was symbolic of both the proliferation of people who deemed mental illness part of their expertise and of the broadening of issues surrounding mental illness. It was becoming increasingly clear that Americans no longer viewed asylum superintendents as the sole arbiters of treatment for the mentally ill. Most states had already usurped much of their power, and the new association's stated beliefs that not all insane persons needed institutionalization and that public distrust could be reduced if mental and general hospitals were less distinct were harbingers of the near future. These critics of the medical superintendents, moreover, constituted an "aggregate of socially concerned and active citizens" who represented a "major political and financial resource which influenced not only governmental administration, but the thinking of public health pioneers and medical educators."[16]

By the late 1880s the controversy was cooling off as a younger generation of neurologists established their specialty in general hospitals and medical schools or pursued their private practices. Additionally, many of the younger members of the psychiatric profession were European educated and receptive to pursuing a broader definition of psychiatric concerns and approaches. This younger generation of asylum doctors gradually gained influence in the Association of Medical Superintendents.[17]

Both in the face of the challenge from neurologists and other critics and in keeping with their own ideas about the realities of treating the insane in the late nineteenth century, in 1888 a number of these younger members reworked the traditional policy of the association on asylum design and management as embodied in the revered 1850s propositions. They reported a new set of resolutions that left little of the earlier policy intact. Citing "social science" as a justification for recommending three types of separate asylums (one for the "acute or active" cases, another for those "permanently impaired," and "training schools for the naturally defective"), they overturned the resolution on keeping the chronically insane housed with other patients. Next, they proposed nothing in regard to construction plans of hospitals for acute cases and, by default, rejected the Kirkbride plan and devastated the "old guard" even more by promoting "diversification in appearance" in the others.[18]

The plan of moral therapy was no longer considered sacrosanct either. Occupational therapy, which had played so important a role in the curative plans of the antebellum members, now, in a subtle but real shift, was urged as "productive" employment. And, above all, the younger members rejected moral treatment as a comprehensive plan of therapy by recommending that there were to be "no inelastic system, or prescribed rules" of treatment. The only policy untouched was the plan of organization within the institution; the medical superintendent was still to hold sway over the asylum, whatever its shape or arrangements.[19]

The suggestions were simply an acknowledgment of circumstances as they actually were and far less drastic than those proposed by critics outside the asylum, yet the association refused to consider the merits of the resolutions. The members voted simply not to reaffirm the old "propositions." As the younger members had anticipated, the association could not yet escape the "human veneration for ancestors, and things ancient."[20]

The inflexibility exhibited by the members of the association, even as they were under attack from all quarters, is explainable in the light of the behavior of those "ancestors"; many of the founders and their protégés were still active members in the 1880s. Their intense loyalty to the profession as they had shaped it had been surpassed only by their regular attendance at association meetings and their consequent impact on its proceedings and character. Before 1860, ninety-five men had been eligible for membership; one-quarter of them attended all the meetings; one-third came to at least 75 percent; and almost two-thirds were present at half.[21]

Even more remarkable was the longevity, and therefore both the real and moral force, of these men in the postwar period. John Curwen, for one, never missed a meeting from 1851, when he took over the Pennsylvania State Lunatic Hospital at Harrisburg, until 1888; he served as the association's secretary until 1893, a term of thirty-five years. Charles Nichols and John Gray were equally conscientious, each missing only five sessions before their deaths in the late 1880s. Isaac Ray attended half the meetings during his seventeen-year retirement from 1864 to 1881, and Thomas Kirkbride went to every convention held in eastern cities before his physical weakness prevented attendance in the last three years of his life. Others who held superintendencies before 1860 and those who trained under them exhibited similar attendance patterns. Consequently, from 1862 to 1873, not only did these veteran members still control the presidency, but they also constituted an absolute majority in the association meetings. For another seven years they made up from one-quarter to one-third of the body and, until 1885, at least one-fifth. They were a considerable voting bloc, but more importantly, they were constant adherents to the association's "glorious past."[22]

The association's refusal to reject traditional policy in 1888 was a last gasp, however. Dissent from within the organization had been evident since the beginning of the decade. Men like Richard Gundry, who believed that the "best means of reform is to let the light in every place," and Henry Hurd had urged the association to move in new directions. Hurd's warning that the "work of construction is over" and that a "new era with new requirements" demanded leaving behind the overriding institutional management concerns would be especially heeded by the younger generation. In 1885 the association had changed its membership rules to include assistant physicians, and, significantly, the discussions of these new members at their meetings turned toward more scientific issues. In 1890, when Edward Cowles once again reminded the members that the "best heritage we can hand down to those who come after us is a spirit of liberal catholicity to progress in our work" and freedom from "hampering traditions," he acknowledged that many of his colleagues were already "responding to the inspiring stimulus of modern progress in neurology and all of the branches of scientific medicine." Two years later, the association members formally recognized the change that had taken place in their specialty and in their professional organization by changing their name to the American Medico-Psychological Association. Although some had feared the loss of professional identity, the name change indicated the demise of the "old guard" and the newer members' willingness to broaden their concerns beyond those of mere institutional management and toward developments in the therapeutics of mental disease.[23]

Psychiatry outside the Asylum Walls

The reorientation of the professional organization of asylum administration was really a belated acknowledgment of the emergence of two distinct traditions in American psychiatry. The medical superintendents' concern had been the institutionalized insane; others, like the neurologists and those who were to follow, developed new theories and methods about the care of the mentally ill outside the state asylums. Neurologists continued to treat some mentally ill and neurasthenic patients in their private practices, while between 1890 and 1920 a number of innovations of the newer psychiatric practitioners diverted attention from the institutionalized insane.

In conjunction with the burgeoning developments in medicine and pathology, the emergence of the modern general hospital, and the European model of scientific research conducted at universities with close affiliations with mental hospitals, some American psychiatrists promoted the establishment of research institutes and psychopathic hospitals. Hoping to integrate medicine and psychiatry, research institutes like the Pathological Institute of the New York State Hospital in New York City (1895) or Illinois's State Psychopathic Institute in Kanakee (1907) conducted studies about the causes of mental illness "from the standpoint of cellular biology" and other sciences and offered courses for asylum doctors. Stressing research and instruction, these institutes and their doctors shifted emphasis from patient care to their laboratory findings.[24]

Psychopathic hospitals, on the other hand, while interested in clinical research and the training of medical students, did not so easily lose sight of patients. Their purpose, however, was to offer short-term, immediate care for acute cases. Originating in 1879 with the Bellevue Hospital's establishment of a pavilion for processing the insane in lieu of sending them to jails while awaiting commitment papers, the experiment spawned a number of such "reception" hospitals in the first decades of the twentieth century. Institutions like the Boston Psychopathic Hospital or the Henry Phipps Psychiatric Clinic in Baltimore treated only voluntary patients whose hospitalization was measured in days rather than years and provided the opportunity to avoid commitment to mental hospitals altogether. Other alternatives to traditional institutional commitment emerged as some general hospitals created psychiatric wards and as mental hospitals organized outpatient clinics. Both provided therapeutic services without institutionalization, and by 1920 outpatient clinics were especially common.[25]

This accumulation of institutional innovations, although not as extensive in numbers of patients treated as in the state mental hospitals, significantly altered perceptions about American psychiatry. Affiliations with medical schools or general hospitals yielded a heightened morale, while the emphasis on research created a rising optimism about mental illness and mental health. People interested in pursuing careers in psychiatry by the 1930s no longer had to practice in state mental hospitals, and having no chronic patients to deal with made the profession more attractive. All this, however, merely reinforced the image of the state mental hospital as a receptacle for the incurably insane.

Another development in the early twentieth century that distracted people from the long-term hospitalized patient was the mental hygiene movement. Clifford Beers's emergence into the public spotlight in 1908 with the publication of *The Mind That Found Itself,* his tale of three years in a series of private and state hospitals, was the beginning. Beers's aim, at first, had been merely to improve conditions in mental hospitals, but on the advice of a number of the newer psychiatrists like Adolf Meyer and Thomas Salmon, he extended his ideas about reform to include the establishment of a national organization that would disseminate information to promote mental health in general. Emphasizing prevention, although vague about practical measures, Beers formed the National Committee for Mental Hygiene in 1909 and worked assiduously to create state affiliates. Influenced by nativist sentiment and hereditarian theories, the committee moved to addressing broader social problems like truancy, vagrancy, sexual immorality, dependency, and crime and soon became deeply involved in promoting legislation on marriage regulation, immigration restriction, and involuntary sterilization. To all intents and purposes, Beers's organization had moved many Americans' concerns from mental illness to mental health and some psychiatrists' involvement from a focus on institutional means (whatever the form) to community activity and political action.[26]

While some psychiatrists worked with Beers because of their interest in the effects of defective habits, life-styles, or personalities on mental health, others took quite different routes. As Gerald Grob has pointed out, American psychiatrists in the early twentieth century as a group "remained highly eclectic and fragmented." Indicative of this fragmentation were those who were receptive to psychoanalytic theories. Adolf Meyer was "reserved but not unfriendly" to the new concepts, and William Alanson White played a major role in promoting psychoanalysis both through his writings and through his editorship of the *Psychoanalytical Review*. American psychoanalysis was beleaguered for decades, however, because some thought it originated in a "decadent" and "immoral" European society and were discomfited by its seeming preoccupation with sex. For state hospital doctors, psychoanalysis had little practical application since Freud and his followers centered their therapies on neurotic patients rather than the hardest of cases. As Smith Ely Jelliffe, the founder with White of the *Psychoanalytical Review*, put it, "one has not the time, nor are the patients in the main the type for whom [psychoanalysis] can be used." Additionally, the somatic approach of many psychiatrists precluded their acceptance of Freudian theories.[27]

E. E. Southard, for instance, continued to emphasize brain pathology while others developed studies of autointoxication, analyzed blood and body chemicals, or delved into immunology. This interest in pathology led Southard to advise his students to "look beyond the individual patient." For him and others, "not to see the woods for the trees, not to observe disease principles in the rush of individual patients" was the "fallacy."[28]

Yet Southard was as eclectic in his professional person, as were his colleagues in their scientific pursuits and, with Mary Jarrett at the Boston Psychopathic Hospital, helped to establish psychiatric social work. Basing their theories on a growing interest in the life history of patients and a sense that aftercare would help prevent recurrence of mental illness, many psychiatrists attached to psychopathic hospitals and outpatient clinics encouraged the use of social workers to keep contact with patients. Jarrett, eventually a prime mover in the formation of the American Association of Psychiatric Social Workers, thought that most psychiatrists lacked the knowledge of community conditions necessary for helping patients and suggested that specialists like psychiatric social workers could provide the service. The gathering of information about family and community environment inevitably led psychiatric social workers to involvement with child guidance clinics, educational institutions, and family welfare agencies as they mobilized community resources to aid their patients' adjustment. Psychiatric social workers, however, were only one group of new mental health professionals; clinical psychologists, social and behavioral scientists, occupational therapists, and psychiatric nurses similarly addressed broad issues of mental hygiene and in some way concerned themselves with the mentally ill, while distancing themselves from institutionalized patients.[29]

Redefining the functions of psychiatry through psychopathic hospitals, psychiatric wards in general hospitals, and the mental hygiene movement had created a fertile soil for the emergence of these mental health professions. But the widening of career choices devoted to the treatment of acute cases made institutional psychiatry less attractive, and the emphasis on individual social adjustment and social problems amounted to an abandonment of the chronically hospitalized patient.

"The myth of the therapeutic community"

As Gerald Grob has so effectively illustrated, in the face of the optimism generated by the new institutional structures, the community's involvement with preventive measures and support systems for maintaining mental health, and psychiatry's closer ties to medical innovation, the mentally ill patient in the state hospital became "invisible." Many of those patients suffered from underlying somatic problems for which the new psychiatrists had few solutions and were the types of cases in whom psychiatrists were less interested because they needed care more than active psychiatric treatment.[30]

The reality, however, was that state hospitals cared for the bulk of the mentally ill. While in 1875 state hospitals accounted for nearly 20,000 patients, by 1900 that number had risen to 150,000 and by 1950 to nearly half a million. The asylum superintendents, moreover, had long lost the battle against large asylums. In 1875, 42 of the 53 state hospitals cared for 500 or fewer patients; by 1939 only 12 of the 182 state institutions held fewer than 500 patients, 92 held over 1,500, and 24 cared for between 3,000 and 5,000 people.[31]

Most psychiatrists still worked in institutions, but the psychiatric profession deserted the state hospital in its organizational aims in the 1920s and 1930s. In 1921 the American Medico-Psychological Association became the American Psychiatric Association, and Owen Copp captured the tenor of the change in his presidential address when he declared that "the path of mental hygiene starts and ends in the community." Copp's analysis that mental hygiene's "course leads through the home, the school, the hospital, out again into the widening network of supervisory and helpful agencies in the community" was a recognition of the broadened aspects of the practice of psychiatry and the diminution of the role of the hospital. New committees on psychiatric social work, public education, and graduate education and the section on social problems created within the association's structure reinforced the profession's clinical, scientific, and educational pursuits.[32]

In 1934 the American Psychiatric Association joined with the American Neurological Association in establishing a certifying board for practitioners, marking another move away from institutional patients and toward a community clientele. Throughout the decade, the psychiatric profession had increasingly identified with the larger and more prestigious medical profession. While it had behooved the founders of the association in the 1840s and 1850s to distance themselves from the AMA, in the early twentieth century such aloofness had become detrimental. Both the medical profession's growing identification with science and the AMA's efforts to reorganize medical education had enhanced the prestige of medicine and the AMA. With their efforts to integrate instruction in their specialty in medical school curricula, psychiatrists further stressed working relationships with psychopathic hospitals, outpatient clinics, general hospitals, child guidance clinics, and other community services, adding yet another reinforcement to the shift toward private practice and these other agencies (multiplied in the late thirties by the federal government social welfare policies) and away from state mental hospitals.[33]

The mental hospital with its custodial function and massive patient population continued to operate much as it had in the nineteenth century, however. Despite their loss of authority and status, medical superintendents still managed the asylum, sometimes seeing as little of their charges on a daily basis as had their predecessors of a century or more before, but coordinating the lives of thousands of patients and dealing with a multitude of social workers, government watchdog agencies, and political magnates. They agonized over their budgets, tried to cajole their staffs to an acceptable level of performance, and worked toward an efficient operation of their hospitals. They, like Pliny Earle in the 1840s, remained committed to the "movements of the internal and somewhat complicated machinery" of the institution. And, like Earle, they too were caught in the frequently contradictory demands of the bureaucratic necessities of their role as manager of those thousands of chronically ill patients and what they continued to perceive as the therapeutic purposes of their institutions.[34]

That the state hospitals were any longer "therapeutic communities," of course, was a myth. But the optimism generated by the services of the psychopathic hospitals and similar institutional alternatives and the omnipresence in the community of other mental health facilities and personnel led the public (and the psychiatrists themselves) to perceive psychiatry as promising solutions for the social problem of mental illness. Indeed, in the 1920s and 1930s there was a good deal of therapeutic experimentation even within state hospitals. Fever therapy was widely used for paretic patients, and, after psychiatrists allied themselves more closely with scientific medicine and technology, other aggressive therapies seemed ready to fulfill the promise. New drugs led some to hope that a chemical cure for insanity was at hand, and the use of insulin and metrazol shock treatments, electroshock therapy, and prefrontal lobotomies initially sparked renewed enthusiasm for the recovery of long-term psychotic patients. Unpredictable diabetic comas that increased death risks, induced convulsions that resulted in serious injuries, and psychosurgery that left many patients in a vacuous state, however, created suspicions about the new methods. The experimental nature of the treatments, moreover, raised serious ethical questions, and disappointing results in recovery rates in the long run merely gave new fodder to those who saw state mental hospitals not only as institutions of last resort, but increasingly as repressive and brutalizing environments.[35]

Institutional psychiatrists continued to depict their hospitals as therapeutic rather than custodial, but the accumulation of patients, the sheer size of their institutions, the inadequate staffing and funding, and their meager recovery rates belied their portrayal. By the late 1930s there existed considerable discontent with the growing cost of state mental hospitals, pessimism about the ever increasing numbers of patients not likely to leave the institutions, and dismay at the dismal conditions of treatment and care. This "disjuncture between image and reality" of state mental hospitals ultimately called "into doubt their very legitimacy."[36]

Drastic action was delayed by the outbreak of World War II, but the long-term effects of the desertion of institutional psychiatry by the profession, the discovery of antipsychotic drugs, the rise in status of newer systems of treatment like psychoanalysis and psychotherapy, and an emerging interest in civil rights in the late 1940s and 1950s fostered sentiments for the rejection of the asylum. Harry Truman signed the National Mental Health Act creating the National Institute of Mental Health in 1946, and in 1955 Congress created the Joint Commission on Mental Illness and Health. Its recommendation in 1961 for the dismantling of large state mental hospitals, coupled with the passage of the Aid to the Disabled and Community Mental Health Centers acts, began the deinstitutionalization movement. States created community mental health centers, encouraged a variety of other services such as halfway houses, board and care homes, cooperative apartments, and emergency crisis shelters and systematically discharged patients from their state hospitals. In 1960, 536,000 patients had been institutionalized; by 1981 that number had dropped to 125,000.[37]

Deinstitutionalization produced successful programs hailed by the public and the profession and, inspired by court decisions in the 1970s about the "least restrictive setting" for treatment and patients' rights to refuse treatment, patient advocates worked to release thousands of institutionalized patients. In Lansing, Michigan, for example, only 50 patients now reside in state hospitals out of a catchment area of more than 400,000, and for the residents of Johnston County, North Carolina, the comprehensive mental health services that are available in Smithfield mean that no one has to leave the county for help. In the state of Vermont (with a population of only 500,000), where the patient population at the one state hospital dropped from nearly 1,200 in 1966 to only 176 in 1983, the 10 community health agencies covering the state geographically play the major role in the delivery of mental health services. Even in the wake of a condemnation of the conditions at the state hospital in late 1984, neither the hospital administrators, the governor, the state legislators, psychiatrists in private practice, nor former patients attacked the community mental health system. For thousands of former patients across the nation and for those now functioning in the community who may have been confined in an earlier time, deinstitutionalization has improved the quality of life.[38]

The decision to locate care outside the hospital, however, has set off another, less promising "chain reaction of consequences."

In an atmosphere that Saul Feldman, a former administrator at the National Institute of Mental Health, has called "oversell and overkill," patients were released before services were in place. Many communities still provide inadequate facilities or no services at all. While 768 communities have received federal funds, 500 others targeted for government financing have not. Moreover, state budget allocations lag behind the times; seven out of every ten mental health dollars nationwide still go into the maintenance of state hospitals.[39]

The complexity of the system has presented other as yet unsolved problems. Constitutional questions, not only about patients' rights but also about the separation of powers, can arise when courts dictate to legislatures about reallocations of state budgets; political and professional disputes have emerged between the new administrators of community mental health funds and the old state hospital bureaucracies; and Medicare and Medicaid regulations that pay inpatient costs implicitly undermine the government's mandate for outpatient care. Additionally, the fragmentation endemic in the variety of agencies providing services (both private and governmental) perpetuates the "turf problems" that abound.[40]

The most helpless victims of that complexity and fragmentation are the patients, especially the chronically ill. Susan Sheehan's poignant tale of Sylvia Frumkin, the young New York woman who had been treated in forty-five different settings in her eighteen years as a mental patient, is only one of the more "celebrated" cases. Others, as John Talbott, the current president of the American Psychiatric Association, points out, have been "transinstitutionalized" into nursing homes or privately owned residential care facilities, while short-term inpatient stays and high readmission rates mark the lives of many alcoholics and psychotic patients. And as newspapers, and even the professional literature, increasingly indicate, the system's failure to recognize the need for "asylum" and some of the services once offered by "the asylum" (sometimes as basic as food, shelter, clothing, and medicine easily attained; sometimes as personal as a sense of identity) has peopled our cities' streets.[41]

The fact that deinstitutionalization has not worked perfectly is not reason to abandon the policy; nor should its successes lead us to glorify it. Twentieth-century deinstitutionalization is both as simple and as complex as the discovery of the asylum in the early nineteenth century.

The experiences of the founders of American psychiatry can be instructive for the planners and implementers of deinstitutionalization. Just as those early moral therapists reacted against the abuse the insane suffered in jails and almshouses and perceived their asylum system as the universal remedy, the social climate of the 1960s led many to place their hope in the equally singular solution of deinstitutionalization as a reaction against the custodialism and repression of the antiquated and outmoded state hospital. Panaceas and reactive behavior, however, have their pitfalls, as we have seen in the case of the nineteenth-century asylum administrators.

In their optimism about asylum treatment, they created an expectation about curability they ultimately could not meet. Because their professional identity was so intertwined with that asylum as they had shaped it in the plan of moral treatment and their role as medical superintendents, they clung to a complete faith in its viability and legitimacy as *the* answer for the care and treatment of the mentally ill long after it no longer worked. That commitment made them unreceptive to alternative means or services and largely oblivious to the fact that they no longer met the needs of all the mentally ill or even all patients in their asylums.

The promoters of deinstitutionalization need only learn the lessons that their forebears in the care of the mentally ill ignored. They must recognize the need to cast aside professional rivalries, to lobby more intensively for public support and adequate funding, and to remain open to the complexities of providing comprehensive treatment and care not only for the many who can return to the community but also for those who cannot. Avoiding the pitfalls of the one "ideal" solution can perhaps fulfill the promise of the 1960s as articulated by John Kennedy when he told Congress that "if we apply our medical knowledge and social insights fully, all but a small portion of the mentally ill can eventually achieve a wholesome and constructive social adjustment."

Appendix
Pre-1860 American Asylum Administrators

(Asterisks indicate service as assistant physicians)

Career Administrators
Allen, John R. Kentucky Lunatic Asylum, Lexington, 1843–54.

Athon, James S. Indiana Hospital for the Insane, Indianapolis, 1853–61.

Awl, William M. Ohio Lunatic Asylum, Columbus, 1838–51.

Bancroft, Jesse P. New Hampshire Asylum for the Insane, Concord, 1857–82.

Barkdull, J. D. Louisiana Insane Asylum, Jackson, 1857–65.

Barstow, John W. Sanford Hall, Flushing, N.Y., 1854–74.

Bates, James. Maine Insane Asylum, Augusta, 1845–51.

Bell, Luther V. McLean Asylum, Charlestown, Mass., 1836–56.

Bemis, Merrick. Worcester State Lunatic Hospital, Worcester, Mass., *1848–55, 1856–72.

Benedict, Nathan D. Blockley Almshouse, Philadelphia, Pa., 1846–49. New York State Lunatic Asylum, Utica, 1849–54.

Booth, Chauncey. Vermont Asylum for the Insane, Brattleboro, *1837–40. Maine Insane Asylum, Augusta, *1840–43. McLean Asylum, Charlestown, Mass., *1843–56.

Brigham, Amariah. Hartford Retreat for the Insane, Hartford, Conn., 1840–42. New York State Lunatic Asylum, Utica, 1842–49.

Brown, David Tilden. Blackwell's Island Almshouse, Blackwell's Island, N.Y., 1844. Vermont Asylum for the Insane, Brattleboro, *1845–46. New York State Lunatic Asylum, Utica, *1846–47. Bloomingdale Asylum, Bloomingdale, N.Y., 1852–77.

Bryce, Peter. South Carolina Lunatic Asylum, Columbia, *1859–60. New Jersey State Lunatic Asylum, Trenton, *1860. Alabama Insane Hospital, Tuscaloosa, 1860–92.

Buel, Henry W. Sanford Hall, Flushing, N.Y., 1849–54. Spring Hill, Litchfield, Conn., 1854–93.

Butler, John S. Boston Lunatic Hospital, Boston, Mass., 1839–42. Hartford Retreat for the Insane, Hartford, Conn., 1843–73.

Buttolph, Horace A. New York State Lunatic Asylum, Utica, *1842–47.

Career Administrators (*cont.*)

New Jersey State Lunatic Asylum, Trenton, 1847–76. State Asylum at Morristown, Morristown, N.J., 1876–85.

Carriel, Henry F. New Jersey State Lunatic Asylum, Trenton, *1858–69. Illinois State Hospital for the Insane, Jacksonville, 1870–93.

Chandler, George. Worcester State Lunatic Hospital, Worcester, Mass., *1834–42. New Hampshire Asylum for the Insane, Concord, 1842–45. Worcester State Lunatic Hospital, Worcester, Mass., 1846–56.

Chapin, Edward R. Maine Insane Asylum, Augusta, *1843. Vermont Asylum for the Insane, Brattleboro, *1855–57. Long Island State Hospital, Brooklyn, N.Y., 1857–73.

Cheatham, William. Central Hospital for the Insane, Nashville, Tenn., 1852–62.

Chipley, William S. Kentucky Lunatic Asylum, Lexington, 1855–70. Cincinnati Sanitarium, Cincinnati, Ohio, 1875–80.

Choate, George C. S. Taunton State Hospital, Taunton, Mass., 1855–70.

Cleaveland, Joseph M. New York State Lunatic Asylum, Utica, *1857–67. Hudson River State Hospital, Poughkeepsie, N.Y., 1867–93.

Cook, George. New York State Lunatic Asylum, Utica, *1848–54. Brigham Hall, Canandaigua, N.Y., 1855–76.

Curwen, John. Pennsylvania Hospital for the Insane, Philadelphia, *1844–49. Pennsylvania State Lunatic Hospital, Harrisburg, 1851–81. State Hospital for the Insane, Warren, Pa., 1881–1900.

Cutter, Nehemiah. [Private Asylum], Pepperell, Mass., 1834–53.

Earle, Pliny. Friends' Asylum for the Insane, Frankford, Pa., 1840–44. Bloomingdale Asylum, Bloomingdale, N.Y., 1844–49. Northampton State Lunatic Hospital, Northampton, Mass., 1864–85.

Firestone, Leander. Cleveland State Hospital, Cleveland, Ohio, 1853–56. Ohio Lunatic Asylum, Columbus, 1878–81.

Fisher, Edward C. Western Lunatic Hospital, Staunton, Va., *1850–51. State Hospital, Raleigh, N.C., 1853–68. Western Lunatic Hospital, Staunton, Va., *1871–81, *1884–90.

Fisher, William. Maryland Hospital for the Insane, Baltimore, 1836–46.

Fonerden, John. Maryland Hospital for the Insane, Baltimore, 1846–69.

Fuller, Silas. Hartford Retreat for the Insane, Hartford, Conn., 1834–40.

Galt, John M. Eastern Lunatic Hospital, Williamsburg, Va., 1841–62.

Gray, John P. New York State Lunatic Asylum, Utica, *1850–54, 1854–86.

Green, Thomas F. Georgia State Sanitarium, Milledgeville, 1846–79.

Gundry, Richard. Ohio Lunatic Asylum, Columbus, *1855–56. Southern Ohio Lunatic Asylum, Dayton, *1857–61, 1861–72. Athens State Hospital, Athens, Ohio, 1872–77. Ohio Lunatic Asylum, Columbus, 1877–1878. Maryland Hospital for the Insane, Baltimore, 1878–91.

Harlow, Henry M. Vermont Asylum for the Insane, Brattleboro, *1844. Maine Insane Asylum, Augusta, *1845–50, 1850–83.

Hawthorne, James C. Hawthorne Asylum, Portland, Oreg., 1858–78.

Higgins, J. M. Illinois State Hospital for the Insane, Jacksonville, 1848–1853.

Hills, R. Ohio Lunatic Asylum, Columbus, 1856–64. West Virginia Hospital for the Insane, Weston, 1864–71.

Hopkins, R. C. Ohio Lunatic Asylum, Columbus, *1844–48. Cleveland State Hospital, Cleveland, Ohio, 1856–57.

Ingraham, T. M. Long Island State Hospital, Brooklyn, N.Y., pre–1855.

Jarvis, Edward. [Private Asylum], Dorchester, Mass., 1845–84.

Kells, Robert. State Insane Hospital, Jackson, Miss., 1859–66.

Kendrick, Oscar C. Ohio Lunatic Asylum, Columbus, *1852–54. Cleveland State Hospital, Cleveland, Ohio, 1858–64.

Kirkbride, Thomas S. Friends' Asylum for the Insane, Frankford, Pa., 1832–33. Pennsylvania Hospital for the Insane, Philadelphia, 1840–83.

Langdon, Oliver M. Longview Hospital, Cincinnati, Ohio, 1848–56, 1859–70.

Lee, J. Edwards. New York State Lunatic Asylum, Utica, *1847–48. Pennsylvania Hospital for the Insane, Philadelphia, *1851–56. Wisconsin State Hospital for the Insane, Mendota, 1859–60. Pennsylvania Hospital for the Insane, Philadelphia, *1862–68.

MacDonald, James. Bloomingdale Asylum, Bloomingdale, N.Y., 1825–30, 1831–37. Sanford Hall, Flushing, N.Y., 1841–49.

McFarland, Andrew. New Hampshire Asylum for the Insane, Concord, 1845–52. Illinois State Hospital for the Insane, Jacksonville, 1854–70. Oaklawn Retreat, Jacksonville, Ill., 1870–91.

McIlhenny, J. J. Southern Ohio Lunatic Asylum, Dayton, 1856–62.

McNairy, John S. Central Hospital for the Insane, Nashville, Tenn., 1843–49.

Mead, Edward. [Private Asylum], Chicago, Ill., 1847–51. [Private Asylum], Cincinnati, Ohio, 1852–69. [Private Asylum], Winchester, Mass., 1872. [Private Asylum], Roxbury, Mass., 1873.

Nichols, Charles H. New York State Lunatic Asylum, Utica, *1848–49. Bloomingdale Asylum, Bloomingdale, N.Y., 1849–52. Government Hospital for the Insane (St. Elizabeths), Washington, D.C., 1852–77. Bloomingdale Asylum, Bloomingdale, N.Y., 1877–89.

Ogden, Benjamin. Bloomingdale Asylum, Bloomingdale, N.Y., 1837–39. Sanford Hall, Flushing, N.Y., 1852–60.

Parker, John W. South Carolina Lunatic Asylum, Columbia, 1836–70, *1876–82.

Patterson, Richard J. Ohio Lunatic Asylum, Columbus, *1842–47. Indiana Hospital for the Insane, Indianapolis, 1847–53. Iowa Asylum for the Insane, Mount Pleasant, 1860–65.

Pond, Preston. Louisiana Insane Asylum, Jackson, 1848–55.

Prince, William H. Northampton State Lunatic Hospital, Northampton, Mass., 1858–64.

Career Administrators (*cont.*)

Ranney, Mark H. Butler Hospital for the Insane, Providence, R.I., *1849–1854. McLean Asylum, Charlestown, Mass., *1854–65. Iowa Asylum for the Insane, Mount Pleasant, 1865–73. Wisconsin State Hospital for the Insane, Mendota, 1873–74. Iowa Asylum for the Insane, Mount Pleasant, 1875–82.

Ranney, Moses. Blackwell's Island Almshouse, Blackwell's Island, N.Y., 1848–64.

Ray, Isaac. Maine Insane Asylum, Augusta, 1841–45. Butler Hospital for the Insane, Providence, R.I., 1845–66.

Reed, Joseph A. Dixmont Hospital for the Insane, Dixmont, Pa., 1857–84.

Rockwell, William H. Hartford Retreat for the Insane, Hartford, Conn., *1827–36. Vermont Asylum for the Insane, Brattleboro, 1836–73.

Sawyer, John. Butler Hospital for the Insane, Providence, R.I., *1858–59. Wisconsin State Hospital for the Insane, Mendota, *1861–67. Butler Hospital for the Insane, Providence, R.I., 1867–85.

Smith, S. Hanbury. Ohio Lunatic Asylum, Columbus, *1840–43, 1850–52.

Smith, Turner R. H. Missouri State Hospital, Fulton, 1851–65. City Sanitarium, St. Louis, Mo., 1872–73. Missouri State Hospital, Fulton, 1873–1885.

Stedman, Charles H. Boston Lunatic Hospital, Boston, Mass., 1842–51.

Steuart, Richard S. Maryland Hospital for the Insane, Baltimore, 1869–1876.

Stokes, William H. Maryland Hospital for the Insane, Baltimore, 1834–35. Mount Hope Institution, Baltimore, Md., 1842–87.

Stribling, Francis T. Western Lunatic Hospital, Staunton, Va., 1836–74.

Taylor, Edward. Friends' Asylum for the Insane, Frankford, Pa., 1823–32.

Todd, Eli. Hartford Retreat for the Insane, Hartford, Conn., 1824–33.

Tyler, John E. New Hampshire Asylum for the Insane, Concord, 1852–57. McLean Asylum, Charlestown, Mass., 1858–71.

Van Anden, Charles E. State Lunatic Asylum for Insane Convicts, Auburn, N.Y., *1859–62, 1862–70.

Van Deusen, Edwin H. New York State Lunatic Asylum, Utica, *1853–58. Michigan Asylum for the Insane, Kalamazoo, 1858–78.

Walker, Clement A. Boston Lunatic Hospital, Boston, Mass., 1851–81.

White, George H. [Private Asylum], Hudson, N.Y., 1845–?.

White, Samuel. [Private Asylum], Hudson, N.Y., 1830–45.

Woodward, Samuel B. Worcester State Lunatic Hospital, Worcester, Mass., 1832–46.

Worthington, Joshua H. Friends' Asylum for the Insane, Frankford, Pa., 1842–77.

Wyman, Rufus. McLean Asylum, Charlestown, Mass., 1818–35.

Short-term Administrators*

Annan, Samuel. Western Lunatic Asylum, Hopkinsville, Ky., 1854–58.

Aylett, W. D. Insane Asylum of California, Stockton, 1857–61.

Baiseley, Robert B. Long Island State Hospital, Brooklyn, N.Y., 1855–56.

Blanchard, E. S. Long Island State Hospital, Brooklyn, N.Y., 1855.

Bullock, Francis. Long Island State Hospital, Brooklyn, N.Y., 1850–53.

Campbell, A. B. Blockley Almshouse, Philadelphia, Pa., 1854–55, 1856–57.

Clements, Joshua P. Southern Ohio Lunatic Asylum, Dayton, 1856. Vermont Asylum for the Insane, Brattleboro, *1856–58.

Cooper, David. Georgia State Sanitarium, Milledgeville, 1843–46.

Eels, George E. Ohio Lunatic Asylum, Columbus, 1854–56.

Evans, John. Indiana Hospital for the Insane, Indianapolis, 1845–48.

Haines, William S. Blockley Almshouse, Philadelphia, Pa., 1850–53.

Hall, Edward. State Lunatic Asylum for Insane Convicts, Auburn, N.Y., 1858–62.

Kendrick, Elijah. Ohio Lunatic Asylum, Columbus, 1852–54.

Knapp, Cyrus. Maine Insane Asylum, Augusta, 1840.

Laisy, Jacob. Cleveland State Hospital, Cleveland, Ohio, 1857.

Langdon, Samuel. Insane Asylum of California, Stockton, 1856.

Langley, W. S. State Insane Hospital, Jackson, Miss., 1855–57.

Lansing, John V. Long Island State Hospital, Brooklyn, N.Y., 1856–58.

Lee, Thomas G. Hartford Retreat for the Insane, Hartford, Conn., *1832–34. McLean Asylum, Charlestown, Mass., *1834–35.

McClintock, James. Blockley Almshouse, Philadelphia, Pa., 1857–58.

Meyberry, G. Louisiana Insane Asylum, Jackson, 1855–57.

Montgomery, F. G. Western Lunatic Asylum, Hopkinsville, Ky., 1858–62.

Mount, William. Longview Hospital, Cincinnati, Ohio, 1857–59.

Power, Edward C. Louisiana Insane Asylum, Jackson, 1853–54.

Quinn, J. J. Longview Hospital, Cincinnati, Ohio, 1853–56.

Reid, Robert. Insane Asylum of California, Stockton, 1853–56.

Selby, W. H. Louisiana Insane Asylum, Jackson, 1848.

Smith, R. K. Blockley Almshouse, Philadelphia, Pa., 1855–56, 1858–59.

Stewart, Joseph S. Blockley Almshouse, Philadelphia, Pa., 1853–54.

Williamson, W. B. State Insane Hospital, Jackson, Miss., 1857–59.

Winchell, Martin E. Long Island State Hospital, Brooklyn, N.Y., pre–1855. New Jersey State Lunatic Asylum, Trenton, *1855.

Young, John S. Central Hospital for the Insane, Nashville, Tenn., 1849–1852.

Assistant Physicians

Awl, Robert H. Ohio Lunatic Asylum, Columbus, 1848–50.

Barnes, Henry F. Indiana Hospital for the Insane, Indianapolis, 1858–61.

Bartlett, C. K. Northampton State Lunatic Hospital, Northampton, Mass., 1859–69.

Assistant Physicians (*cont.*)

Bayley, Guy C. Bloomingdale Asylum, Bloomingdale, N.Y., 1830–32.

Bethshares, H. H. Central Hospital for the Insane, Nashville, Tenn., 1852–62.

Blackmer, John. Maine Insane Asylum, Augusta, 1859–60.

Booth, Henry M. Vermont Asylum for the Insane, Brattleboro, 1845–46, 1854–56.

Brooks, Daniel. Hartford Retreat for the Insane, Hartford, Conn., post–1836.

Buffum, G. M. Vermont Asylum for the Insane, Brattleboro, 1858–59.

Chapin, J. B. New York State Lunatic Asylum, Utica, 1854–57.

Chase, B. W. Vermont Asylum for the Insane, Brattleboro, 1853–54.

Corey, Charles, Jr., Bloomingdale Asylum, Bloomingdale, N.Y., 1857–65.

Cornett, Charles F. Illinois State Hospital for the Insane, Jacksonville, 1854–59.

Cuttin, Jacob. Vermont Asylum for the Insane, Brattleboro, 1855.

Davis, T. V. L. Western Lunatic Hospital, Staunton, Va., 1858–63.

DeWitt, William R. Pennsylvania State Lunatic Hospital, Harrisburg, 1851–59.

Disney, Charles. Ohio Lunatic Asylum, Columbus, 1853–54.

Dunlap, John M. Indiana Hospital for the Insane, Indianapolis, 1858–63.

Elliot, J. B. New Jersey State Lunatic Asylum, Trenton, 1851–55.

Elliott, Thomas B. Indiana Hospital for the Insane, Indianapolis, 1851–1856.

Ely, D. L. Ohio Lunatic Asylum, Columbus, 1856–63.

Evans, Charles. Friends' Asylum for the Insane, Frankford, Pa., 1832–51.

Favill, John. Wisconsin State Hospital for the Insane, Mendota, 1860.

Fox, John. McLean Asylum, Charlestown, Mass., 1839–43.

Freeland, William. Western Lunatic Asylum, Hopkinsville, Ky., 1858–59.

Fuller, D. Dixmont Hospital for the Insane, Dixmont, Pa., 1857–64.

Gambrill, Richard H. Western Lunatic Hospital, Staunton, Va., 1842–58, 1863–65.

Given, Robert A. Pennsylvania Hospital for the Insane, Philadelphia, 1842–44.

Hamilton, William H. Western Lunatic Hospital, Staunton, Va., 1851–81, 1884.

Hart, S. W. Hartford Retreat for the Insane, Hartford, Conn., post–1836.

Hartshorne, Edward. Pennsylvania Hospital for the Insane, Philadelphia, 1841.

Hatch, Thomas E. Worcester State Lunatic Hospital, Worcester, Mass., post–1842.

Headly, W. S. New York State Lunatic Asylum, Utica, 1852–54.

Hodge, Charles, Jr. New Jersey State Lunatic Asylum, Trenton, 1857–58.

Holman, Francis A. Vermont Asylum for the Insane, Brattleboro, 1846–1850.

Jones, H. K. Illinois State Hospital for the Insane, Jacksonville, 1851–52.

Jones, S. Preston. Government Hospital for the Insane (St. Elizabeths), Washington, D.C., 1858–59. Pennsylvania Hospital for the Insane, Philadelphia, 1859–84.

Kenny, Asa P. Illinois State Hospital for the Insane, Jacksonville, 1860–1864.

Lee, John R. McLean Asylum, Charlestown, Mass., 1837–39. Worcester State Lunatic Hospital, Worcester, Mass., post-1842.

Longshore, William S. Pennsylvania Hospital for the Insane, Philadelphia, 1860–62.

Lovejoy, Oliver S. Vermont Asylum for the Insane, Brattleboro, 1850–53.

Low, Samuel B. Vermont Asylum for the Insane, Brattleboro, 1841–44.

Lukens, Charles. Friends' Asylum for the Insane, Frankford, Pa., 1817–21, 1822–23.

McCrea, James. Friends' Asylum for the Insane, Frankford, Pa., 1833–34.

McCullough, T. P. Ohio Lunatic Asylum, Columbus, 1849–50. Indiana Hospital for the Insane, Indianapolis, 1853–54.

McElwee, Andrew. Ohio Lunatic Asylum, Columbus, 1854–56.

McGregor, John R. Butler Hospital for the Insane, Providence, R.I., 1856–57.

Matlack, Charles F. Friends' Asylum for the Insane, Frankford, Pa., 1821–1822.

Mendenhall, Thomas J. Pennsylvania Hospital for the Insane, Philadelphia, 1849–51.

Merrill, Paul. Maine Insane Asylum, Augusta, 1856–59.

Moore, Edward M. Friends' Asylum for the Insane, Frankford, Pa., 1837–1839.

Morton, Robert. Friends' Asylum for the Insane, Frankford, Pa., 1832–35.

Nash, F. New York State Lunatic Asylum, Utica, 1856–59.

Nutt, J. Indiana Hospital for the Insane, Indianapolis, 1848–51.

Padgett, A. A. Central Hospital for the Insane, Nashville, Tenn., 1852–62.

Perkins, Roger G. Butler Hospital for the Insane, Providence, R.I., 1854–1855.

Pickering, Samuel W. Friends' Asylum for the Insane, Frankford, Pa., 1823–32.

Pierce, Charles R. Ohio Lunatic Asylum, Columbus, 1852–53.

Porter, M. G. New York State Lunatic Asylum, Utica, 1849–51.

Porter, Robert C. Friends' Asylum for the Insane, Frankford, Pa., 1835–37.

Porter, William. Hartford Retreat for the Insane, Hartford, Conn., post-1836.

Ray, B. Lincoln. Butler Hospital for the Insane, Providence, R.I., 1859–1867.

Rowland, Edward. McLean Asylum, Charlestown, Mass., 1835–36.

Sabine, Andrew. Ohio Lunatic Asylum, Columbus, 1858–60.

Smith, Edward A. Pennsylvania Hospital for the Insane, Philadelphia, 1856–62.

Smith, Francis Gurney. Pennsylvania Hospital for the Insane, Philadelphia, 1841.

Smith, Horatio S. Maine Insane Asylum, Augusta, 1845–50.

Smith, Jerome C. Maine Insane Asylum, Augusta, 1854–56. McLean Asylum, Charlestown, Mass., 1856–61.

Spann, N. C. Indiana Hospital for the Insane, Indianapolis, 1856.

Stephens, Bela N. Government Hospital for the Insane (St. Elizabeths), Washington, D.C., 1859–65.

Steuart, James A. Maryland Hospital for the Insane, Baltimore, post–1854.

Swift, H. S. New York State Lunatic Asylum, Utica, 1854.

Thoburn, Joseph. Ohio Lunatic Asylum, Columbus, 1851–52.

Thompson, Austin W. Northampton State Lunatic Hospital, Northampton, Mass., 1858–59.

Thrall, William. Ohio Lunatic Asylum, Columbus, 1854–58.

Tilden, W. P. Insane Asylum of California, Stockton, 1860–63.

Torbett, George A. Indiana Hospital for the Insane, Indianapolis, 1854–1858.

Tourtellott, L. A. New York State Lunatic Asylum, Utica, 1855–62, 1867–1868.

Trimble, Isaac. Friends' Asylum for the Insane, Frankford, Pa., 1834–35.

Weeks, F. C. Vermont Asylum for the Insane, Brattleboro, 1858–62.

Willey, Samuel. Ohio Lunatic Asylum, Columbus, 1851–52.

Wilson, William. Bloomingdale Asylum, Bloomingdale, N.Y., 1837–39.

Wood, Thomas. Friends' Asylum for the Insane, Frankford, Pa., 1839–40.

Woodward, Rufus. Worcester State Lunatic Hospital, Worcester, Mass., post–1842.

Wright, F. M. New York State Lunatic Asylum, Utica, 1859–62.

Young, William P. Government Hospital for the Insane (St. Elizabeths), Washington, D.C., 1855–58.

Source: Compiled by author.

Notes

Abbreviations

Proceedings   Proceedings of the Annual Meeting of the Association of Medical Superintendents of American Institutions for the Insane

    AJI   *American Journal of Insanity*

    AAS   American Antiquarian Society, Worcester, Mass.

    IPH   Institute of the Pennsylvania Hospital, Philadelphia, Pa.

    WSH   Western State Hospital, Staunton, Va.

Preface

1. Thomas Szasz, *Law, Liberty, and Psychiatry* (New York: Macmillan, 1963) and *The Age of Madness* (New York: Jason Aronson, 1974); Thomas Scheff, *Mental Illness and Social Processes* (New York: Harper & Row, 1967); Erving Goffman, *Asylums* (Garden City, N.Y.: Doubleday, 1961).

2. David J. Rothman, *The Discovery of the Asylum* (Boston: Little, Brown, 1971); Michel Foucault, *Madness and Civilization,* trans. Richard Howard (New York: Pantheon Books, 1965), esp. chaps. 2 and 9.

3. Richard Fox, *So Far Disordered in Mind* (Berkeley: University of California Press, 1978), chap. 1.

4. Nancy Tomes, *A Generous Confidence: Thomas Story Kirkbride and the Art of Asylum Keeping* (Cambridge: Cambridge University Press, 1984). Work on similar questions concerning other kinds of institutions has been done by Jamil S. Zainaldin and Peter L. Tyor; see their "Asylum and Society: An Approach to Industrial Change," *Journal of Social History* 13 (Fall 1979):23–48.

5. Grob began his work with an analysis of the origins and development of the first therapeutic state hospital in Massachusetts at Worcester, *The State and the Mentally Ill* (Chapel Hill: University of North Carolina Press, 1966). An interpretive introduction to a reprint of Edward Jarvis's 1855 *Insanity and Idiocy in Massachusetts* (Boston: William White, 1855. Reprint. Cambridge, Mass.: Harvard University Press, 1971) followed. In 1973 Grob extended his analysis in *Mental Institutions in America: Social Policy to 1875* (New York: Free Press) and in 1983 in his work on social policy and the mentally ill, *Mental Illness and Ameri-*

can Society, 1875–1940 (Princeton: Princeton University Press). See also his "Rediscovering the Asylum" in *The Therapeutic Revolution,* ed. Morris J. Vogel and Charles E. Rosenberg, pp. 135–57 (Philadelphia: University of Pennsylvania Press, 1979).

6. See especially Andrew Scull, *Museums of Madness* (New York: St. Martin's Press, 1979), his study of nineteenth-century British psychiatry. Scull sees the rise of therapeutic asylums in much the same light as does Foucault. An emerging market economy demanded restorative confinement. The "more respectable asylum doctors" created a "proto-profession" and promoted the asylum "as a technical, objective, scientific response to the patient's condition" (pp. 90–91). Characterizing "medical men as moral entrepreneurs," Scull traces how "mad-doctors" (increasingly a derogatory term in Britain) secured for themselves a monopoly of a "service market" and "significant status advantages" (chap. 4, esp. p. 29). Scull weaves sociological theory, narrative accounts of asylums, and enactment of reform legislation; but little of the reformers, "mad doctors," or the British professional organization emerges. Jan E. Goldstein, in "French Psychiatry in Social and Political Context: The Formation of a New Profession, 1820–1860" (Ph.D. diss., Columbia University, 1978), suggests a similar element of moral entrepreneurship among French alienists.

7. John Callender, "History and Work of the Association of Medical Superintendents of American Institutions for the Insane—President's Address," *AJI* 40 (July 1883):1–32; Kirkbride to Gov. Hugh [1881?], Kirkbride MSS, IPH.

Introduction

1. Details about the founding session of the Association of Medical Superintendents of American Institutions for the Insane are gleaned from "Medical Association. Meeting of the Medical Superintendents of American Institutions for the Insane," *AJI* 1 (January 1845):253–58; John Curwen, *History of the Association of Medical Superintendents of American Institutions for the Insane* (Harrisburg, Pa.: Theo. F. Scheffer, 1875); Albert Deutsch, *The Mentally Ill in America* (New York: Doubleday, Doran, 1937); D. Hack Tuke, "American Retrospect," *AJI* 41 (January 1886):590–96; Henry M. Hurd, ed., *The Institutional Care of the Insane in the United States and Canada,* 4 vols. (Baltimore: Johns Hopkins Press, 1916); and the numerous letters in the Kirkbride MSS, IPH, Stribling MSS, WHS, and Woodward, Earle, and Chandler MSS, AAS.

2. Butler to Earle, 16 April 1844, Earle MSS, AAS; Bell to Woodward, 25 July 1844, Woodward MSS, AAS.

3. Woodward to Stribling, 26 May 1843, Stribling MSS, WSH.

4. The curability statistics are cited in Deutsch, *Mentally Ill in America,* chap. 8 and can be verified in the annual reports of Eli Todd,

Samuel Woodward, John Galt, William Awl, and others. The predictions of Earle and Woodward are cited in Deutsch, pp. 151–52.

5. John Curwen, *The Original Thirteen Members of the Association of Medical Superintendents of American Institutions for the Insane* (Warren, Pa.: E. Cowan & Co., Printers, 1885), p. 7. Curwen's book includes physical descriptions, as well as those of personality, character, and behavior. Curwen began as an assistant physician under Thomas Kirkbride in 1844, became superintendent of the Pennsylvania State Lunatic Hospital at Harrisburg in 1851, and then never missed a meeting of the association.

6. Howard Kelly and Walter Burrage, *American Medical Biographies* (Baltimore: Norman Remington, 1920), p. 180; Franklin B. Sanborn, *Memoirs of Pliny Earle, M.D.* (Boston: Damrell & Upham, 1898), p. 54.

7. Awl to Kirkbride, 5 December 1857, Kirkbride MSS, IPH.

8. See Gerald N. Grob's careful assessment of Woodward's struggles with legislators' attitudes toward public policy in *The State and the Mentally Ill* (Chapel Hill: University of North Carolina Press, 1966).

9. There is no definitive study of William Awl's career; these conclusions are drawn from his voluminous correspondence with his colleagues.

10. Norman Dain, in *Disordered Minds* (Williamsburg, Va.: Colonial Williamsburg Foundation, 1971), depicts the ongoing rivalry between Galt and Stribling; for the quotation, see Galt to Stribling, 1 July 1844, Stribling MSS, WSH.

11. Ibid.; Curwen, *Original Members*, p. 39; Kirkbride to Stribling, 9 August 1867, Stribling MSS, WSH; Woodward to Chandler, 28 July 1844, Chandler MSS, AAS.

12. "Autobiographical Sketch dictated by Thomas S. Kirkbride, M.D., in 1882," Kirkbride MSS, IPH; Dain, *Disordered Minds*, pp. 69–71.

13. Curwen, *Original Members*, p. 14; Isaac Ray, *Contributions to Mental Pathology* (Boston: Little, Brown & Co., 1873. Reprint, with an Introduction by Jacques M. Quen. New York: Scholars' Facsimiles & Reprints, 1973), pp. v–vi. In England at the trial of Daniel M'Naghten, who wanted to shoot Robert Peel but killed Peel's private secretary instead, the court decided that a person was insane if he could not distinguish right from wrong.

14. Brigham to Kirkbride, 12 June 1849, Kirkbride MSS, IPH.

15. Curwen, *Original Members*, pp. 14, 17, 29. A copy of Earle's graduating thesis from the University of Pennsylvania Medical School, "The Causes, Duration, Termination, and Moral Treatment of Insanity," is in the Earle MSS, housed at the Westchester Division, New York Hospital, White Plains, N.Y.

16. J. H. Pooley, "Memoir of William Maclay Awl, M.D., of Columbus, Ohio," *Transactions of the Thirty-Second Annual Meeting of the Ohio State Medical Society* (Cincinnati: Mallory and Webb, Printers, 1877), pp. 72–74.

17. Sanborn, *Memoirs of Pliny Earle*, pp. 79–80; Pliny Earle, "The

Poetry of Insanity," *AJI* 1 (January 1845):193–224, citation on pp. 204–5.

18. The best sources for the understanding of moral treatment are the annual reports of the asylum doctors. Year after year, they explained the nature of the treatment, published the schedule of activities, and cited cases of people who had been cured by their therapy. Standard secondary works that deal with moral treatment include Hurd, *Institutional Care;* Deutsch, *Mentally Ill in America;* Grob, *The State and the Mentally Ill* and *Mental Institutions in America* (New York: Free Press, 1973); Norman Dain, *Concepts of Insanity in the United States, 1789–1865* (New Brunswick, N.J.: Rutgers University Press, 1964); Leonard K. Eaton, *New England Hospitals, 1790–1833* (Ann Arbor: University of Michigan Press, 1957); J. Sanborne Bockoven, *Moral Treatment in American Psychiatry* (New York: Springer Publishing Co., 1963); Eric T. Carlson and Norman Dain, "The Psychotherapy that was Moral Treatment," *American Journal of Psychiatry* 117 (December 1960):519–24; Norman Dain and Eric T. Carlson, "Milieu Therapy in the Nineteenth Century: Patient Care at the Friends' Asylum, Frankford, Pennsylvania, 1817–1861," *Journal of Nervous and Mental Disease* 131 (October 1960): 277–90.

19. Hurd, *Institutional Care,* 2:602–3; Eaton, *New England Hospitals,* pp. 137–38; Dain and Carlson, "Milieu Therapy," pp. 286–87.

20. Pliny Earle, *History, Description, and Statistics of the Bloomingdale Asylum for the Insane* (New York: Egbert, Hovey, & King, 1848), p. 26.

21. See, for instance, Eaton, *New England Hospitals;* Earle, *History, Description, and Statistics;* and Grob, *The State and the Mentally Ill.*

22. Sanborn, *Memoirs of Pliny Earle,* pp. 59–60. Earle resigned from his job at Bloomingdale and left for a tour of European asylums. In his later account of each of these institutions, he stressed the therapeutic use of labor for patients. See Pliny Earle, *Institutions for the Insane in Prussia, Austria, and Germany* (Utica: New York Asylum, Printers, 1853). Also see chap. 5 below for further discussion of Earle's trials at the Bloomingdale Asylum.

23. Woodward to Chandler, 28 July 1844, Woodward MSS, AAS. While Woodward was dismayed that at Stribling's asylum "each attendant [had] one or more slaves to do his work" and worried about these "serious obstacles to great success," Stribling wanted to alter the situation so that, rather than employ attendants with their slaves, the hospital would purchase its own slaves. See Western Lunatic Hospital, Annual Reports, 1842, 1843, 1844; "Lunatic Asylums of the United States," *AJI* 2 (October 1845):151–58. See also Awl to Kirkbride, 25 October 1849, 24 December 1849, Kirkbride MSS, IPH.

24. See Deutsch, *Mentally Ill in America,* pp. 184–85; the 178 letters from Curwen in the Kirkbride manuscript collection (Curwen was secretary of the association from 1858 to 1893 and published two major histories of its work); Buttolph to Woodward, 5 May 1842, Woodward MSS,

AAS; Buttolph to Kirkbride, 9 January 1847, Kirkbride MSS, IPH.

25. For Jarvis's career, see Gerald N. Grob, *Edward Jarvis and the Medical World of Nineteenth-century America* (Knoxville: University of Tennessee Press, 1978); for evidence of his interest in the founding meeting, see Jarvis to Woodward, 12 October 1844, Woodward MSS, AAS.

Chapter 1   A Changing World

1. Sentiments about the conditions of the insane in almshouses or jails and about the curability of insanity were rampant in various appeals to state legislatures in the early years of the nineteenth century. See especially *Reports and Other Documents relating to the State Lunatic Hospital at Worcester, Mass.*, 1837; *Report in Relation to an Asylum for the Insane Poor*, Pennsylvania, 1839; *Report of the Commissioners, appointed by the Governor of New Jersey, to ascertain the number of Lunatics and Idiots in the State*, 1840; and *Report of the Committee on the Insane Poor in Connecticut*, 1838, all reprinted in *The Origins of the State Mental Hospital in America* (New York: Arno Press, 1973); Henry Hurd, ed., *The Institutional Care of the Insane in the United States and Canada* (Baltimore: Johns Hopkins Press, 1916) 2:93–102, where the petition of the Connecticut Medical Society is reprinted (although with an incorrect date).

2. For genealogical and biographical sources, see below, chap. 2, n. 2 and the Bibliography.

3. For discussions of colonial New England society, see Richard Bushman, *From Puritan to Yankee* (New York: W. W. Norton, 1970); John Demos, *A Little Commonwealth* (New York: Oxford University Press, 1970); Philip J. Greven, Jr., *Four Generations* (Ithaca, N.Y.: Cornell University Press, 1970) and *The Protestant Temperament* (New York: New American Library, 1977); James A. Henretta, *The Evolution of American Society* (Lexington, Mass.: D. C. Heath, 1973) and "Families and Farms: *Mentalité* in Pre-Industrial America," *William and Mary Quarterly* 35 (January 1978):3–32; Edmund Morgan, *The Puritan Family* (New York: Harper & Row, 1966); Donald Scott, *From Office to Profession* (Philadelphia: University of Pennsylvania Press, 1978); Daniel Scott Smith, "Parental Power and Marriage Patterns," in *The American Family in Social-Historical Perspective*, ed. Michael Gordon, pp. 255–68 (New York: St. Martin's Press, 1983).

4. My analysis of Southern society is drawn from John Blassingame, *The Slave Community* (New York: Oxford University Press, 1979); Greven, *Protestant Temperament;* Herbert Gutman, *The Black Family in Slavery and Freedom* (New York: Vintage Books, 1977); Henretta, *Evolution of American Society;* Rhys Isaac, "Evangelical Revolt"; Russell Menard, "From Servant to Freeholder"; Robert Weir, " 'The Harmony We Were Famous For' "; and David Williams, "The Small Farmer in Eighteenth-Century Virginia Politics," in *Colonial America,* ed. Stanley

N. Katz and John M. Murrin, pp. 518–40, 290–313, 421–46, and 410–21, respectively (New York: Alfred A. Knopf, 1983); Daniel Blake Smith, "Autonomy and Affection" in *The American Family in Social-Historical Perspective,* ed. Michael Gordon, pp. 209–28 (New York: St. Martin's Press, 1983).

5. Brian Levy, " 'Tender Plants' " in *Colonial America,* ed. Stanley N. Katz and John M. Murrin, pp. 177–203 (New York: Alfred A. Knopf, 1983); J. Robert Frost, *The Quaker Family in Colonial America* (New York: St. Martin's Press, 1973); Sydney V. James, *A People among Peoples* (Cambridge, Mass.: Harvard University Press, 1963) all discuss Quaker values and life-styles.

6. For an extended discussion of the nature of the colonial economy, see Henretta, *Evolution of American Society* and "Families and Farms."

7. The commonality of the colonists' religious experience is a major theme in Greven's *Protestant Temperament.*

8. See especially Richard Bushman, "The Great Awakening in Connecticut"; Nathan Hatch, "The Origins of Civil Millennialism in America"; Isaac, "Evangelical Revolt," in *Colonial America,* ed. Stanley N. Katz and John M. Murrin, pp. 487–97, 497–518, and 518–40, respectively (New York: Alfred A. Knopf, 1983).

9. See Douglass North, Terry Anderson, and Peter Hill, *Growth and Welfare in the American Past* (Englewood Cliffs, N.J.: Prentice-Hall, 1983); Douglass North, *The Economic Growth of the United States* (New York: W. W. Norton, 1966); and Henretta, "Families and Farms."

10. Henretta, *Evolution of American Society.*

11. Until recently historians have accepted the dated and limited assessment of hostile attitudes toward the insane in the colonial period as put forth by Albert Deutsch in 1937 in his *Mentally Ill in America* (New York: Doubleday, Doran). However, two as yet unpublished doctoral studies offer new information. Dora M. E. Blackmon's "Care of the Mentally Ill in America, 1604–1812, in the Thirteen Original Colonies" (Ph.D. diss., University of Washington, 1964) adheres to an interpretation influenced by the Deutsch conclusions but offers a number of examples of attitudes and treatment that belie her conclusions. Mary Ann Jimenez's "Changing Faces of Madness: Insanity in Massachusetts, 1700–1850" (Ph.D. diss., Brandeis University, 1980) is a thorough examination of a variety of sources dealing with the mad and offers a more convincing analysis of the place of the mad in the colonial social order.

12. Jimenez, "Changing Faces of Madness," pp. 83–86 and 94; Blackmon, "Care of the Mentally Ill," pp. 121–22.

13. For the specific references, see Jimenez, "Changing Faces of Madness," pp. 92–94; Blackmon, "Care of the Mentally Ill," pp. 106–7. For other examples, see Margaret Creech, *Three Centuries of Poor Law Administration: A Study of Legislation in Rhode Island* (Chicago: University of Chicago Press, 1936), pp. 85–89, 314–18; David M. Schneider,

The History of Public Welfare in New York State (Chicago: University of Chicago Press, 1938), pp. 82–83.

14. Jimenez, in "Changing Faces of Madness," traces Coolidge's fate on pp. 88–90, 102, 117–20.

15. Blackmon, "Care of the Mentally Ill," p. 109.

16. For a discussion of the Enlightenment writers' fascination with medicine, see Peter Gay, *The Enlightenment: An Interpretation* (New York: Alfred A. Knopf, 1969), vol. 2, chap. 1. For the role of the "minister-physician," see Whitfield J. Bell, Jr., *The Colonial Physician and Other Essays* (New York: Science History Publications, 1975); John Duffy, *The Healers* (New York: McGraw-Hill, 1976); Maurice B. Gordon, *Aesculapius Comes to the Colonies* (Ventnor, N.J.: Ventnor Publishers, 1949); Richard H. Shryock, *Medicine and Society in America, 1600–1860* (New York: New York University Press, 1960).

17. For discussions of medical theories, see Charles E. Rosenberg, "The Therapeutic Revolution" in *The Therapeutic Revolution,* ed. Morris Vogel and Charles Rosenberg, pp. 3–25 (Philadelphia: University of Pennsylvania Press, 1979), and for their relationship to psychiatric theories, see Norman Dain, *Concepts of Insanity in the United States, 1789–1865* (New Brunswick, N.J.: Rutgers University Press, 1964).

18. Jimenez, in "Changing Faces of Madness," discusses James Otis on pp. 95–97, 102, 111; Archelaus Putnam on pp. 210–12; and the changes in the treatment of the insane in the late eighteenth century on pp. 205–25.

19. For the experiences of Concord and East Sudbury, see Jimenez, "Changing Faces of Madness," pp. 215–25; for the changing attitudes of other communities, pp. 212, 223–25. See also Douglas Lamar Jones, "The Strolling Poor: Transiency in Eighteenth-Century Massachusetts," *Journal of Social History* 8 (Summer 1975):28–54. At least in part, the move to confine the insane in late eighteenth-century America arose from economic and social changes as well as from the growing moral sense that idleness was a corrupting force. In that respect, the American move toward incarceration resembled Foucault's "great confinement" of mid-seventeenth-century Europe. See Michel Foucault, *Madness and Civilization,* trans. Richard Howard (New York: Pantheon Books, 1965), pp. 46–64.

20. As cited in Mary Beth Norton, *Liberty's Daughters* (Boston: Little, Brown, 1980), p. 243.

21. For the changing American scene in the early nineteenth-century, see Richard Brown, *Modernization: The Transformation of American Life* (New York: Hill & Wang, 1976); David Brion Davis, *Antebellum American Culture* (Lexington, Mass.: D. C. Heath, 1979); John Kasson, *Civilizing the Machine: Technology and Republican Values, 1776–1900* (New York: Penguin, 1977); Edward Pessen, *Jacksonian America* (Homewood, Ill.: Dorsey Press, 1969); Leonard L. Richards, *The Advent of*

American Democracy (Glenview, Ill.: Scott, Foresman, 1977); and Ronald G. Walters, *American Reformers* (New York: Hill & Wang, 1978).

22. Henretta, *Evolution of American Society,* p. 214; Brown, *Modernization,* chap. 5; Alexis de Tocqueville, *Democracy in America,* trans. Henry Reeve (New York: Dearborn, 1838. Reprint, rev. and ed. Phillips Bradley, 2 vols. New York: Vintage Books, 1945), 2:144–45.

23. Walters, *American Reformers;* Gary B. Nash, "Up From the Bottom in Franklin's Philadelphia" in *The Private Side of American History,* ed. Gary B. Nash, pp. 163–78 (New York: Harcourt Brace Jovanovich, 1983) and "Urban Wealth and Poverty" in *Colonial America,* ed. Stanley N. Katz and John M. Murrin, pp. 447–83 (New York: Alfred A. Knopf, 1983); Benjamin J. Klebaner, "Poverty and Its Relief in American Thought, 1815–1861," *Social Service Review* 38 (December 1964): 382–99.

24. The time periods upon which these population trends are based vary. I studied the population statistics for the decades in which each man lived in his hometown, as well as those for two decades before and after his residence there. In the case of the New Englanders, twenty-three of their hometowns barely grew, and nineteen actually lost population.

For descriptions of this type of population depletion, see Lois K. Mathews Rosenberry, *The Expansion of New England* (New York: Russell & Russell, 1962); Stewart H. Holbrook, *Yankee Exodus* (Seattle: University of Washington Press, 1968); Lewis D. Stilwell, *Migration from Vermont* (Montpelier: Vermont Historical Society, 1948); David M. Ludlum, *Social Ferment in Vermont, 1791–1850* (Montpelier: Vermont Historical Society, 1948); Rowland Berthoff, *An Unsettled People: Social Order and Disorder in American History* (New York: Harper & Row, 1971); and Whitney R. Cross, *The Burned-over District* (New York: Harper & Row, 1965).

25. For Samuel Bell's early experiences in Francestown, see W. R. Cochrane and George K. Wood, *History of Francestown, N.H.* (Nashua, N.H.: James H. Barker, Printer, 1895), p. 447. Bell eventually rose to prominence in New Hampshire politics, becoming governor (1819–23) and United States senator (1823–35). For the others, see William S. Hall, "John Waring Parker," *Journal of the South Carolina Medical Association* 69 (October 1973):381–89; William Wesley Woollen, *Biographical and Historical Sketches of Early Indiana* (Indianapolis: Hammond & Co., 1883), pp. 478–80.

26. Eric T. Carlson, "Amariah Brigham: I. Life and Works," *American Journal of Psychiatry* 112 (April 1956):831–36; Howard Kelly and Walter Burrage, *American Medical Biographies* (Baltimore: Norman Remington, 1920), p. 1184. Of fifty-one traceable families, twenty-one exhibited similar patterns.

27. For the family of Charles Stedman, see Henry S. Nourse, ed., *The Birth, Marriage and Death Register, Church Records and Epitaphs of Lancaster, Mass.* (Clinton, Mass.: W. J. Coulter, Printer, 1890); for Jarvis's family, see Gerald Grob, *Edward Jarvis and the Medical World of*

Nineteenth-century America (Knoxville: University of Tennessee Press, 1978), pp. 1–56. Captain Daniel White's will is in the probate records housed in the Connecticut State Library at Hartford. For the Cutters' experience, see Daniel B. Cutter, *History of the Town of Jaffrey, New Hampshire, 1749–1880* (Concord, N.H.: Republican Press Association, 1881).

28. For a more detailed discussion of these experiences, see below, chap. 2.

29. In chap. 3, below, I discuss the lives of Samuel Woodward, Francis Stribling, and William Awl in detail.

30. I have adopted a method similar to the one Sidney H. Aronson used in *Status and Kinship in the Higher Civil Service* (Cambridge, Mass.: Harvard University Press, 1964) to determine socioeconomic class. Using occupations of fathers, status of colleges, status of medical schools, expected cost of medical education, probable expenditure for medical training, genealogical description, and education of siblings, I find that none of these men falls into Aronson's Class 1, "rich and illustrious," or Class 4, "poor or destitute." Most of them are in the "prosperous and highly respectable" Class 2 and some in the "average means and respectability" Class 3.

Of thirty-seven fathers whose occupations are known, sixteen were professional men (ten doctors, three lawyers, and three ministers), sixteen owned farmlands, two were merchants, and three were skilled artisans.

31. Paul Johnson, *A Shopkeeper's Millennium* (New York: Hill & Wang, 1978); Mary Ryan, *The Cradle of the Middle Class* (Cambridge: Cambridge University Press, 1981); Anthony Wallace, *Rockdale* (New York: W. W. Norton, 1981); Walters, *American Reformers;* Alice Felt Tyler, *Freedom's Ferment* (New York: Harper & Row, 1962); Charles I. Foster, *An Errand of Mercy* (Chapel Hill: University of North Carolina Press, 1960); C. S. Griffin, *The Ferment of Reform, 1830–1860* (New York: Thomas Y. Crowell, 1967) and *Their Brothers' Keepers* (New Brunswick, N.J.: Rutgers University Press, 1960).

32. See below, chaps. 2 and 3.

33. Theodric Romeyn Beck, *An Inaugural Dissertation on Insanity* (New York: J. Seymour, 1811), pp. 23–24.

34. Isaac Ray, *Mental Hygiene* (Boston: Ticknor & Fields, 1863), pp. 224, 225, 262; Proceedings, Twelfth Annual Meeting, *AJI* 14 (July 1857):86.

35. Proceedings, Thirteenth Annual Meeting, *AJI* 15 (July 1858): 126–28.

36. Amariah Brigham, *Remarks on the Influence of Mental Cultivation and Mental Excitement upon Health,* 2d ed. (Boston: Marsh, Capen & Lyon, 1833), pp. 80–81; for Jarvis's comments, Proceedings, Thirteenth Annual Meeting, *AJI* 15 (July 1858):127.

37. Amariah Brigham, *Observations on the Influence of Religion upon the Health and Physical Welfare of Mankind* (Boston: Marsh, Capen &

Lyon, 1835), pp. 143–44, 149, 265–66, 275; Pliny Earle, "On the Causes of Insanity," *AJI* 4 (July 1848):206–7.

38. As cited in Amariah Brigham, *An Inquiry concerning the Diseases and Functions of the Brain, the Spinal Cord, and the Nerves* (New York: George Adlard, 1840), pp. 289–90. Isaac Ray agreed and blamed the newspapers for getting people involved. "The appeals of an aspiring demagogue, the debates of an excited convention, the platform of a political party, exercise the minds of millions, who, without this agency, would have moved on to their dying hour in happy ignorance of them all." Ray, *Mental Hygiene,* p. 237.

39. Ohio Lunatic Asylum, Annual Report, 1850, p. 14.

40. See Leonard K. Eaton, *New England Hospitals, 1790–1833* (Ann Arbor: University of Michigan Press, 1957), p. 32; Hurd, *Institutional Care,* 2:93–102; *Reports and Other Documents relating to the State Lunatic Hospital at Worcester, Mass.* in *The Origins of the State Mental Hospital in America.*

41. See Gay, *Enlightenment,* 2:13, 15–16; Jimenez, "Changing Faces of Madness," pp. 227–30; Constance M. McGovern, "The Insane, the Asylum, and the State in Nineteenth-Century Vermont," *Vermont History* 52 (Fall 1984):206–8.

42. On Pinel, see Jan E. Goldstein, "French Psychiatry in Social and Political Context: The Formation of a New Profession, 1820–1860" (Ph.D. diss., Columbia University, 1978); Dain, *Concepts of Insanity;* Constance M. McGovern, " 'Mad Doctors' " (Ph.D. diss., University of Massachusetts, 1976); René Semelaigne, *Les Pionniers de la psychiatrie française avant et après Pinel,* 2 vols. (Paris: Librairie J.-B. Baillière et Fils, 1930–32); Philippe Pinel, *A Treatise on Insanity,* trans. D. D. Davis (Sheffield, England: W. Todd, 1806).

43. On Tuke, see Andrew Scull, *Museums of Madness* (New York: St. Martin's Press, 1979); William L. Parry-Jones, *The Trade in Lunacy* (London: Routledge & Kegan Paul, 1972); Dain, *Concepts of Insanity;* McGovern, " 'Mad Doctors' "; Samuel Tuke, *Description of the Retreat* (York, England: Thomas Wilson and Sons, Printers, 1813).

44. On Rush, see Eric T. Carlson, Jeffrey L. Wollock, and Patricia S. Noel, eds., *Benjamin Rush's Lectures on the Mind* (Philadelphia: American Philosophical Society, 1981); Dain, *Concepts of Insanity.*

45. Hurd, *Institutional Care,* 3:137, 442; Eaton, *New England Hospitals,* pp. 67–68, 118, 125.

46. See Eaton, *New England Hospitals,* passim.

47. Eaton, *New England Hospitals,* pp. 29–55, 69–79; Gerald N. Grob, *The State and the Mentally Ill* (Chapel Hill: University of North Carolina Press, 1966), pp. 26–29.

48. Hurd, *Institutional Care,* 2:30; *Report and Memorial of the County Superintendents of the Poor of New York State on Lunacy and Its Relation to Pauperism, and for the Relief of the Insane Poor* in *The Origins of the State Mental Hospital in America* (New York: Arno Press,

1973); Norman Dain, *Disordered Minds* (Williamsburg, Va.: Colonial Williamsburg Foundation, 1971), p. 62; *Report of the Directors to whom was committed the charge of erecting A Lunatic Asylum for the State of Ohio*, Ohio Lunatic Asylum, Annual Report, 1838, p. 5.

Chapter 2   An Uncertain Profession

1. "Obituaries," [Samuel White], *AJI* 1 (April 1845):384; Norman Dain, *Disordered Minds* (Williamsburg, Va.: Colonial Williamsburg Foundation, 1971), pp. 70–71; Howard Kelly and Walter Burrage, *American Medical Biographies* (Baltimore: Norman Remington, 1920), pp. 48, 91; Gerald N. Grob, *The State and the Mentally Ill* (Chapel Hill: University of North Carolina Press, 1966), pp. 43–48.

There were at least 115 men who held a medical superintendency (or its equivalent) before 1860 (see Appendix), but I have limited my study to the eighty-three who held a post for more than five years. This tenure seems to indicate a serious interest in the profession.

2. The genealogical, ethnic, religious, and educational data upon which the rest of this chapter relies have been gleaned from a variety of biographical works including Henry Hurd, ed., *The Institutional Care of the Insane in the United States and Canada* (Baltimore: Johns Hopkins Press, 1916); Kelly and Burrage, *American Medical Biographies;* James G. Wilson and John Fiske, eds., *Appleton's Cyclopaedia of American Biography* (New York: D. Appleton and Company, 1887); *The National Cyclopaedia of American Biography* (London: James T. White and Company, 1892); *Dictionary of American Biography* (New York: Charles Scribner's Sons, 1828–1959); the obituaries and memorials in *AJI;* many other journal articles and monographs on specific individuals; unpublished or privately printed biographies from the institutions in which these men served; and extant local histories. (See Bibliography.)

Prestigious colleges are defined as those founded in the pre-Revolutionary period as cited in Sidney H. Aronson, *Status and Kinship in the Higher Civil Service* (Cambridge, Mass.: Harvard University Press, 1964).

3. See Kelly and Burrage, *American Medical Biographies,* p. 217; Thomas Earle to Pliny Earle, 8 September 1831, Earle MSS, AAS; Gerald N. Grob, Introduction to Edward Jarvis, *Insanity and Idiocy in Massachusetts* (Boston: William White, 1855. Reprint. Cambridge, Mass.: Harvard University Press, 1971), p. 40.

4. Others went to Castleton Medical College, Castleton, Vermont; the Medical Department of Dartmouth College, Hanover, New Hampshire; the Medical Department of the University of New York, New York City; the Medical Department of Transylvania University, Lexington, Kentucky; the Medical College of South Carolina, Charleston; Louisville Medical Institute, Kentucky; the Medical College of Ohio, Cincinnati; the Medical College of Philadelphia; the Medical School of Maine at

Bowdoin College, Brunswick, Maine; Geneva Medical College, Geneva, New York; and Woodstock Clinical School of Medicine, Woodstock, Vermont.

5. Notable preceptors are defined as those who are mentioned in standard histories of medicine in America, such as William F. Norwood, *Medical Education in the United States before the Civil War* (Philadelphia: University of Pennsylvania Press, 1944) or Francis R. Packard, *History of Medicine in the United States,* 2 vols. (New York: Hafner, 1963). The rest studied with less famous, although not necessarily less capable, local doctors.

6. For a discussion of the importance of foreign study on career success, see Courtney R. Hall, "The Rise of Professional Surgery in the United States, 1800–1865," *Bulletin of the History of Medicine* 26 (Summer 1952):238–39.

7. For the history of medical licensing, see Joseph F. Kett, *The Formation of the American Medical Profession* (New Haven, Conn.: Yale University Press, 1968), chap. 1; William G. Rothstein, *American Physicians in the Nineteenth Century* (Baltimore: Johns Hopkins Press, 1972), pp. 63–81; Henry B. Shafer, *The American Medical Profession, 1783–1850* (New York: Columbia University Press, 1936), pp. 200–214; and Richard H. Shryock, *Medical Licensing in America, 1650–1965* (Baltimore: Johns Hopkins Press, 1967), pp. 3–42.

Among the more zealous who joined medical societies were William Awl, who initiated the annual state convention in Ohio, and Samuel Woodward, who participated in nearly every early move in New England to establish a national medical association.

8. Norwood, *Medical Education,* gives an excellent sense of the growth and widespread lack of quality of medical schools in the antebellum period. The material on medical education in this chapter is based on an analysis of Norwood's description of each individual school. The availability of clinical facilities in medical schools is as follows:

	pre-1800	1800s	1810s	1820s	1830s	1840s	Total by 1850
Clinical facilities	3	2	0	5	11	5	26
No clinical facilities	1	0	4	8	3	15	31

9. Despite other drawbacks, schools noted for their outstanding faculties were the College of Physicians and Surgeons of the Western District of the State of New York, Fairfield; the Medical School of Maine at Bowdoin College, Brunswick, Maine; Geneva Medical College, Geneva, N.Y.; Albany Medical College, Albany, N.Y.; the University of Pennsylvania School of Medicine, Philadelphia; the Medical School of Harvard University, Cambridge, Mass.; and Jefferson Medical College, Philadelphia. Only the Medical Department of the University of Virginia, Charlottes-

ville, provided salaries for its professors in the 1830s. The University of Michigan Medical School, Ann Arbor, experimented with salaries when it opened in 1850, but before 1860 the practice was not accepted generally.

10. As cited in Franklin B. Sanborn, *Memoirs of Pliny Earle, M.D.* (Boston: Damrell & Upham, 1898), pp. 56–57.

11. As cited in Shafer, *American Medical Profession*, p. 166.

12. See Thomas Kirkbride's Account Book, 28 May 1835–4 January 1839, Kirkbride MSS, IPH. Nancy Tomes, in *A Generous Confidence: Thomas Story Kirkbride and the Art of Asylum-Keeping* (Cambridge: Cambridge University Press, 1984), argues that Kirkbride was well on his way to a lucrative practice. Yet his one extant account book covers less than four years, and his records show little increase in income from year to year. Kirkbride also noted the accounts he had turned over to bill collectors. These meager records and, in addition, Kirkbride's choice of asylum administration when at the same time he received the offer of the cherished surgical post at the Pennsylvania Hospital, his description of the preferred salary for the asylum job as "liberal," and his noting (through his parents' remarks) that the psychiatric post offered him professional "certainty" all substantiate the very real doubts Kirkbride himself had about his professional prospects in general or surgical practice. For further discussion, see below, chap. 3.

Furthermore, typical incomes for physicians of the period are difficult to ascertain. Aronson, *Status and Kinship*, p. 48, says a good physician could make between $4,000 and $5,000 annually. Aronson bases his figure on Evarts B. Greene, *The Revolutionary Generation* (New York: Macmillan, 1943), p. 93, who, in turn bases his figure on the one example of Benjamin Rush's income of £900. Both Daniel H. Calhoun, *The American Civil Engineer* (Cambridge, Mass.: Harvard University Press, 1960), p. 172, and Rothstein, *American Physicians,* use Shafer's *American Medical Profession* incomes but opt for his lowest figures. Shafer does not attempt to draw conclusions about average or typical incomes but remarks that his sources of citations, day books and account books, "are those of prominent and successful doctors, and not those of the small country doctor or impoverished city doctor who could hardly afford to keep accounts" (p. 169). Charles E. Rosenberg cites a beginning New York City doctor's income at $400 and that of an established physician at $1,500–2,000 in the 1860s. "The Practice of Medicine in New York a Century Ago," *Bulletin of the History of Medicine* 41 (Summer 1967): 223–53. For other analyses of incomes, see Barnes Riznik, "The Professional Lives of Early Nineteenth-century New England Doctors," *Journal of the History of Medicine and Allied Sciences* 19 (January 1964):1–16; George Rosen, *Fees and Fee Bills* (Baltimore: Johns Hopkins Press, 1946), pp. 7–19. Despite every effort, there is little agreement among historians as to what constituted "typical" incomes for nineteenth-century physicians.

13. The AMA 1847 report is cited in Rothstein, *American Physicians,* p. 98. The combined ratios from Riznik's and my studies are:

1790s	1:668	1820s	1:575
1800s	1:795	1830s	1:542
1810s	1:597	1840s	1:668

The ratios of doctors to population are taken from Barnes Riznik's computer study, which he used as the basis for his article, "The Professional Lives of Early Nineteenth-century New England Doctors" and for his longer and more detailed paper of the same title (typescript, Old Sturbridge Village Library, Sturbridge, Mass.) and from Constance M. McGovern, " 'Mad Doctors': American Psychiatrists, 1800–1860" (Ph.D. diss., University of Massachusetts, 1976). Ratios in my study were determined by consulting the U.S. Census for the years in which the men practiced in the communities, and the number of doctors was determined by counting those listed in city directories or by analyzing lists of physicians in local histories. In both sources, the error is more likely to be on the side of underestimation of the number of doctors serving any given community.

14. Jaffrey's doctor-patient ratio zigzagged throughout the first half of the nineteenth century:

	Doctors	Ratio		Doctors	Ratio
1790s	2	1:618	1820s	1	1:1,339
1800s	3	1:447	1830s	2	1:677
1810s	3	1:445	1840s	1	1:1,411

For the results of the study of the psychiatrists' towns, see McGovern, " 'Mad Doctors.' " Data were gathered from twenty-five published city directories (see Bibliography), although relying on these sources for information sometimes misrepresents the situation inasmuch as compilers frequently missed people in their listings. For other communities, I relied upon the results of Riznik's manuscript computer study. The majority of the communities selected were those that were either birthplaces or places of business of the men who form the main subject of this book. The choice of communities was sometimes limited by the availability of the data.

15. Percentages are based on the number of known men: nine older men, all rural-born; and fifty-one younger men, six urban-born and forty-five rural-born. For William Rockwell's experience, see William Chauncey Fowler, *History of Durham, Connecticut* (Hartford, Conn.: Press of Wiley, Waterman & Eaton, 1866).

16. See Gerald N. Grob, *Edward Jarvis and the Medical World of Nineteenth-century America* (Knoxville: University of Tennessee Press, 1978), pp. 29–56.

17. Rothstein, *American Physicians,* p. 179.

18. For the treatment of the Thomsonian movement in detail, see James Harvey Young, *The Toadstool Millionaires* (Princeton, N.J.: Princeton University Press, 1961), pp. 44–57; Rothstein, *American Physicians*, pp. 125–51; Kett, *Formation of the American Medical Profession*, pp. 97–131. Kett is especially insightful in his handling of the political and cultural repercussions of the movement.

19. See Kett, *Formation of the American Medical Profession*, pp. 132–64 for the best historical scholarship on homeopathy. The growth of eclecticism is outlined in Rothstein, *American Physicians*, pp. 218–22, and Grahamism and hydropathy as social forces are treated in Richard H. Shryock, *Medicine in America* (Baltimore: Johns Hopkins Press, 1966), pp. 111–25.

20. James Chandler to George Chandler, 10 August 1840, Chandler MSS, AAS; Jones to Kirkbride, 23 February 1837, Kirkbride MSS, IPH; Joseph A. Waddell, *Annals of Augusta County, Virginia*, 2d ed. (Bridgewater, Va.: C. J. Carrier, 1958), p. 432; Western Lunatic Hospital, Annual Report, 1836, p. 12; John Curwen, *History of the Association of Medical Superintendents of American Institutions for the Insane* (Harrisburg, Pa.: Theo. F. Scheffer, 1875), p. 97.

21. See such works as John Demos, *A Little Commonwealth* (New York: Oxford University Press, 1970); Philip J. Greven, Jr., *Four Generations* (Ithaca, N.Y.: Cornell University Press, 1970); Michael Katz, *The People of Hamilton, Canada West: Family and Class in a Mid-Nineteenth Century City* (Cambridge, Mass.: Harvard University Press, 1975).

22. The breakdowns of average marriage age for lawyers, ministers, and doctors, derived from my study of college graduates, " 'Mad Doctors,' " are as follows:

	Older (pre-1820)	Younger (post-1820)
Lawyers	28.1 years ($N = 70$)	29.2 years ($N = 158$)
Ministers	28.4 years ($N = 61$)	29.8 years ($N = 186$)
Doctors	26.2 years ($N = 17$)	29.1 years ($N = 67$)
Psychiatrists	28.9 years ($N = 8$)	31.1 years ($N = 24$)

23. The following table, derived from McGovern, " 'Mad Doctors,' " shows the average number of years between the start of professional practice and marriage:

	Older	Younger
Lawyers	5.7 years ($N = 72$)	5.3 years ($N = 161$)
Ministers	2.4 years ($N = 57$)	3.5 years ($N = 158$)
Doctors	4.7 years ($N = 17$)	4.7 years ($N = 66$)
Psychiatrists	6.4 years ($N = 8$)	7.3 years ($N = 24$)

24. The average national decline in the American birthrate between 1830 and 1860 was approximately 20 percent. For a brief review of the literature on demographic transition and the hypothesis that relates declining economic opportunity to a lowered birthrate, see Robert V. Wells,

"Family History and Demographic Transition," *Journal of Social History* 9 (Fall 1975):1–19. For the national birthrate decline, see Yasukichi Yasuba, *Birth Rates of the White Population in the United States, 1800–1860* (Baltimore: Johns Hopkins Press, 1962), esp. chap. 2. Yasuba (pp. 68–72) notes that Maine (33.6 percent), New Hampshire (37.5 percent), Vermont (38.5 percent), Kentucky (22.8 percent), and Tennessee (25.3 percent) had the greatest declines in crude birth ratios, although other New England and frontier states also had large declines. For the thirty psychiatrists about whom there are data, the decrease in the birth ratio was 47.8 percent; three were born in New Hampshire and one in Maine. For the thirteen for whom there is paired data (that is, the number of children of both fathers and their sons), the decrease was 59.5 percent. One was born in Vermont, three in New Hampshire, two in Maine, and one in Kentucky. The majority were born in states with more slowly declining birthrates, and therefore the disparity between the birthrates of antebellum Americans in general and of psychiatrists in particular remains significant. Delayed marriage is more likely to affect birthrate, of course, when women marry later; unfortunately, there is little available information on the ages of psychiatrists' wives. For discussion of this factor, see Daniel Scott Smith, "Family Limitation, Sexual Control, and Domestic Feminism in Victorian America," in *Clio's Consciousness Raised*, ed. Mary Hartman and Lois Banner, pp. 119–36 (New York: Harper & Row, 1974), and Robert V. Wells, "Demographic Change and the Life Cycle of American Families," in *The Family in History*, ed. Theodore K. Rabb and Robert I. Rotberg, pp. 85–94 (New York: Harper & Row, 1971).

25. My study of 597 (of 880) graduates of Middlebury College, 1800–60, in " 'Mad Doctors,' " shows that on the average the decline in the birthrate among other professionals was only 19 percent. The following table depicts the breakdown, according to profession, of the average number of children and the rate of decline:

	Older	Younger	Decline
Lawyers	4.9 ($N =$ 64)	4.0 ($N =$ 89)	18.4%
Ministers	5.6 ($N =$ 105)	4.6 ($N =$ 182)	17.9%
Doctors	5.2 ($N =$ 19)	4.5 ($N =$ 22)	13.5%
Others	5.4 ($N =$ 29)	3.9 ($N =$ 87)	24.1%

26. Grob, *The State and the Mentally Ill*, pp. 44–45.

27. See Awl to Kirkbride, 6 June 1848, 7 July 1849; S. H. Smith to Kirkbride, 8 March 1852; Nichols to Kirkbride, 3 March 1852, Kirkbride MSS, IPH. For Stribling, see Western Lunatic Hospital, Annual Report, 1842.

28. Porter to Woodward, 5 October 1832, Woodward MSS, AAS.

29. For a sampling of this kind of concern on the part of Woodward, see the following letters to him: Miner, June 1834; Sumner, 22 February

1840; Salter, 2 March 1840; Awl, 18 April 1842; Batchelder, 18 April 1842; King, 12 May 1842; Taft, 10 December 1842; and Woodward to Mann, 26 February 1840, Woodward MSS, AAS; Woodward to Earle, 11 October 1840, Earle MSS, AAS; Woodward to Chandler, 12 May 1842, Chandler MSS, AAS; Woodward to Kirkbride, 2 September 1842, Kirkbride MSS, IPH.

30. E. K. Hunt, "Memorial of Dr. Amariah Brigham," *AJI* 14 (July 1857):13–14; Sumner to Woodward, 17 April 1840, Woodward MSS, AAS; and Hurd, *Institutional Care,* 4:360–62.

31. The fate of Earle's young cousin Mary is described in a poignant letter to Franklin B. Sanborn from another of Earle's cousins, Rebecca Spring, 14 July 1897, Earle MSS, AAS. Spring also pointed out that, at one time, Earle was "interested in a lady of Salem, and she in him, but he told me he could not marry her on account of there being insanity in her family also." Earle never married. His brother was described by Samuel May in a letter to Sanborn, 26 May 1897, Earle MSS, AAS. Earle's sister eventually entered the Northampton State Lunatic Hospital in Massachusetts for psychiatric treatment while Earle was superintendent there. See Sanborn, *Memoirs of Pliny Earle,* pp. 220, 293 and Northampton State Lunatic Hospital Register, 1885. For his brother's advice, see Thomas Earle to Pliny Earle, 9 September 1831, Earle MSS, AAS.

32. Proceedings, Fourteenth Annual Meeting, *AJI* 16 (July 1859): 44–46; J. H. Pooley, "Memoir of William Maclay Awl, M.D., of Columbus, Ohio," *Transactions of the Thirty-Second Annual Meeting of the Ohio State Medical Society* (Cincinnati: Mallory and Welsh, Printers, 1877), p. 76.

33. Ronald G. Walters, *American Reformers* (New York: Hill & Wang, 1978), p. 6.

34. Eric T. Carlson, "Edward Mead and the Second American Psychiatric Journal," *American Journal of Psychiatry* 113 (April 1956):561; Sanborn, *Memoirs of Pliny Earle,* pp. 24–26.

35. The quotation is from "Autobiographical Sketch dictated by Thomas S. Kirkbride, M.D., in 1882," pp. 10–12, Kirkbride, MSS, IPH.

36. The lack of formal class instruction does not necessarily indicate total ignorance of works written about mental disease. Medical students gained knowledge about the nervous system through their anatomy lectures, and, as Tomes, in *Generous Confidence,* p. 60, points out, Thomas Kirkbride was quite familiar with Benjamin Rush's book on diseases of the mind. Samuel Woodward's father assigned Rush's book to his apprentices, and the younger Woodward had copies of similar treatises in his library. See Riznik, "Professional Lives" (typescript), and the will of Samuel Bayard Woodward housed at the Hampshire County Courthouse, Northampton, Massachusetts. In their careers as psychiatrists, too, they were aware of many of the books published on the Continent. In the second issue of his journal, Amariah Brigham printed a list of

eighty-eight books on insanity published in the previous one hundred years. "List of Books," *AJI* 1 (October 1844): 186–92.

37. Superintendents' salaries in some institutions:

Vermont Asylum for the Insane (Brattleboro)	1836	$1,000
	1842	1,200
Indiana Hospital for the Insane (Indianapolis)	1847	1,200
Friends' Asylum for the Insane (Frankford, Pa.)	1849	1,000
Pennsylvania Hospital for the Insane (Philadelphia)	1850	3,000
Ohio Lunatic Asylum (Columbus)	1850	1,200
New York State Lunatic Asylum (Utica)	1850	2,000
Hartford Retreat for the Insane (Hartford, Conn.)	1850	1,500
New Jersey State Lunatic Asylum (Trenton)	1850	1,500
McLean Asylum (Charlestown, Mass.)	1850	1,500
Western Lunatic Hospital (Staunton, Va.)	1850	2,500
Louisiana Insane Asylum (Jackson, La.)	1850	800
Pennsylvania State Lunatic Hospital (Harrisburg)	1851	1,500
Iowa Asylum for the Insane (Mount Pleasant)	1861	1,600

38. Shafer, *American Medical Profession,* pp. 169, 166–67; Riznik, "Professional Lives," typescript.

39. See Awl to Kirkbride, 27 May 1847; Benedict to Kirkbride, 31 January 1855; Lee to Kirkbride, 11 December 1865, Kirkbride MSS, IPH.

The following table shows the length of service in psychiatry of 79 of the 83 early superintendents:

	Died in office	Retired after 60	Others
40+ years	5	2	0
30–39 years	6	5	0
20–29 years	7	3	6
10–19 years	7	1	14
9– years	4	3	16

40. See Patterson to Kirkbride, 20 February 1852, Nichols to Kirkbride, 3 March 1852, 19 March 1852, 22 April 1852, Kirkbride MSS, IPH; Sanborn, *Memoirs of Pliny Earle,* pp. 159–60; Bell to Earle, 22 January 1858, Earle MSS, AAS.

41. For both men the late-in-life moves to other institutions were mixed blessings. Buttolph went from the New Jersey State Lunatic Asylum at Trenton to the new State Lunatic Asylum at Morristown, N.J., in 1876; he resigned that position in 1885 (at the age of seventy) in protest over the managers' plan to separate the medical department from the business department. John Curwen was forced out of his post at the Pennsylvania State Lunatic Hospital at Harrisburg in 1881 when he refused to accept the trustees' appointment of a woman doctor on the staff;

he spent the next thirteen years working at the State Hospital for the Insane at Warren, Pa., retiring at the age of seventy-nine.

42. Hurd, *Institutional Care*, 2:84.

43. Kirkbride, "Autobiographical Sketch," pp. 10–12.

Chapter 3   The Organizers

1. See Woodward to Stribling, 26 May 1843, Stribling MSS, WSH, in which Woodward included the text of a letter from James Barnard suggesting the exchange of European and American annual reports and mentioning the formation of the British association of asylum administrators in 1841. Both Stribling (in 1843) and Awl (in 1842) had noted the desirability of such a gathering in their annual reports. See also Kirkbride to Stribling, 1 June 1844, 5 July 1844, 28 August 1844; Woodward to Stribling, 5 August 1844, ibid.; Woodward to Earle, 26 July 1844, Earle MSS, AAS.

2. Awl to Kirkbride, 27 May 1847, Kirkbride MSS, IPH; Woodward to Mann, 11 March 1844, Woodward MSS, AAS.

3. Nancy Tomes, *A Generous Confidence: Thomas Story Kirkbride and the Art of Asylum-keeping* (Cambridge: Cambridge University Press, 1984), chap. 5.

4. "Medical Association. Meeting of the Medical Superintendents of American Institutions for the Insane," *AJI* 1 (January 1845):254.

5. Kirkbride to Awl, 27 June 1843, 24 July 1844, Kirkbride MSS, IPH.

6. See Tomes, *Generous Confidence,* chap. 4 for a more detailed discussion of Kirkbride's judgment about the unsuitability of the new hospital; see Kirkbride to Brigham, 23 November 1844, Kirkbride MSS, IPH, for the quotation.

7. John Curwen described Kirkbride's patience in the "Obituary Notice of Thomas S. Kirkbride, M.D.," which he read before the American Philosophical Society, 16 January 1885. See copy in Kirkbride MSS, IPH, p. 225; Tomes, *Generous Confidence,* pp. 223–26, cites patients' descriptions of Kirkbride's other attributes.

8. For an insightful view of the gradual transition of Quaker benevolence to general philanthropy, see Sydney V. James, *A People among Peoples* (Cambridge, Mass.: Harvard Universtiy Press, 1963).

9. The most reliable information on Thomas Kirkbride's youth and early career are his "Autobiographical Sketch dictated by Thomas S. Kirkbride, M.D., in 1882" and Tomes, *Generous Confidence.* See Curwen, "Obituary," p. 226 for Kirkbride's attitude toward his Quaker heritage and Kirkbride to Butler, 31 January 1864, Kirkbride MSS, IPH, for his assessment of his father's character.

10. Kirkbride to Butler, 31 January 1864, Kirkbride MSS, IPH. Kirkbride wrote this letter to Lizzie Butler (who became his second wife two years later) on the occasion of his father's death.

11. Kirkbride, "Autobiographical Sketch," pp. 3–5.

12. See Thomas Kirkbride's Account Book, 28 May 1835–4 January 1839, Kirkbride MSS, IPH. Many of his prepaid patients necessitated only seven to twelve visits a year, but others were more time consuming. Kirkbride recorded, for instance, fifty-one visits in 1837 and forty-seven in 1838 for one family. For further discussion of the use of doctors' account books, especially Kirkbride's, see above, chap. 2, n. 12.

13. Kirkbride, "Autobiographical Sketch," pp. 9–10.

14. Ibid., pp. 10–12.

15. See Tomes, *Generous Confidence*, pp. 157–63; Pennsylvania Hospital for the Insane, Annual Reports, 1842, 1843; Kirkbride to Awl, 24 July 1844, Kirkbride MSS, IPH.

16. As late as the 1880s, the Pennsylvania Hospital for the Insane was referred to as "Kirkbride's." See, for instance, such references in the board of trustee minutes and casebooks of the Pennsylvania State Lunatic Hospital at Harrisburg. After 1869 (when the law was changed to guarantee patients' rights to legal counsel), Kirkbride often appeared in court, and even cases that entailed no fault on the part of the hospital or its staff were blown out of proportion by the press. Generally, however, few questioned the good character of Kirkbride himself. See Tomes, *Generous Confidence*, pp. 243–56.

17. It is impossible to list all the letters concerning these subjects that crossed Thomas Kirkbride's desk, but for examples see the following letters to him: Earle, 27 June 1846; Fonerden, 10 July 1846; Buttolph, 9 July 1847; Ray, 16 January 1847; Awl, 1 December 1847; Commissioners of Indiana, 24 March 1848; Lopes, 17 April 1852; Lind, 15 April 1853; McFarland, 24 March 1855; T. R. H. Smith, 19 March 1859; Green, 27 September 1859; Curwen, 31 July 1860, Kirkbride MSS, IPH.

18. Fonerden to Kirkbride, 10 May 1850; Awl to Kirkbride, 7 July 1849; and Ray to Kirkbride, 19 May 1858, ibid.; Kirkbride to Stribling, 17 May 1846, 7 July 1855, 9 August 1867, Stribling MSS, WSH.

19. For example, see the following letters to Kirkbride: Awl, 27 May 1847; MacDonald, 25 May 1848; Earle, 9 December 1848; S. Hanbury Smith, 8 March 1852; Nichols, 19 March 1852, 30 March 1852, 22 April 1852; Brown, 3 May 1853; McFarland, 24 March 1855; Curwen, 31 July 1860; Isaac Ray, 9 May 1861; Patterson, 20 February 1852, Kirkbride MSS, IPH; Kirkbride to Stribling, 1854, and 7 July 1855, Stribling MSS, WSH.

20. Dix to Stribling, 7 February 1852, ibid.; Nichols to Kirkbride, 3 March 1852, Kirkbride MSS, IPH. For Kirkbride's regular contacts with Stribling, see Kirkbride to Stribling, 1 June 1844, 5 July 1844, 28 August 1844, Stribling MSS, WSH.

21. Western Lunatic Hospital, Annual Report, 1836, pp. 1–9.

22. Norman Dain, *Disordered Minds* (Williamsburg, Va.: Colonial Williamsburg Foundation, 1971), pp. 113–27, traces the dispute with par-

ticular emphasis on Galt and the Eastern Lunatic Hospital. The rivalry is also evident in Galt to Stribling, 12 April 1843, 16 December 1843, 13 November 1844, 24 September 1845; as well as in the manuscript copies of their respective "reports to the legislature," Stribling MSS, WSH. See also Woodward to Chandler, 28 July 1844, Chandler MSS, AAS.

23. Biographical and genealogical material on Stribling is in Hugh Milton McIlhany, Jr., *Some Virginia Families being Genealogies of the Kinney, Stribling, Trout, McIlhany, Milton, Rogers, Tait, Snickers, McCormick, and Other Families of Virginia* (Staunton, Va.: Stoneburner & Prufer, 1903. Reprint. Baltimore: Genealogy Publishing Company, 1962); Nancy Feys Dunne, "The Era of Moral Therapy at Western State Hospital" (M.A. thesis, DePaul University, 1968); Joseph A. Waddell, *Annals of Augusta County, Virginia*, 2d. ed. (Bridgewater, Va.: C. J. Carrier, 1958). On Robley Dunglison, see William F. Norwood, *Medical Education in the United States before the Civil War* (Philadelphia: University of Pennsylvania Press, 1944), p. 263; Dunglison to Court of Directors, 18 May 1836, Stribling MSS, WSH. Complete minutes and votes of the court of directors are contained in the manuscript copy of the Records of the Directory of the Western Lunatic Hospital from 1825 to 1837.

24. See Western Lunatic Hospital, Annual Report, 1836, p. 7.

25. Ibid., pp. 1–9.

26. Between 1828 and 1835, twelve patients had been cured by William Boys, Stribling's predecessor. In the last six months of 1836, Stribling released five, and each year after that the number of cures increased. Systematic discharges are evident if one analyzes the Western Lunatic Hospital Register, which contains information on patients from 1828 through 1845. Stribling also noted his reasons for discharging patients in his annual reports.

27. See Western Lunatic Hospital, Annual Reports, 1837, p. 12; 1838; and 1839, pp. 15–18. For evidence of the success of Stribling's tactics, see Hull to Stribling, 13 January 1845; Boyer to Stribling, 18 June 1844; Garden to Stribling, 25 July 1847, Stribling MSS, WSH.

28. See Western Lunatic Hospital, Annual Report, 1837, p. 12.

29. See Woodward to Chandler, 14 May 1843, Chandler MSS, AAS; Kirkbride to Stribling, 1 June 1844, Stribling MSS, WSH; Awl to Woodward, 18 April 1842; Jarvis to Woodward, 12 October 1844, Woodward MSS, AAS; Butler to Earle, 16 April 1844, Earle MSS, AAS; and Western Lunatic Hospital, Annual Report, 1843, pp. 16–17.

30. "Medical Association," p. 257.

31. See the following letters to Stribling: Kirkbride, 31 March 1850; Awl, 15 March 1850; Benedict, 16 March 1850; Butler, 16 March 1850; Buttolph, 16 March 1850; Bell, 26 March 1850, Stribling MSS, WSH. Galt's feelings about the salary raise are cited in Dain, *Disordered Minds*, p. 153. See this work also for a fuller treatment of Galt's personality and work.

32. Report of the Investigating Committee of the Western Lunatic Asylum, 1851, Records, WSH; Western Lunatic Hospital, Annual Report, 1853.

33. See particularly Brown to Kirkbride, 3 May 1853, Kirkbride MSS, IPH, in which Brown denounced Galt: "by his own pen, would Galt be 'condemned,' for his last paper throughout. But is it worthwhile & is he 'of any account' as they say in his country . . . he is a 'windmill'—well enough to let alone." See also below, chap. 5 for a more detailed account of Galt's fall from grace. Dain, *Disordered Minds,* pp. 122–23 notes the story about Galt's new director contacting Stribling.

34. Ohio Lunatic Asylum, Annual Report, 1842, p. 57; *Journal of the Proceedings of the Convention of Physicians of Ohio* (Cincinnati: A. Pugh, 1835), pp. 3–6.

35. Biographical data on William Awl is in J. H. Pooley, "Memoir of William Maclay Awl, M.D., of Columbus, Ohio," *Transactions of the Thirty-Second Annual Meeting of the Ohio State Medical Society* (Cincinnati: Mallory and Webb, Printers, 1877), pp. 69–80; Alfred E. Lee, *History of the City of Columbus, Capital of Ohio* (New York: Munsell & Co., 1892), 2:591–94; Henry M. Wynkoop, *Picturesque Lancaster: Past and Present* (Lancaster, Ohio: Republican Printing Company, 1897), p. 11; Osman Castle Hooper, *History of the City of Columbus, Ohio* (Columbus, Ohio: Memorial Publishing Company, 1920), p. 37; William T. Martin, *History of Franklin County* (Columbus, Ohio: Follett, Foster, & Company, 1858), pp. 90–92; and Alden B. Steele, *The History of Clark County, Ohio* (Chicago: W. H. Beers & Co., 1881), pp. 596, 633, and passim.

36. See Joseph Kett, *The Formation of the American Medical Profession* (New Haven, Conn.: Yale University Press, 1968), pp. 79–96.

37. *Journal of the Proceedings of the Convention of Physicians of Ohio,* pp. 3–6; Lee, *History of Columbus,* p. 592.

38. For the directors' trip, see Lee, *History of Columbus,* p. 592; *Report of the Directors to whom was committed the charge of erecting a Lunatic Asylum for the State of Ohio* in Ohio Lunatic Asylum, Annual Report, 1838, p. 5; Awl to Woodward, 5 September 1838, Woodward MSS, AAS. This is not the letter asking for a recommendation, but one thanking Woodward for his "kind and very friendly letter" to Dr. Parsons.

39. Ohio Lunatic Asylum, Annual Report, 1839, pp. 26–27.

40. Ohio Lunatic Asylum, Annual Report, 1841, p. 57; Albert Deutsch, *The Mentally Ill in America* (New York: Doubleday, Doran, 1938), p. 153.

41. Todd to Woodward, 15 September 1843, Woodward MSS, AAS; Woodward to Chandler, 14 May 1843, Chandler MSS, AAS; and Ohio Lunatic Asylum Annual Report, 1841, pp. 82–86.

42. Patterson to Kirkbride, 20 February 1852, Kirkbride MSS, IPH.

Patterson's full remark was "that these state institutions are *horrible* establishments, & no *sensitive* man—none but one who had the skin of a *rhinocerous* [*sic*] has any business in one of them. I speak of those in the West particularly." At the time Patterson administered the Indiana Hospital for the Insane, but he spoke from long experience at the Ohio Lunatic Asylum also. For the association's resolution, see Proceedings, Third Annual Meeting, *AJI* 5 (July 1848):91.

43. Awl to Kirkbride, 19 June 1846, 24 March 1847, 27 May 1847, 30 August 1847, 7 July 1849, 24 December 1849, Kirkbride MSS, IPH.

44. For help in assessing Ohio politics in the 1840s and 1850s, see Eugene H. Roseboom and Francis P. Weisenburger, *A History of Ohio* (New York: Prentice-Hall, 1934); Paul Kleppner, *The Cross of Culture* (New York: Free Press, 1970); John S. C. Abbott, *The History of the State of Ohio* (Detroit: Northwestern Publishing Company, 1875).

45. For Awl's complaints, see his letters to Kirkbride, 24 March 1847, 27 May 1847, 30 August 1847, 2 August 1849, Kirkbride MSS, IPH. For the materials on S. Hanbury Smith, see Dix to Stribling, 2 April 1850, Stribling MSS, WSH; Patterson to Kirkbride, 20 February 1852; S. Hanbury Smith to Kirkbride, 8 March 1852; Nichols to Kirkbride, 30 March 1852, 22 April 1852, Kirkbride MSS, IPH. And for comments on Awl's retirement see Pooley, "Memoir of William Maclay Awl," pp. 79–80; Jacob H. Studer, *Columbus, Ohio: Its History, Resources, and Progress* (Columbus: W. Richies, 1873); and Awl to Kirkbride, 2 August 1849, Kirkbride MSS, IPH.

46. See Awl to Kirkbride, 7 July 1849, 7 April 1851, ibid.

47. Biographical material on Samuel Woodward, father of Samuel Bayard Woodward, is gleaned from Samuel Orcutt, *History of Torrington, Connecticut* (Albany, N.Y.: J. Munsell, Printer, 1878); Barnes Riznik, "The Professional Lives of Early Nineteenth-century New England Doctors," *Journal of the History of Medicine and Allied Sciences* 19 (January 1964):5.

48. For discussion of the humanitarian spirit emerging from the Second Great Awakening, see Charles R. Keller, *The Second Great Awakening in Connecticut* (New Haven, Conn.: Yale University Press, 1942); Sidney E. Mead, "Denominationalism: The Shape of Protestantism in America," *Church History* 1 (December 1954):291–320; H. Richard Niebuhr, *The Social Sources of Denominationalism* (New York: H. Holt, 1929); Donald G. Mathews, "The Second Great Awakening Considered as an Organizing Process, 1780–1830, An Hypothesis," *American Quarterly* 21 (Spring 1969):23–43. For Woodward's youthful writings, see Gerald N. Grob, *The State and the Mentally Ill* (Chapel Hill: University of North Carolina Press, 1966), pp. 43–46.

49. See Orcutt, *History of Torrington*, pp. 627–30; Henry R. Stiles, *The History of Ancient Wethersfield, Connecticut* (New York: Grafton

Press, 1904), vol. 1; Howard Kelly and Walter Burrage, *American Medical Biographies* (Baltimore: Norman Remington, 1920), pp. 1263–64.

Stiles listed the doctors in Wethersfield from the time of the town's founding to 1904. In a chapter on the history of Rocky Hill (the southern section of Wethersfield), Dr. Rufus Griswold reported the results of his study of account books of doctors who were contemporaries of Woodward. Even by 1843, local doctors received no more than thirty-three cents for an ordinary visit. It would appear that Woodward sold medicines in his store, as well as more general merchandise—expanding his possibilities for income. In 1827, when the prisoners were transferred to the Connecticut State Prison from the old Newgate Prison, there were 127 inmates. See notice of appointment, 3 August 1831, Woodward MSS, AAS.

50. For Woodward's training of medical apprentices, see Riznik, "The Professional Lives of Early Nineteenth-century New England Doctors," typescript, pp. 101–2.

51. In 1832 when Woodward left Wethersfield to take the superintendency of the Worcester State Lunatic Hospital, 150 townspeople, representing 669 of their family members, signed a farewell scroll expressing gratitude for his service. See Testimonial Letter in Woodward MSS, AAS.

52. Woodward probably acquired his interest in the deaf from Mason Cogswell, who promoted education and training for those unfortunates as a result of his own daughter's loss of hearing. Woodward frequently expressed his concern for the inmates of the Connecticut State Prison at Wethersfield. See esp. *Reports and other Documents relating to the State Lunatic Hospital at Worcester, Mass.,* in *The Origins of the State Mental Hospital in America* (New York: Arno Press, 1973).

53. For the origins of the Hartford Retreat for the Insane and the role of the Connecticut Medical Society and its individual members, see Leonard K. Eaton, *New England Hospitals, 1790–1833* (Ann Arbor: University of Michigan Press, 1957), chap. 3.

54. For Woodward's appointment, see Eaton, *New England Hospitals,* pp. 232–33; Grob, *The State and the Mentally Ill,* pp. 38–41. See also Porter to Woodward, 5 October 1832, Woodward MSS, AAS. For a different interpretation of Woodward's motives, see Grob, *The State and the Mentally Ill,* p. 48 and *Mental Institutions in America: Social Policy to 1875* (New York: Free Press, 1973), p. 135.

55. Woodward's career at Worcester and the problems with which he had to cope are documented in Grob, *The State and the Mentally Ill,* chap. 3.

56. Henry Hurd, ed., *The Institutional Care of the Insane in the United States and Canada* (Baltimore: Johns Hopkins Press, 1916), vols. 2 and 3.

57. Constance M. McGovern, " 'Mad Doctors': American Psychiatrists, 1800–1860" (Ph.D. diss., University of Massachusetts, 1976), chap. 5.

58. Grob, *The State and the Mentally Ill*, chap. 3.

59. Woodward to Stribling, 5 August 1844, Stribling MSS, WSH; Woodward to Earle, 26 July 1844, Earle MSS, AAS.

60. "Medical Association," pp. 253–58.

61. See Thomas Kirkbride's account of his trip north in 1845; Ray to Kirkbride, 16 January 1847; Woodward to Kirkbride, 31 December 1845, Kirkbride MSS, IPH. Thomas Kirkbride had remarked also on Woodward's heavy reliance on drugs; see Earl W. Bond, *Dr. Kirkbride and His Mental Hospital* (Philadelphia: J. P. Lippincott, 1947), p. 39.

62. See the following letters to Samuel Woodward: Mann, 15 January 1839, 26 February 1840, 11 March 1844; Miner, June 1834; Gallaudet, 21 February 1840; Sumner, 22 February 1840; Salter, 2 March 1840; Awl, 18 April 1842; Batchelder, 18 April 1842; Fisher, 30 April 1842; King, 12 May 1842; Taft, 10 December 1842, Woodward MSS, AAS; Woodward to Chandler, 12 May 1842, Chandler MSS, AAS; Woodward to Kirkbride, 2 September 1842, Kirkbride MSS, IPH.

63. For Woodward's retirement plans, see Kelly and Burrage, *American Medical Biographies*, pp. 1262–63; Awl to Kirkbride, 19 June 1846, Kirkbride MSS, IPH.

64. See Woodward to Earle, 26 July 1844, Earle MSS, AAS; Woodward to Kirkbride, 21 November 1844, Kirkbride MSS, IPH.

Chapter 4 The Organization

1. Kirkbride to Stribling, 28 August 1844, Stribling MSS, WSH; John Curwen, *History of the Association of Medical Superintendents of American Institutions for the Insane* (Harrisburg, Pa.: Theo. F. Scheffer, 1875), p. 5; Woodward to Kirkbride, 21 November 1844, Kirkbride MSS, IPH. The only established hospitals not represented at some meeting by 1860 were those opened in that year, the county asylums of Iowa and Wisconsin, and the state hospitals in California and Oregon.

2. Medical superintendents could not rely on twentieth-century professionalization techniques like licensing bureaus, specialized systems of medical education, or state-imposed standards and sanctions. Rather, as Gerald Grob notes in "The Social History of Medicine and Disease in America: Problems and Possibilities," *Journal of Social History* 10 (Summer 1977):391–409, they stressed "character" and considered themselves neither a "classless" profession nor "free-wheeling entrepreneurs," as other professions did. See Paul Mattingly, *The Classless Profession: American Schoolmen in the Nineteenth Century* (New York: Springer, 1963); Daniel H. Calhoun, *The American Civil Engineer* (Cambridge, Mass.: Harvard University Press, 1960). They were fully conscious of the status-conferring aspects of middle-class origins and a liberal education, however, and, starting out as salaried officials, they used that system to carve out a place for themselves. The professional milieu they created

resembled the "shop culture" that Monte A. Calvert describes in *The Mechanical Engineer in America, 1830–1910* (Baltimore: Johns Hopkins Press, 1967).

3. See "Notice," *AJI* 2 (April 1846):396.

4. Awl to Kirkbride, 27 May 1847, Kirkbride MSS, IPH; Harrison to Stribling, 23 March 1847, Stribling MSS, WSH; William Rothstein, *American Physicians in the Nineteenth Century* (Baltimore: Johns Hopkins Press, 1972), pp. 199–204.

5. Proceedings, Eighth Annual Meeting, *AJI* 10 (July 1853):85.

6. Mayberry to Kirkbride, 12 April 1858; Nichols to Kirkbride, 9 May 1865, Kirkbride MSS, IPH.

7. Eric T. Carlson, "Theodric Romeyn Beck, M.D.," *American Journal of Psychiatry* 114 (February 1958):754–55, and "The Unfortunate Dr. Parkman," ibid. 123 (December 1966):725–27; Witmore to Stribling, 6 February 1850, Stribling MSS, WSH.

8. Gerald N. Grob, *Edward Jarvis and the Medical World of Nineteenth-century America* (Knoxville: University of Tennessee Press, 1978), pp. 49–55; Eric T. Carlson, "Edward Mead and the Second Psychiatric Journal," *American Journal of Psychiatry* 113 (December 1956):561.

9. See Proceedings, Annual Meetings, *AJI*, 1849–53.

10. Proceedings, Third Annual Meeting, *AJI* 5 (July 1848):92 and Proceedings, Fourth Annual Meeting, *AJI* 6 (July 1849):53.

11. Proceedings, Second Annual Meeting, *AJI* 3 (July 1846):90.

12. When Stribling did return to the fold in 1868, the association rewarded him not with an office but with the honor of holding the next annual meeting in Staunton, Va., the only southern city to host a meeting in the antebellum period. Meetings had been held in Baltimore in 1853 and in Lexington, Ky., in 1859 (and would be held in Baltimore again in 1873 and in Nashville in 1874), but Staunton was the only truly southern city in which the association met.

13. Nichols to Kirkbride, 22 April 1852, Kirkbride MSS, IPH.

14. Woodward to Stribling, 5 August 1844, Stribling MSS, WSH.

15. William Fisher of the Maryland Insane Hospital told Stribling that he simply could not leave his asylum because of his "peculiar situation." See Fisher to Stribling, 10 July 1844, ibid. David Cooper of the Georgia State Sanitarium at Milledgeville was renowned for being an eccentric. See Kirkbride to Stribling, 30 March 1845, ibid. And it is possible that Stribling had not written to William Stokes, the resident physician of the Mount Hope Institution (Baltimore) run by the Sisters of Charity, or that Stokes simply did not have time to attend since a new building was being occupied in 1844. John Allen of the Kentucky Lunatic Asylum in Lexington, had just taken over and was in the process of instituting moral therapy for the first time, and John McNairy of the Central Hospital for the Insane in Nashville, Tenn., was working in a small, inadequate building.

16. Most of these other northeastern members served on a committee

at either their third or fourth meeting. Two men, D. T. Brown and Andrew McFarland, did not serve until their fifth meeting, and Mark Ranney did not receive the honor until he attended his eighth. If some from the South were ignored, it was generally because they attended only once. The exceptions to this were William Stokes and John Galt. There may have been a bias against Stokes because he headed an essentially private (and Catholic Church–supported) asylum. John Galt has a story all his own; see below, chap. 5. For the most part, the only westerners ignored were those from Ohio. This bias probably stemmed from both the pattern of short-term appointments and the long-standing policy of the state legislature to interfere in asylum administration.

17. Another form of control, linked to that of the makeup of the business committee, was the assignment of papers by the president of the association. The presidency itself was another area dominated by the founding members.

18. I determined the proportion of meetings attended by counting only those held while any particular hospital was in existence. For instance, the Indiana Hospital for the Insane did not receive its first patients until 1848, therefore it could be represented at only twelve "possible" meetings of the fifteen before the Civil War. Richard Patterson attended four meetings, and James Athon came to seven, and therefore Indiana was represented at 92 percent of the "possible" meetings.

19. The other exceptions in the West, of course, were Oregon and California. The locations of annual meetings and the percentages of delegates from the Northeast, 1844–60, are as follows:

1844	77%	Philadelphia	1854	60%	Washington
1846	70%	Washington	1855	83%	Boston
1848	80%	New York	1856	38%	Cincinnati
1849	87%	Utica, N.Y.	1857	72%	New York
1850	68%	Boston	1858	58%	Quebec
1851	65%	Philadelphia	1859	38%	Lexington, Ky.
1852	81%	New York	1860	67%	Philadelphia
1853	65%	Baltimore			

20. Woodward to Chandler, 14 May 1843, Chandler MSS, AAS.

21. The following analysis, particularly of discussion participation, omits the meetings of 1844, 1846, 1848, 1850–53, and 1856 because there are either no records or incomplete ones of the discussion as published in *AJI*.

22. Although I cite the actual numbers of papers presented, the ranking of this "quantity" of participation is based also on the "possible" meetings at which each man could have presented a paper.

23. Proceedings, Tenth Annual Meeting, *AJI* 12 (July 1855):98–100; Proceedings, Ninth Annual Meeting, *AJI* 11 (July 1854):54; Proceedings, Fifteenth Annual Meeting, *AJI* 17 (July 1860):35–43.

24. Proceedings, Fourteenth Annual Meeting, *AJI* 16 (July 1859):66–79; William Chipley, "Sitomania: Its Causes and Treatment," *AJI* 16 (July 1859):1–42; Proceedings, Fifteenth Annual Meeting, *AJI* 17 (July 1860):72–73.

Participants in discussion and the frequency of participation per member are as follows:

	Participants	Frequency
Southwesterners	4	9.0
Northeasterners	33	8.5
Westerners	9	7.0
Southerners	8	4.4

25. Northeasterners made up 55 percent of the active membership, delivered 80 percent of the papers, controlled 68 percent of the discussion, and held 89 percent of the offices.

26. John Butler, for instance, reminded Stribling of old battles fought and won together. He wrote nostalgically:

You know we Massachusetts folks remember the day when their two noble states stood together against the world in '76. How goes the old song!

"Massachusetts all afire
Old Virginy never tire
Yankee doodle dandy."

Butler to Stribling, 1 February 1851, Stribling MSS, WSH.

27. See the following letters to Stribling: Awl, 18 August 1849; Butler, 16 March 1850, 10 July 1850; Stedman, 20 April 1850; Kirkbride, 26 September 1850, Stribling MSS, WSH.

28. See the following letters to Kirkbride: Nichols, 4 November 1860; Buttolph, 30 October 1860; Curwen, 22 May 1861, Kirkbride MSS, IPH; Stribling, 26 March 1859, Stribling MSS, WSH.

29. Awl also had described Cutter as "curious." See Ray to Kirkbride, 23 July 1849, Awl to Kirkbride, 27 May 1847, 5 December 1857, Kirkbride MSS, IPH.

30. Awl to Woodward, 18 April 1842, Woodward MSS, AAS; Brigham to Kirkbride, 12 June 1849; Nichols to Kirkbride, 30 March 1852, Kirkbride MSS, IPH; Proceedings, Tenth Annual Meeting, *AJI* 12 (July 1855):98–100.

31. Isaac Ray, "The Statistics on Insane Hospitals," *AJI* 6 (July 1849):23–27.

32. Brigham to Kirkbride, 12 June 1849, Kirkbride MSS, IPH.

33. "On Statistics, Applied to Mental Diseases," *AJI* 5 (April 1849):322–27.

34. "Statistics on Insanity," *AJI* 6 (October 1849):141–45; "Reports of

Asylums," *AJI* 7 (October 1850):189, 194. The latter includes the statement of James Bates of the Maine Insane Asylum in which he points out that numbers "may mislead by disguising the truth," but he would continue to include them in his reports and hoped others would use them "honestly." The editor responded by suggesting that the tables not be discarded but simply improved.

35. Proceedings, Tenth Annual Meeting, *AJI* 12 (July 1855):98–100.

36. Ray to Kirkbride, 9 March 1853, Kirkbride MSS, IPH.

37. For the complete discussion, see Proceedings, Eighth Annual Meeting, *AJI* 10 (July 1853):84–85. One annual meeting was cancelled— that of 1861—but that was because of the outbreak of the Civil War.

38. For examples, see Commissioners of Indiana to Kirkbride, 24 March 1848; Nichols to Kirkbride, 22 April 1852, 25 September 1853, Kirkbride MSS, IPH; Gerald N. Grob, *The State and the Mentally Ill* (Chapel Hill: University of North Carolina Press, 1966), p. 40.

39. Nichols to Kirkbride, 25 September 1853, Kirkbride MSS, IPH.

40. See Curwen to Kirkbride, 1851 onward, Kirkbride MSS, IPH. For the Chandler-Woodward connections, see Fletcher to Chandler, 6 May 1840; Woodward to Chandler, 12 May 1842, Chandler MSS, AAS; Woodward to Chandler, 5 May 1846, Woodward MSS, AAS. For Fisher and Nichols, see Report of the Investigating Committee of the Western Lunatic Asylum, 1851, Records, WSH; Henry Hurd, ed., *The Institutional Care of the Insane in the United States and Canada* (Baltimore: Johns Hopkins Press, 1916), 2:144.

41. The various twists of Patterson's fate are gleaned from the Awl, Woodward, and Kirkbride correspondence, local histories that mention both Fisher and McGugin, and from clues in Hurd, *Institutional Care*, vols. 2 and 3. See esp. Awl to Kirkbride, 1 December 1847, 6 June 1848; Sunderland to Kirkbride, 31 September 1860; Buttolph to Kirkbride, 30 October 1860, Kirkbride MSS, IPH.

42. Benedict to Kirkbride, 21 June 1851; Awl to Kirkbride, 24 December 1849, ibid.

43. Buttolph to Woodward, 5 May 1842, Woodward MSS, AAS (Woodward had just received the news of the appointment eighteen days before); Buttolph to Kirkbride, 9 January 1847, Kirkbride MSS, IPH.

44. For the assessment of Booth, see the association's eulogy of him in Curwen, *History of the Association*, pp. 42–45.

45. Nichols to Kirkbride, 3 March 1852, 19 March 1852, 30 March 1852, 22 April 1852, Kirkbride MSS, IPH.

46. Hurd, *Institutional Care*, 2:657; Ray to Kirkbride, 28 August 1853, Kirkbride MSS, IPH.

47. Mead to Kirkbride, 15 May 1860; Patterson to Kirkbride, 20 February 1852, ibid. See also "Summary," *AJI* 11 (April 1855):390, for the admonition when the appointment to the Cleveland State Hospital of Leander Firestone was "hailed with pride by Democratic friends."

48. Earle to Kirkbride, 29 March 1858, Kirkbride MSS, IPH.

49. Proceedings, Fifteenth Annual Meeting, *AJI* 17 (July 1860):58–59.

50. For examples of their personal relationships, see Woodward to Chandler, 14 May 1843, 28 July 1844, Chandler MSS, AAS; Awl to Kirkbride, 27 May 1847, 20 March 1849, 25 April 1849, 25 May 1854, Kirkbride MSS, IPH; Kirkbride to Earle, 8 July 1845, Earle MSS, AAS; Earle to Stribling, 16 August 1847, Bell to Stribling, 7 December 1847, Stribling MSS, WSH; Kirkbride to Woodward, 25 December 1845, Woodward MSS, AAS.

51. Ray to Kirkbride, 20 June 1851; Earle to Kirkbride, 9 November 1857; Curwen to Kirkbride, 25 November 1857, Kirkbride MSS, IPH.

52. For examples of their deep concern for one another and their families, see Awl to Kirkbride, 23 January 1847, Brown to Kirkbride, 11 May 1855, ibid.; Awl to Stribling, 18 August 1849, Stribling MSS, WSH. For reaction to the Nichols's tragedy, see Brown to Kirkbride, 8 February 1860; for concern about Bemis, see Jarvis to Kirkbride, 8 February 1866, Curwen to Kirkbride, 28 February 1866; for reaction to Kirkbride's injury, see Bates to Kirkbride, 22 October 1849; and for a sampling of the concern about Pliny Earle, see Nichols to Kirkbride, 30 March 1852, Kirkbride MSS, IPH.

53. Nichols to Kirkbride, 19 March 1852, ibid.

54. See the Proceedings of the association meetings in the *AJI*, 1844–60. The phrase that these hospitals were examined "with great interest and satisfaction" is repeated regularly.

55. For examples of the ways in which the association members expressed their thoughts about these other institutions, see Proceedings, Third Annual Meeting, *AJI* 5 (July 1848):90–91; Proceedings, Sixth Annual Meeting, *AJI* 8 (July 1851):91–92; Proceedings, Seventh Annual Meeting, *AJI* 9 (July 1852):72; Proceedings, Twelfth Annual Meeting, *AJI* 14 (July 1857):108–9; Proceedings, Fifteenth Annual Meeting, *AJI* 17 (July 1860):72. See also the following letters to Thomas Kirkbride: Earle, 7 December 1848; Nichols, 3 March 1852, 19 March 1852, 30 March 1852; Brown, 3 May 1853, Kirkbride MSS, IPH; "Dr. William Stokes, of the Mount Hope Institution, near Baltimore, Maryland, and the *American Journal of Insanity*," *AJI* 5 (January 1849):262–76.

Chapter 5 Asylum Management

1. Woodward to Earle, 26 July 1844, Earle MSS, AAS; New Hampshire Asylum for the Insane, Annual Report, 1846, for Andrew McFarland's remark.

2. Earle to Stribling, 16 August 1847, Stribling MSS, WSH.

3. Kirkbride's dissatisfaction with the layout of the Pennsylvania Hospital for the Insane, his early interest in "moral architecture," and his use of annual reports to convey a positive image of the asylum are discussed in Nancy Tomes, *A Generous Confidence: Thomas Story Kirkbride and*

the Art of Asylum-Keeping (Cambridge: Cambridge University Press, 1984), chap. 4. Kirkbride did publish his thoughts in the *American Journal of the Medical Sciences* in 1846 (see notice of this in the "Miscellany" section, *AJI* 4 [July 1847]:95) and frequently expressed his ideas on the same subject at association meetings. The first edition of his book, *On the Construction, Organization, and General Arrangements of Hospitals for the Insane* (Philadelphia: Lindsay and Balkiston) appeared in 1854.

4. Almost to a man, medical superintendents agreed with Kirkbride's techniques as evidenced in the reports of Stribling, Awl, Brigham, Ray, and others. For the association's actions, see Proceedings, Fourth Annual Meeting, *AJI* 6 (July 1849):66–68; Proceedings, Fifth Annual Meeting, *AJI* 7 (July 1850):82–83; Proceedings, Sixth Annual Meeting, *AJI* 8 (July 1851):86–88; for the specific recommendations, see John Curwen, *History of the Association of Medical Superintendents of American Institutions for the Insane* (Harrisburg, Pa.: Theo. F. Scheffer, 1875), pp. 24–26. For an example of their reaction to compliance with their policy, see "Reports of American Asylums," *AJI* 10 (October 1853):169, where the editor expressed delight that, in establishing the Missouri State Hospital, the planners had written their by-laws to "correspond with the opinions of the Association of Medical Superintendents, as expressed in their proceedings, and in the twenty-six Resolutions of this body passed in 1851, all of which Dr. Smith has printed in his report."

5. See the following letters to Kirkbride: Earle, 7 December 1848; Fonerden, 10 May 1850; Patterson, 20 February 1852; Nichols, 19 March 1852, 30 March 1852; McFarland, 24 March 1855, Kirkbride MSS, IPH; Fisher to Stribling, 10 July 1844; Nichols to Stribling, 25 December 1854, Stribling MSS, WSH.

6. Awl to Kirkbride, 19 June 1846; Nichols to Kirkbride, 22 April 1852; Brown to Kirkbride, 3 May 1853, Kirkbride MSS, IPH.

7. From the first three propositions of those the association adopted on the "Organization of Hospitals for the Insane," as cited in Curwen, *History of the Association*, p. 29.

8. The members prefaced every proposition concerning other officers and staff with this reminder of the superintendent's authority. See ibid., p. 30.

9. Proceedings, Eighth Annual Meeting, *AJI* 10 (July 1853):88.

10. From the fifth proposition on the "Organization of Hospitals for the Insane," as cited in Curwen, *History of the Association*, p. 30.

11. The Hartford Retreat for the Insane paid a low salary of $200 to its assistant physician, while Stribling's assistant at the Western Lunatic Hospital in Staunton, Va., received $750. Provision for room and board was added, although only for the assistant, not for his family. At the Pennsylvania Hospital for the Insane, the New Jersey State Lunatic Asylum, and the Hartford Retreat for the Insane in 1850 the steward

was paid more than the assistant physician. See the series of letters to Stribling in 1850 that list salaries, Stribling MSS, WSH.

12. See Pliny Earle's graduating thesis at the New York Hospital, Westchester Division, White Plains, N.Y.; unsigned typescript copy of "Sketch of the Life and Work of Dr. Horace A. Buttolph," 3 June 1942, at the New Jersey State Lunatic Asylum (now the Trenton State Hospital), Trenton, N.J.; Autobiographical Note, Chandler MSS, AAS.

13. For examples of the ways in which they used these informal methods to train both their assistants and new men in the field, see the following letters to Kirkbride: Woodward, 9 September 1842; Awl, 19 June 1846, 1 December 1847; Fonerden, 10 July 1846, 10 May 1850; Lopes, 17 April 1852; Nichols, 22 April 1852, 25 September 1853; Lind, 15 April 1853; Green, 7 October 1856, Kirkbride MSS, IPH; Kirkbride to Woodward, 25 December 1845, Woodward MSS, AAS; Kirkbride to Earle, 8 July 1845, Earle MSS, AAS. Beginning in 1858, a few assistant physicians attended annual meetings as observers.

14. See Morrill Wyman, Jr., *A Brief Record of the Lives and Writings of Dr. Rufus Wyman and His Son Dr. Morrill Wyman* (Cambridge, Mass.: privately printed, 1908).

15. See esp. Woodward to Mann, 15 January 1839, Woodward MSS, AAS; Kirkbride to Managers of the Penna. Hospital, 30 June 1862, Kirkbride MSS, IPH.

16. Ray to Kirkbride, 19 May 1858, ibid.; Proceedings, Fifteenth Annual Meeting, *AJI* 17 (July 1860):53–60.

17. "Bibliography: Notice of John Curwen, *A Manual for Attendants in Hospitals for the Insane*," *AJI* 8 (January 1852):288–90; *Rules and Regulations for the Attendants, &c., at the Pennsylvania Hospital for the Insane, near Philadelphia* (Philadelphia: Brown, Bicking & Guilbert, 1841). The anonymous reviewer for the *AJI* cited Curwen's explicit warnings to attendants thus:

You have no doubt considered the difficulties and responsibility, together with the nature of those duties which you will be called upon to perform. Unless you have made up your mind to submit to much self-denial and many privations; unless you enter on the discharge of your duties with a full determination to perform those duties with hearty good will and a sincere desire to benefit those who may be placed under your care; unless you feel thoroughly inbued with the disposition to assist to the utmost of your ability in one of the most benevolent undertakings to which men can be called, it will be the part of prudence, as well as sound discretion, to retrace your steps, and turn your attention to some other vocation.

18. Proceedings, Seventh Annual Meeting, *AJI* 9 (July 1852):67. Although the manual was authored by Curwen, many members made suggestions. In 1851 "interleaved" copies of the proposals with room for remarks had been provided to the members. See Proceedings, Sixth Annual Meeting, *AJI* 8 (July 1851):89.

19. Proceedings, Fifteenth Annual Meeting, *AJI* 17 (July 1860):54–55.

20. See these remarks in the Vermont Asylum for the Insane, Annual Report, 1837, pp. 19–21.

21. Woodward described his attitude in Worcester State Lunatic Hospital, Annual Report, 1833; Gerald N. Grob, *The State and the Mentally Ill* (Chapel Hill: University of North Carolina Press, 1966), p. 70, uses similar language.

22. Rockwell's notes on patients in the casebooks at the Vermont Asylum for the Insane indicate this kind of concern and close attention in the early years. See Patient Records, Vermont Asylum for the Insane (now the Brattleboro Retreat), Brattleboro, Vermont, 1836 through the 1840s. See also the Vermont Asylum for the Insane, Annual Report, 1837, pp. 16–17.

23. To a great extent, the medical superintendents' talk about family and parental images had always been far more indicative of their sense of the ideal than representative of what they could put into practice. Michel Foucault's indictment of the repressive nature of the patriarchal asylum system misses this point. Foucault linked the legal "minority" status of the insane with society's view of madness as childhood. He judged that the asylum not only "alienated" the "concrete liberty" of the mad person, but that the "family mode" in the asylum was the "truly alienating situation" in that violence then became an "incessant attack against the Father." See Michel Foucault, *Madness and Civilization,* trans. Richard Howard (New York: Pantheon Books, 1965), pp. 253–55. Men like William Rockwell, however, dropped the family image early; by the early 1840s, for instance, Rockwell was far more concerned about the classification of patients and the efficient (and curative) aspects of the therapy regime than he was about convincing anyone that an asylum of over 100 patients any longer resembled a family.

24. Pliny Earle, *A Visit to Thirteen Asylums for the Insane in Europe* (Philadelphia: J. Dobson, 1841), pp. 135–36.

25. Vermont Asylum for the Insane, Patient Records, 1830s.

26. Samuel Woodward in Worcester State Lunatic Hospital, Annual Report, 1836, p. 185.

27. Samuel Woodward as cited by Pliny Earle, *Thirteen Asylums,* p. 137.

28. Awl to Kirkbride, 7 July 1849; Kirkbride to Managers of the Penna. Hospital, 30 June 1862, Kirkbride MSS, IPH. For Kirkbride's regular appearance at the tea parties, see Tomes, *Generous Confidence,* p. 208.

29. The fourth proposition on the "Organization of Hospitals for the Insane," as cited in Curwen, *History of the Association,* pp. 29–30.

30. This and the following description of the various methods Thomas Kirkbride used to involve everyone in his plan of moral treatment and asylum functioning is from Tomes, *Generous Confidence,* esp. chaps. 4 and 5.

31. Henry Hurd, ed., *The Institutional Care of the Insane in the*

United States and Canada (Baltimore: Johns Hopkins Press, 1916), 3: 140–41.

32. William Russell, *The New York Hospital* (New York: Columbia University Press, 1945), pp. 221–43; Earle to Stribling, 16 August 1847, Stribling MSS, WSH; Earle to Kirkbride, 9 December 1848, Kirkbride MSS, IPH.

In 1854, Earle commented on the situation at the Bloomingdale Asylum. He said that in the early years the managers had been "gifted with a prescience of which the building erected by their direction remains a monumental witness." But they had "rested too long upon their original work." Other asylums had created the position of medical superintendent with sole authority, yet "Bloomingdale is the only one which still clings to that relic of the past—a collection of executive officers acting nearly independent of each other." See Earle's unsigned comments to Kirkbride about the 1854 "report of the Bloomingdale Asylum," Kirkbride MSS, IPH.

33. Notes on Medical Lectures, Earle MSS, AAS; Earle to Kirkbride, 7 December 1848, Kirkbride MSS, IPH.

34. Nichols to Kirkbride, 22 April 1852, ibid.; Ray to Dix, 8 December 1851, Dix MSS, Houghton Library, Harvard University. In 1877, twenty-five years after he left Bloomingdale for St. Elizabeths, Nichols returned to the post in New York, but only with the stipulation that he would have the full authority of a medical superintendent. See Hurd, *Institutional Care,* 3:141.

35. Earle, *Thirteen Asylums,* passim; Constance M. McGovern, "The Early Career of Pliny Earle: a Founder of American Psychiatry," (M.A. thesis, University of Massachusetts, 1971); Kirkbride to Earle, 16 August 1860; Bell to Earle, 22 January 1858, Earle MSS, AAS.

36. Earle to Prince, 22 April 1864, ibid.

37. Earle's 1854 unsigned comments on Bloomingdale, Kirkbride MSS, IPH; Earle's diaries, 1863–81, Dix to Earle, 1 August 1886, Earle MSS, AAS; Northampton State Lunatic Hospital, Annual Reports, 1864–86; Franklin B. Sanborn, *Memoirs of Pliny Earle, M.D.* (Boston: Damrell & Upham, 1898), pp. 262–64.

In his 1854 comments, Earle had described the "most nearly perfect" asylum as one "in which the executive power is vested solely in the superintendent." The asylum directors would have "practically acknowledged that [the superintendent] more fully understands the wants and necessities of the patients than it is possible for any other person officially connected with the institution to understand them." The superintendent's suggestions, "derived from experience, observation, reading, or his own inventive talent," would be "most generally adopted" and "most cheerfully and immediately carried into effect." Earle made Northampton, in his eyes, the "most nearly perfect asylum."

38. See the following letters (among others) to Earle: Wells, 13 Febru-

ary 1877; Corson, 10 March 1877; Ray, 18 February 1872; Brown, 31 January 1872, Earle MSS, AAS.

39. The following description of John Galt and his inability to exercise full control over the Eastern Lunatic Hospital is from Norman Dain's analysis in *Disordered Minds* (Williamsburg, Va.: Colonial Williamsburg Foundation, 1971), esp. chaps. 3 and 5. Galt's sister is cited by Dain, p. 70.

40. Ibid., p. 141.

41. Ibid., p. 134.

42. Even in 1851, when S. Hanbury Smith read a paper for the absent Galt, the association members reacted favorably to his remarks "On the impropriety of treating the Insane and persons affected with other disorders in the same building." See Proceedings, Sixth Annual Meeting, *AJI* 8 (July 1851):84, 86.

43. See John M. Galt, *The Treatment of Insanity* (New York: Harper & Brothers, 1846).

44. Curwen, *History of the Association,* p. 7. This resolution does not appear in the Proceedings, First Annual Meeting, *AJI* 1 (January 1845), but Curwen picked it up from the secretary's notes, and the members referred to it frequently in later meetings.

45. John M. Galt, *Essays on Asylums for Unsound Minds* (Richmond, Va.: H. K. Ellyson's Power Press, 1850); Proceedings, Fifth Annual Meeting, *AJI* 7 (July 1850):79.

46. Proceedings, Eighth Annual Meeting, *AJI* 10 (July 1853):72, 74, and 78. Friends' Asylum still accepted patients' pledges not to escape, but their rate of absconders was high. See Norman Dain and Eric T. Carlson, "Milieu Therapy in the Nineteenth Century: Patient Care at the Friends' Asylum, Frankford, Pennsylvania, 1817–1861," *Journal of Nervous and Mental Disease* 131 (October 1960):280–88.

47. John M. Galt, "The Farm of St. Anne," *AJI* 11 (April 1855):352–57.

48. Proceedings, Tenth Annual Meeting, *AJI* 12 (July 1855):42 and 47.

49. Ibid., p. 42 for the Brown comment and pp. 44–46 for Nichols's remarks.

50. Brown to Kirkbride, 3 May 1853, 11 May 1855, Kirkbride MSS, IPH. Interestingly, in the meeting, Kirkbride's language is exactly that of Brown's. See Proceedings, Tenth Annual Meeting, *AJI* 12 (July 1855): 43–44.

51. Ibid., p. 48.

Chapter 6   Selling the Profession

1. [T. R. Beck], "Notice of the Meeting of the Association of Medical Superintendents of American Institutions for the Insane," *AJI* 9 (April 1853):397; Bell to Woodward, 25 July 1844, Woodward MSS, AAS; Kirkbride to Stribling, 5 July 1844, 17 May 1844, and 1856; Woodward to

Stribling, 5 August 1844, Stribling MSS, WSH; Brigham to Kirkbride, 19 February 1848, Kirkbride MSS, IPH.

2. New York State Lunatic Asylum, Annual Report, 1845, p. 25.

3. Ibid., p. 25; Butler Hospital for the Insane, Annual Report, 1850, pp. 22–23; Maine Insane Asylum, Annual Report, 1841, pp. 8–9.

4. [C. B. C.], "Memoir of Amariah Brigham," *AJI* 6 (October 1849): 189; Witmore to Stribling, 6 February 1850, Stribling MSS, WSH; Brigham to Kirkbride, 3 March 1845, Kirkbride MSS, IPH.

5. "Medical Association. Meeting of the Medical Superintendents of American Institutions for the Insane," *AJI* 1 (January 1845):258; Kirkbride to Stribling, 17 May 1846, Stribling MSS, WSH.

6. Proceedings, Second Annual Meeting, *AJI* 3 (July 1846):92; Proceedings, Third Annual Meeting, *AJI* 5 (July 1848):92; Kirkbride to Stribling, 17 May 1846; Brigham to Stribling, 1 March 1849, Stribling MSS, WSH; MacDonald to Kirkbride, 25 May 1848; Brigham to Kirkbride, 1 March 1849, Kirkbride MSS, IPH. The *Vermont Phoenix,* for instance, regularly printed in full William Rockwell's annual reports for the Vermont Asylum for the Insane in the late 1830s and early 1840s.

7. Proceedings, Ninth Annual Meeting, *AJI* 11 (July 1854):44–45.

8. See discussions of the attitudes about etiology and nosology of antebellum psychiatrists in Norman Dain, *Concepts of Insanity* (New Brunswick, N.J.: Rutgers University Press, 1964) and John Chynoweth Burnham, *Psychoanalysis and American Medicine, 1894–1918: Medicine, Science, and Culture.* Psychological Issues, vol. 5, no. 4, monograph 20 (New York: International Universities Press, 1967).

9. Remarks about Cutter's rather dubious manner of depicting the specialty appear in Ray to Kirkbride, 23 July 1849, and Awl to Kirkbride, 5 December 1857, Kirkbride MSS, IPH. Awl, in an earlier correspondence with Kirkbride, had described Cutter's personality after hearing him speak at a meeting of the AMA. Awl to Kirkbride, 27 May 1847, ibid.

10. See Batchelder to Woodward, 26 April 1842, Woodward MSS, AAS; Nichols to Kirkbride, 19 March 1852; Stedman to Kirkbride, 17 May 1852, Kirkbride MSS, IPH, for references to "mad doctors." The correspondence between the psychiatrists reveals that they referred to one another and their specialty in the manner described. They did not use the term *psychiatrist,* or even *alienist,* although *psychological medicine* does begin to appear in journal articles, largely European reprints, before 1860.

11. Proceedings, Third Annual Meeting, *AJI* 5 (July 1848):93–95; Proceedings, Ninth Annual Meeting, *AJI* 11 (July 1854):55–56; Proceedings, Twelfth Annual Meeting, *AJI* 14 (July 1857):90.

12. Proceedings, Twelfth Annual Meeting, *AJI* 14 (July 1857):90; Edward Jarvis, "Distribution of Lunatic Hospital Reports," *AJI* 14 (January 1858):248–53, and 310.

13. Of the 112 papers presented between 1844 and 1860, 45 dealt with moral and medical treatment, 36 with the general subjects of construction and hospital regimen, 8 with the causes of insanity, and 23 with a series of miscellaneous questions—all in some way related to public image.

14. Ray had established his reputation in this area, even before he became an asylum superintendent, with his 1838 publication of *A Treatise on the Medical Jurisprudence of Insanity,* 3d ed. (Boston: Little, Brown, 1853). He also worked for years to fashion a law on commitment that would safeguard the position of the superintendent while still protecting the rights of the patients. Rhode Island, Ray's residence, passed such legislation in 1850; other states were slower to act. See "Legislation for the Insane," *AJI* 8 (October 1851):147–49.

15. Isaac Ray, "Project of a Law for Determining Legal Relations," *AJI* 7 (January 1851):215–33, and "Hints to Medical Witnesses in Questions of Insanity," *AJI* 8 (July 1851):49–61; John Galt, "On the Medical Question of the Confinement of the Insane," *AJI* 9 (January 1853):217–23; William Stokes, "On a Court of Medical Experts in Cases of Insanity," *AJI* 10 (October 1853):112–22; Proceedings, Eighth Annual Meeting, *AJI* 10 (July 1853):86. Indeed, hardly an issue of the journal appeared that did not contain some article about courtroom trials.

16. The best account of the long struggle for legislation endorsed by the association is in John Curwen, *History of the Association of Medical Superintendents of American Institutions for the Insane* (Harrisburg, Pa.: Theo. F. Scheffer, 1875), pp. 67–74.

17. Ray, "Hints to Medical Witnesses," pp. 49–61, and "Medical Experts," in Isaac Ray, *Contributions to Mental Pathology,* pp. 409–32 (Boston: Little, Brown & Co., 1873. Reprint, with an Introduction by Jacques M. Quen. New York: Scholars' Facsimiles & Reprints, 1973).

18. Isaac Ray, "On the Popular Feeling towards Insane Hospitals," *AJI* 9 (July 1852):36–65.

19. Proceedings, Sixth Annual Meeting, *AJI* 8 (July 1851):82–93.

20. Curwen to Kirkbride, 31 January 1852; Nichols to Kirkbride, 30 March 1852, 22 April 1852, Kirkbride MSS, IPH; Dix to Stribling, 2 April 1850, Stribling MSS, WSH; Ohio Lunatic Asylum, Annual Reports, 1849, 1850; and Proceedings, Seventh Annual Meeting, *AJI* 9 (July 1852):68.

21. S. Hanbury Smith to Kirkbride, 8 March 1852, Kirkbride MSS, IPH.

22. See Proceedings, Ninth Annual Meeting, *AJI* 11 (July 1854):48; Proceedings, Tenth Annual Meeting, *AJI* 12 (July 1855):94–96; Proceedings, Eleventh Annual Meeting, *AJI* 13 (July 1856):83; Gerald N. Grob, *Edward Jarvis and the Medical World of Nineteenth-century America* (Knoxville: University of Tennessee Press, 1978).

23. Proceedings, Fifteenth Annual Meeting, *AJI* 17 (July 1860):35–42.

24. Proceedings, Eighth Annual Meeting, *AJI* 10 (July 1853):75–78;

"Reports of Hospitals for the Insane," *AJI* 8 (October 1851):182–84, for the death toll in the Maine fire.

25. Proceedings, Eighth Annual Meeting, *AJI* 10 (July 1853):78.

26. Proceedings, Tenth Annual Meeting, *AJI* 12 (July 1855):52–61. Some of the psychiatrists who objected to the use of the crib-bedstead because of its appearance nevertheless still occasionally used it for lack of a better device to gain the desired result.

27. Proceedings, Twelfth Annual Meeting, *AJI* 14 (July 1857):72–81.

28. Proceedings, Tenth Annual Meeting, *AJI* 12 (July 1855):64–66.

29. Amariah Brigham, editor of *AJI*, was personally interested in such topics and published Buttolph's paper in the *Journal*, although he publicly spoke out against many of Buttolph's propositions. See Dain, *Concepts of Insanity*, pp. 61–63.

30. See John D. Davies, *Phrenology: Fad and Science* (New Haven, Conn.: Yale University Press, 1955); Ronald G. Walters, *American Reformers* (New York: Hill & Wang, 1978), chap. 9.

31. Proceedings, Fourth Annual Meeting, *AJI* 6 (July 1849):56–58 and Proceedings, Eighth Annual Meeting, *AJI* 10 (July 1853):78–79.

32. Proceedings, Ninth Annual Meeting, *AJI* 11 (July 1854):48. Bell's paper was simply "ordered to lie upon the table." This was the only reference to it in the 1854 proceedings. Every other paper presented at that meeting was summarized and the discussion reported in detail.

33. Kirkbride to Stribling, 1854, Stribling MSS, WSH; Benedict to Kirkbride, 31 January 1855; Brown to Kirkbride, 4 July 1855, Kirkbride MSS, IPH.

34. Proceedings, Tenth Annual Meeting, *AJI* 12 (July 1855):68–78, 81–83. Gray, Cutter, and Nichols asked stilted informational questions. Butler, Tyler, and Fisher simply stated their faith in Bell as a person without taking a stand on the issue. Given the law of gravity, Worthington found it difficult to believe in the phenomena. Workman thought it might be good to investigate, but that would take too much time. Jarvis thought it best to wait.

35. One of the best discussions of the popularization of both phrenology and spiritualism in the antebellum period is in Walters, *American Reformers*, chap. 9.

36. Jackson Vail, *Rockwell Castle or a Thirty Days Trip from Highgate Springs to Boston including Ten Days Confinement in the Brattleboro Prison or the Vermont Asylum for the Insane and Adventures Along the Way* (Montpelier, Vt.: n.p., n.d.); Vermont Asylum for the Insane, Annual Report, 1852, pp. 10–11. For other exposés, see Gerald N. Grob, *Mental Institutions in America: Social Policy to 1875* (New York: Free Press, 1973), pp. 263–65.

37. See, for instance, Woodward to Mann, 15 January 1839, 26 February 1840, 11 March 1844, Woodward MSS, AAS; Nichols to Kirkbride, 3 March 1852; Brown to Kirkbride, 3 May 1853, Kirkbride MSS, IPH;

John Curwen, *The Original Thirteen Members of the Association of Medical Superintendents of American Institutions for the Insane* (Warren, Pa.: E. Cowan & Co., Printers, 1885) for contemporary descriptions of Awl, Stedman, and Stribling; Norman Dain, *Disordered Minds* (Williamsburg, Va.: Colonial Williamsburg Foundation, 1971) for Galt's envy of Stribling's political prowess; and the hundreds of letters in the Kirkbride correspondence.

38. See the *Springfield* (Massachusetts) *Republican,* 1830–50. The *Springfield Republican,* under the ownership and editorship of Samuel Bowles, was, of course, much more than a local newspaper in this period. But even local newspapers like the *Hampshire Gazette* (Massachusetts) carried positive news stories about the local asylum in Northampton. And a newspaper as remote from the Vermont Asylum for the Insane in Brattleboro as the *Burlington Free Press* printed articles in a similar vein. For the attitudes of periodicals' editors, see articles in the *North American Review,* esp. "American Hospitals for the Insane," 79 (July 1854):66–90; "Statistics on Insanity in Massachusetts," 82 (January 1856):78–100; "Report of the Trustees of the Massachusetts General Hospital for the Year 1858," 89 (October 1859):316–39. See also the following articles in the *Boston Medical and Surgical Journal:* "On the Management of the Insane," 22 (29 July 1840):389–92; "Connecticut Retreat for the Insane," 39 (27 September 1848):184; and "Lunatic Asylums in Massachusetts," 39 (31 January 1849):545. See Dain, *Concepts of Insanity,* pp. 148–60, for further evidence of the success of their campaign.

39. See the various Proceedings of the association meetings in the *AJI* both for remarks about greetings from the "city fathers" and for the text of their occasional addresses to the association. Pliny Earle began giving lectures on "medical psychology" at the Berkshire Medical Institute in the early 1860s, as did Henry Harlow at Woodstock and D. T. Brown at the College of Physicians and Surgeons in New York.

40. See "Reports of American Asylums," *AJI* 10 (October 1853):169; Alabama Insane Hospital, Annual Report, 1852, pp. 5–8; South Carolina Lunatic Asylum, Annual Report, 1853, pp. 3–8; "Bibliographic Notices," *Boston Medical and Surgical Journal* 62 (22 March 1860):166–68.

Chapter 7   The Demise of the Asylum

1. The quotations about the benefits of the asylum for chronic patients are from William Rockwell, Vermont Asylum for the Insane, Annual Reports, 1838, 1839, and are representative of the admonitions of other medical superintendents.

2. For much of the material in this chapter, I am indebted to Gerald N. Grob and his *Mental Illness and American Society* (Princeton: Princeton University Press, 1983)—the most important and comprehensive study of developments in American psychiatry since the 1880s. See also

Grob, "Rediscovering the Asylum" in *The Therapeutic Revolution,* ed. Morris J. Vogel and Charles E. Rosenberg, pp. 135–57 (Philadelphia: University of Pennsylvania Press, 1979); David J. Rothman, *Conscience and Convenience* (Boston: Little, Brown, 1980); Richard Fox, *So Far Disordered in Mind* (Berkeley: University of California Press, 1980); and Constance M. McGovern, "The Insane, the Asylum, and the State in Nineteenth-Century Vermont," *Vermont History* 52 (Fall 1984):205–24 for these multiple uses of the asylum in the late nineteenth century.

3. John Curwen, *History of the Association of Medical Superintendents of American Institutions for the Insane* (Harrisburg, Pa.: Theo. F. Scheffer, 1875), pp. 60–62.

4. For the story of the Willard Asylum for the Chronic Insane, see Grob, *Mental Illness,* pp. 76–77; John A. Pitts, "The Association of Medical Superintendents of American Institutions for the Insane, 1844–1892: A Case Study of Specialism in American Medicine" (Ph.D. diss., University of Pennsylvania, 1979), pp. 108–10.

5. These arguments were presented by Amariah Brigham in the first issue of the *AJI* and regularly repeated thereafter by his colleagues. See "Asylums Exclusively for the Incurable Insane," *AJI* 1 (July 1844):44–45; Proceedings, Tenth Annual Meeting, *AJI* 12 (July 1855):86, 96–97; Curwen to Kirkbride, 28 February 1866, Kirkbride MSS, IPH.

6. Gerald N. Grob, *Mental Institutions in America: Social Policy to 1875* (New York: Free Press, 1973), p. 317; Curwen, *History of the Association,* pp. 82–83; Henry Hurd, ed., *The Institutional Care of the Insane in the United States and Canada* (Baltimore: Johns Hopkins Press, 1916), 1:153; Grob, *Mental Illness,* pp. 91–92, 315–17.

7. For the heated rhetoric of the attack on the asylum superintendents, see Dorman B. Eaton, "Despotism in Lunatic Asylums," *North American Review* 132 (March 1881):263–75; Charles E. Rosenberg, *The Trial of the Assassin Guiteau* (Chicago: University of Chicago Press, 1968); for the activities of Elizabeth Packard, see Myra Himelhoch and Arthur Shaffer, "Elizabeth Packard: Nineteenth-Century Crusader for the Rights of Mental Patients," *Journal of American Studies* 13 (December 1979):343–75.

8. Grob, *Mental Institutions,* pp. 257–302; Pitts, "The Association of Medical Superintendents," chap. 5.

9. Ibid., pp. 116–21.

10. Ibid., pp. 121–36.

11. John Callender, "History and Work of the Association of Medical Superintendents of American Institutions for the Insane—President's Address," *AJI* 40 (July 1883):1–32.

12. On the impact of the Pennsylvania Lunacy Commission, see Nancy Tomes, *A Generous Confidence: Thomas Story Kirkbride and the Art of Asylum-keeping* (Cambridge: Cambridge University Press, 1984), pp. 306–8.

13. Grob, *Mental Illness,* pp. 50–62; Rosenberg, *Trial of the Assassin Guiteau,* chap. 3; Pitts, "The Association of Medical Superintendents," chap. 6; Bonnie Blustein, "A New York Medical Man: William Alexander Hammond, Neurologist" (Ph.D. diss., University of Pennsylvania, 1979); Jacques M. Quen, "Asylum Psychiatry, Neurology, Social Work, and Mental Hygiene: An Exploratory Study in Interprofessional History," *Journal of the History of the Behavioral Sciences* 13 (January 1977):3–11. For the quotations, see Eaton, "Despotism in Lunatic Asylums," p. 269.

14. For a perceptive and balanced account of the neurologists' entrepreneur-like attacks on the psychiatrists, see esp. Bonnie Blustein, " 'A Hollow Square of Psychological Science': American Neurologists and Psychiatrists in Conflict," in *Madhouses, Mad-Doctors, and Madmen,* ed. Andrew Scull, pp. 241–70 (Philadelphia: University of Pennsylvania Press, 1981). Blustein notes elsewhere that these tactics on the part of the neurologists were so aggressive that the next generation depicted them as "egotistically restless and in their neurological efforts little better than commercial adventurers." Blustein, "New York Neurologists and the Specialization of American Medicine," *Bulletin of the History of Medicine* 53 (Summer 1979):180. See also Rothman, *Conscience and Convenience,* pp. 36–40.

15. Grob, *Mental Illness,* pp. 49–50, 55–58; Quen, "Asylum Psychiatry, Neurology, Social Work, and Mental Hygiene," p. 10.

16. Ibid., p. 10.

17. Pitts, "The Association of Medical Superintendents," pp. 198–204; William Malamud, "The History of Psychiatric Therapies," in *One Hundred Years of American Psychiatry, 1844–1944,* ed. J. K. Hall, pp. 273–323 (New York: Columbia University Press, 1944).

18. "Report of the Special Committee on Revision of the 'Propositions of the Association,' " *AJI* 44 (July 1888):50–57.

19. Ibid.

20. Proceedings, Forty-Second Annual Meeting, *AJI* 44 (July 1888): 127–44.

21. This figure does not include the seven men who were asylum superintendents before the founding of the association; the ten men who were physicians at the Blockley Almshouse in Philadelphia or in the wards at the Long Island State Hospital in Brooklyn, New York; or the three short-term administrators from California.

22. The presidency was in the hands of antebellum men even longer. Charles Nichols held the post 1873–79; Clement Walker, 1879–82; John Gray, 1883–84; Pliny Earle, 1884–85; Horace Buttolph, 1886–87; John Chapin, 1888–89; and John Curwen, 1893–94. Starting in 1882, the term became a one-year one, and most of these men served in old age.

23. Quotations are as cited in Grob, *Mental Illness,* p. 59 and Pitts, "The Association of Medical Superintendents," pp. 193, 218–19.

24. See Grob, *Mental Illness*, pp. 126–35.

25. Grob, *Mental Illness*, pp. 135–42 and Nathan Hale, *Freud and the Americans: The Beginnings of Psychoanalysis in the United States, 1876–1917* (New York: Oxford University Press, 1971), chap. 4.

26. For the mental hygiene movement, see Grob, *Mental Illness*, chap. 6; Albert Deutsch, "The History of Mental Hygiene" in *One Hundred Years of American Psychiatry, 1844–1944*, ed. J. K. Hall, pp. 367–84 (New York: Columbia University Press, 1944). The most recent biography of Beers is Norman Dain's *Clifford W. Beers: Advocate for the Insane* (Pittsburgh: University of Pittsburgh Press, 1980).

27. Quotations are as cited in Grob, *Mental Illness*, pp. 120, 121; for American responses to early psychoanalysis, see John Chynoweth Burnham, *Psychoanalysis and American Medicine, 1894–1918: Medicine, Science, and Culture*. Psychological Issues, vol. 5, no. 4, monograph 20 (New York: International Universities Press, 1967), chaps. 2 and 3; Hale, *Freud and the Americans*, chap. 11; Jacques M. Quen and Eric T. Carlson, eds., *American Psychoanalysis: Origins and Development* (New York: Brunner/Mazel, 1978).

28. Grob, *Mental Illness*, p. 132.

29. On psychiatric social work, see Grob, *Mental Illness*, chap. 9; Roy Lubove, *The Professional Altruist* (Cambridge, Mass.: Harvard University Press, 1965), chaps. 3 and 4. For comments on the emergence of a number of other mental health professions and their interactions with psychiatry, see Quen, "Asylum Psychiatry, Neurology, Social Work, and Mental Hygiene"; John Chynoweth Burnham, "Psychiatry, Psychology, and the Progressive Movement," *American Quarterly* 12 (Winter 1960): 457–65.

30. Grob, *Mental Illness*, chap. 7.

31. Data on the numbers of patients and size of hospitals are derived from tables in Grob, *Mental Institutions*, pp. 374–94, and the later figures are from Grob, *Mental Illness*, pp. 315–17.

32. As cited in Quen, "Asylum Psychiatry, Neurology, Social Work, and Mental Hygiene," p. 10; the American Psychiatric Association also created a section on psychoanalysis in 1933.

33. Grob, *Mental Illness*, pp. 269–86.

34. The quotation is from Earle to Stribling, 16 August 1847, Stribling MSS, WSH.

35. Grob, *Mental Illness*, pp. 291–308; Malamud, "The History of Psychiatric Therapies."

36. Grob, *Mental Illness*, p. 200.

37. The figures on the declining numbers of institutionalized patients are from Grob, *Mental Illness*, p. 317; and from "Wards without Walls," Associated Press articles that appeared in the *Burlington Free Press*, 2 and 9 December 1984.

38. The Michigan and North Carolina successes are described in

"Wards without Walls." The condemnation of the conditions at the Vermont State Hospital at Waterbury and the public and professional reactions appeared in the *Burlington Free Press* 18, 20, and 27 November, 3 and 6 December 1984.

39. See Leona Bachrach, "Asylum and Chronically Ill Psychiatric Patients," *American Journal of Psychiatry* 141 (August 1984):975–78; "Wards without Walls."

40. See Bachrach, "Asylum and Chronically Ill Psychiatric Patients," p. 975 for the quotation; for the suggestion about constitutional problems, see James H. Jones, review of *The Willowbrook Wars*, by David J. Rothman and Sheila M. Rothman, *New York Times Book Review*, 25 November 1984, p. 32.

41. Susan Sheehan, *Is There No Place on Earth for Me?* (Boston: Houghton Mifflin, 1982). For samples of the most recent professional literature addressing the problems of the chronically ill under the deinstitutionalization system, see Bachrach, "Asylum and Chronically Ill Psychiatric Patients" and *Deinstitutionalization: An Analytical Review and Sociological Perspective* (Rockville, Md.: National Institute of Mental Health, 1976); Merlin Taber, *The Social Context of Helping: A Review of the Literature on Alternative Care for the Physically and Mentally Handicapped* (Rockville, Md.: National Institute of Mental Health, 1980); Thomas Craig, Ann Goodman, Carole Siegel, and Joseph Wanderling, "The Dynamics of Hospitalization in a Defined Population during Deinstitutionalization," *American Journal of Psychiatry* 141 (June 1984): 782–85; Stanley R. Platman and Thomas C. Booker, "The New Long-term Patient in the Public Mental Health Hospital," ibid., 794–95; Luis R. Marcos and Rosa M. Gil, "Psychiatric Catchment Areas in an Urban Center: A Policy in Disarray," ibid. 141 (July 1984):875–77; Jonathan F. Borus, "Strangers Bearing Gifts: A Retrospective Look at the Early Years of Community Mental Health Center Consultation," ibid., 868–71; John A. Talbott, "Response to the Presidential Address: Psychiatry's Unfinished Business in the 20th Century," ibid. 141 (August 1984):927–30. Newspapers like the *New York Times* (see esp. "The Discharged: Mental Patients and the Community," 18, 19, and 20 November 1979; "A Plan for Discharged Mental Patients," 6 July 1981) and the *Washington Post* (see "Streets Called 'Asylums of the '80s' at Conference on Homeless," 26 April 1984), as well as other local and syndicated newspapers, have abounded with reports about the problems faced by some of the deinstitutionalized.

Selected Bibliography

Primary Sources

Manuscripts and Collections

Chandler, George. MSS. American Antiquarian Society, Worcester, Mass.
Church Records. Connecticut State Library, Hartford, Conn.
Dix, Dorothea. MSS. Houghton Library, Harvard University, Cambridge, Mass.
Earle, Pliny. MSS. American Antiquarian Society, Worcester, Mass.
———. MSS. Westchester Division, New York Hospital, White Plains, N.Y.
Harvard Quinquennial File. Harvard University Archives, Cambridge, Mass.
Jarvis, Edward. MSS. Countway Medical Library, Harvard University, Cambridge, Mass.
Kirkbride, Thomas. MSS. Institute of the Pennsylvania Hospital, Philadelphia, Pa.
Probate Records. Connecticut State Library, Hartford, Conn.
Probate Records. Hampshire County Courthouse, Northampton, Mass.
Ray, Isaac. MSS. Payne Whitney Psychiatric Clinic, New York Hospital, New York, N.Y.
Sibley's Collectanea Biographica Harvardiana. Harvard University Archives, Cambridge, Mass.
Stribling, Francis. MSS. Western State Hospital, Staunton, Va.
Woodward, Samuel. MSS. American Antiquarian Society, Worcester, Mass.
Yale University Alumni Files. Yale University, New Haven, Conn.

Hospital Annual Reports and Records

Alabama Insane Hospital, Tuscaloosa, Ala. Annual Report, 1852.
Bloomingdale Asylum, New York, N.Y. Annual Reports and Records, 1844–49.
Boston Lunatic Hospital, Boston, Mass. Annual Reports, 1848–54.
Butler Hospital for the Insane, Providence, R.I. Annual Reports, 1849–66.
Government Hospital for the Insane (St. Elizabeths), Washington, D.C. Annual Reports, 1856–65.
Kentucky Lunatic Asylum, Lexington, Ky. Annual Reports, 1846–51.

Illinois State Hospital for the Insane, Jacksonville, Ill. Annual Reports, 1851–63.
Indiana Hospital for the Insane, Indianapolis, Ind. Annual Reports, 1851–63.
Maine Insane Asylum, Augusta, Me. Annual Reports, 1841–50.
Maryland Insane Hospital, Baltimore, Md. Annual Reports, 1841–50.
New Hampshire Asylum for the Insane, Concord, N.H. Annual Reports, 1836–59.
New Jersey State Lunatic Asylum, Trenton, N.J. Annual Reports, 1848–61.
New York State Lunatic Asylum, Utica, N.Y. Annual Reports, 1843–56.
Northampton State Lunatic Hospital, Northampton, Mass. Annual Reports and Records, 1856–85.
Ohio Lunatic Asylum, Columbus, Ohio. Annual Reports and Records, 1838–52.
Pennsylvania Hospital for the Insane, Philadelphia, Pa. Annual Reports and Records, 1840–60.
Pennsylvania State Lunatic Hospital, Harrisburg, Pa. Annual Reports and Records, 1851–70.
South Carolina Lunatic Asylum, Columbia, S.C. Annual Report, 1853.
Vermont Asylum for the Insane, Brattleboro, Vt. Annual Reports and Records, 1836–72.
Western Lunatic Hospital, Staunton, Va. Annual Reports and Records, 1828–60.
Worcester State Lunatic Hospital, Worcester, Mass. Annual Reports, 1833–37.

Books and Articles

"American Hospitals for the Insane." *North American Review* 79 (July 1854):66–90.
"Asylums Exclusively for the Incurable Insane." *AJI* 1 (July 1844):44–45.
Beck, Theodric Romeyn. *An Inaugural Dissertation on Insanity.* New York: J. Seymour, 1811.
[Beck, T. R.]. "Notice of the Meeting of the Association of Medical Superintendents of American Institutions for the Insane." *AJI* 9 (April 1853):397.
Bell, Luther V. "On the Coercive Administration of Food to the Insane." *AJI* 6 (January 1850):223–35.
"Bibliographic Notices." *Boston Medical and Surgical Journal* 62 (22 March 1860):166–68.
"Bibliography: Notice of John Curwen, *A Manual for Attendants in Hospitals for the Insane*." *AJI* 8 (January 1852):288–90.
Brigham, Amariah. *An Inquiry concerning the Diseases and Functions of the Brain, the Spinal Cord, and the Nerves.* New York: George Adlard, 1840.

———. *Observations on the Influence of Religion upon the Health and Physical Welfare of Mankind*. Boston: Marsh, Capen & Lyon, 1835.

———. *Remarks on the Influence of Mental Cultivation and Mental Excitement upon Health*. 2d ed. Boston: Marsh, Capen & Lyon, 1833.

Buttolph, Horace A. "Modern Asylums for the Insane." *AJI* 3 (April 1847):364–78.

———. "The Relation between Phrenology and Insanity." *AJI* 6 (October 1849):127–36.

Callender, John. "History and Work of the Association of Medical Superintendents of American Institutions for the Insane—President's Address." *AJI* 40 (July 1883):1–32.

[C.B.C.]. "Memoir of Amariah Brigham." *AJI* 6 (October 1849):185–92.

Channing, Walter. "Some Remarks on the Address Delivered to the American Medico-Psychological Association, by S. Weir Mitchell, M.D., May 16, 1894." *AJI* 51 (October 1894):171–81.

Chapin, John B. "Public Complaints Against Asylums for the Insane, and the Commitment of the Insane." *AJI* 40 (July 1883):33–49.

Chipley, William. "Sitomania: Its Causes and Treatment." *AJI* 16 (July 1859):1–59.

———. *A Warning to Fathers, Teachers and Young Men, in Relation to a Fruitful Cause of Insanity and Other Serious Disorders of Youth*. Louisville, Ky.: L. A. Civill & Wood, Publishers, 1861.

"Connecticut Retreat for the Insane." *Boston Medical and Surgical Journal* 39 (27 September 1848):184.

Curwen, John. *History of the Association of Medical Superintendents of American Institutions for the Insane*. Harrisburg, Pa.: Theo. F. Scheffer, 1875.

———. *A Manual for Attendants in Hospitals for the Insane*. Philadelphia: Martien, 1851.

———. *The Original Thirteen Members of the Association of Medical Superintendents of American Institutions for the Insane*. Warren, Pa.: E. Cowan & Co., Printers, 1885.

Curwen, John; Nichols, Charles H.; and Callender, John H. *Memoir of Thomas S. Kirkbride, M.D., L.L.D.* Warren, Pa.: E. Cowan & Co., 1885.

"Dr. William Stokes, of the Mount Hope Institution, near Baltimore, Maryland, and the *American Journal of Insanity*." *AJI* 5 (January 1849):262–76.

Earle, Pliny. *The Curability of Insanity*. Philadelphia: J. B. Lippincott Company, 1887.

———. "Gheel." *AJI* 8 (July 1851):62–72.

———. *History, Description, and Statistics of the Bloomingdale Asylum for the Insane*. New York: Egbert, Hovey, & King, 1848.

———. *Institutions for the Insane in Prussia, Austria, and Germany*. Utica: New York Asylum, Printers, 1853.

———. "On the Causes of Insanity." *AJI* 4 (July 1848):185–211.

———. "The Poetry of Insanity." *AJI* 1 (January 1845):193–224.

————. *A Visit to Thirteen Asylums for the Insane in Europe.* Philadelphia: J. Dobson, 1841.

Eaton, Dorman B. "Despotism in Lunatic Asylums." *North American Review* 132 (March 1881):263–75.

Everts, Orpheus P. "The American System of Public Provisions for the Insane, and Despotism in Lunatic Asylums." *AJI* 38 (October 1881): 113–39.

Galt, John M. *Essays on Asylums for Unsound Minds.* Richmond, Va.: H. K. Ellyson's Power Press, 1850.

————. "The Farm of St. Anne." *AJI* 11 (April 1855):352–57.

————. "On the Medical Question of the Confinement of the Insane." *AJI* 9 (January 1853):217–23.

————. "On the Propriety of Admitting the Insane of the Two Sexes into the Same Lunatic Asylum." *AJI* 11 (January 1855):224–30.

————. "Report on the Organization of Asylums for the Insane." *AJI* 7 (July 1850):38–44.

————. *The Treatment of Insanity.* New York: Harper & Brothers, Publishers, 1846.

Higgins, J. M. "On the Necessity of a Resident Medical Superintendent in an Institution for the Insane." *AJI* 7 (July 1850):54–58.

Hunt, E. K. "Memorial of Dr. Amariah Brigham." *AJI* 14 (July 1857): 1–29.

Jarvis, Edward. "Distribution of Lunatic Hospital Reports." *AJI* 14 (January 1858):248–53.

————. "On the Proper Functions of Private Institutions or Homes for the Insane." *AJI* 16 (July 1860):19–31.

Journal of the Proceedings of the Convention of Physicians of Ohio. Cincinnati: A. Pugh, 1835.

Kirkbride, Thomas S. *On the Construction, Organization, and General Arrangements of Hospitals for the Insane.* Philadelphia: Lindsay and Balkiston, 1854.

"Legislation for the Insane." *AJI* 8 (October 1851):147–49.

"List of Books." *AJI* 1 (October 1844):186–92.

"Lunatic Asylums in Massachusetts." *Boston Medical and Surgical Journal* 39 (31 January 1849):545.

"Lunatic Asylums in the United States." *AJI* 2 (October 1845):151–58.

"Medical Association. Meeting of the Medical Superintendents of American Institutions for the Insane." *AJI* 1 (January 1845):253–58.

"Miscellany." *AJI* 4 (July 1847):95.

"Notice." *AJI* 2 (April 1846):396.

"Obituaries," [Samuel White]. *AJI* 1 (April 1845):384.

"On Statistics, Applied to Mental Disease." *AJI* 5 (April 1849):322–27.

"On the Management of the Insane." *Boston Medical and Surgical Journal* 22 (29 July 1840):389–92.

Pinel, Philippe. *A Treatise on Insanity.* Translated by D. D. Davis. Sheffield, England: W. Todd, 1806.

Pooley, J. H. "Memoir of William Maclay Awl, M.D., of Columbus, Ohio." *Transactions of the Thirty-Second Annual Meeting of the Ohio State Medical Society.* Cincinnati: Mallory and Webb, Printers, 1877.

Ray, Isaac. *Contributions to Mental Pathology.* Boston: Little, Brown & Co., 1873. Reprint, with an Introduction by Jacques M. Quen. New York: Scholars' Facsimiles & Reprints, 1973.

———. "Hints to Medical Witnesses in Questions of Insanity." *AJI* 8 (July 1851):49–61.

———. *Mental Hygiene.* Boston: Ticknor & Fields, 1863.

———. "Observations on the Principal Hospitals for the Insane in Great Britain, France, and Germany." *AJI* 2 (April 1846):289–390.

———. "On the Popular Feeling towards Insane Hospitals." *AJI* 9 (July 1852):36–65.

———. "Project of a Law for Determining Legal Relations." *AJI* 7 (January 1851):215–33.

———. "The Statistics of Insane Hospitals." *AJI* 6 (July 1849):23–52.

———. *A Treatise on the Medical Jurisprudence of Insanity.* 3d ed. Boston: Little, Brown & Co., 1853.

"Report of the Special Committee on Revision of the 'Propositions of the Association.'" *AJI* 44 (July 1888):50–57.

"Report of the Trustees of the Massachusetts General Hospital for the Year 1858." *North American Review* 89 (October 1859):316–39.

"Reports of American Asylums." *AJI* 10 (October 1853):169.

"Reports of Asylums." *AJI* 7 (October 1850):173–98.

"Reports of Hospitals for the Insane." *AJI* 8 (October 1851):182–84.

Rules and Regulations for Attendants, &c., at the Pennsylvania Hospital for the Insane, near Philadelphia. Philadelphia: Brown, Bicking & Guilbert, 1841.

"Statistics on Insanity." *AJI* 6 (October 1849):141–45.

"Statistics on Insanity in Massachusetts." *North American Review* 82 (January 1856):78–100.

Stokes, William. "On a Court of Medical Experts in Cases of Insanity." *AJI* 10 (October 1853):112–22.

"Summary." *AJI* 11 (April 1855):390.

Tuke, D. Hack. "American Retrospect." *AJI* 41 (January 1886):590–96.

———. *Chapters in the History of the Insane in the British Isles.* London: Kegan Paul, Trench & Co., 1882.

———. *The Insane in the United States and Canada.* London: H. K. Lewis, 1885.

Tuke, Samuel. *Description of the Retreat.* York, England: Thomas Wilson and Sons, Printers, 1813.

Vail, Jackson. *Rockwell Castle or a Thirty Days Trip from Highgate Springs to Boston including Ten Days Confinement in the Brattleboro Prison or the Vermont Asylum for the Insane and Adventures Along the Way.* Montpelier, Vt.: n.p., n.d.

"A Village of Lunatics." *AJI* 4 (January 1848):217–22.

White, G. H. "On the Importance of Establishing Separate Institutions for the Different Sexes of the Insane." *AJI* 6 (October 1849): 136–40.

Woodward, Samuel B. *Hints for the Young on a Subject Relating to the Health of Body and Mind.* Boston: Weeks, Jordan & Co., 1838.

Secondary Sources

Abbott, John S. C. *The History of the State of Ohio.* Detroit: Northwestern Publishing Company, 1875.

Ackerknecht, Erwin H. *A Short History of Psychiatry.* Translated by Sula Wolff. New York: Hafner, 1968.

Adams, James, Jr. *The Portland Directory & Register.* Portland, Maine: n.p., 1827.

Allen, Henry Mott. *A chronicle of early Auburn, N.Y., 1793–1860.* Edward J. Peet, 1849.

Allen, William. *The History of Norridgewock.* Norridgewock, Maine: Edward J. Peet, 1849.

Altschule, Mark D., and Russ, Evelyn. *Roots of Modern Psychiatry.* New York: Grune & Stratton, 1957.

Armstrong, J. R. *The Columbus Business Directory for 1843–4.* Columbus, Ohio: Samuel Medary, 1843.

Aronson, Sidney H. *Status and Kinship in the Higher Civil Service.* Cambridge, Mass.: Harvard University Press, 1964.

Atkinson, William B., ed. *A Biographical Dictionary of Contemporary American Physicians and Surgeons.* 2d ed. Philadelphia: D. G. Brinton, 1880.

Atwater, Edward. "The Medical Profession in a New Society, Rochester, New York, 1811–1860." *Bulletin of the History of Medicine* 47 (Summer 1973):221–35.

Bachrach, Leona. "Asylum and Chronically Ill Psychiatric Patients." *American Journal of Psychiatry* 141 (August 1984):975–78.

———. *Deinstitutionalization: An Analytical Review and Sociological Perspective.* Rockville, Md.: National Institute of Mental Health, 1976.

Barrows, John Stuart. *Fryeburg, Maine. A Historical Sketch.* Fryeburg: Pequaket Press, 1938.

Beeson, Leola Selman. *History Stories of Milledgeville and Baldwin Counties.* Macon, Ga.: J. W. Burke, 1943.

Bell, Whitfield J., Jr. *The Colonial Physician and Other Essays.* New York: Science History Publications, 1975.

Berthoff, Rowland. *An Unsettled People: Social Order and Disorder in American History.* New York: Harper & Row, 1971.

Bidwell, Percy W., and Falconer, John I. *History of Agriculture in the Northern United States, 1620–1860.* Washington, D.C.: Carnegie Institution of Washington, 1925.

Biographical Directory of the American Congress, 1774–1971. Washington, D.C.: U.S. Government Printing Office, 1971.

Blackmon, Dora M. E. "The Care of the Mentally Ill in America, 1604–1812, in the Thirteen Original Colonies." Ph.D. diss., University of Washington, 1964.

Blassingame, John. *The Slave Community.* New York: Oxford University Press, 1979.

Bledstein, Burton J. *The Culture of Professionalism.* New York: W. W. Norton, 1976.

Blustein, Bonnie. " 'A Hollow Square of Psychological Medicine': American Neurologists and Psychiatrists in Conflict." In *Madhouses, Mad-Doctors, and Madmen,* pp. 241–70. Edited by Andrew Scull. Philadelphia: University of Pennsylvania Press, 1981.

———. "A New York Medical Man: William Alexander Hammond, Neurologist." Ph.D. diss., University of Pennsylvania, 1979.

———. "New York Neurologists and the Specialization of American Medicine." *Bulletin of the History of Medicine* 53 (Summer 1979): 170–83.

Bockoven, J. Sanborne. *Moral Treatment in American Psychiatry.* New York: Springer, 1963.

Bond, Earl W. *Dr. Kirkbride and His Mental Hospital.* Philadelphia: J. P. Lippincott, 1947.

Boorstin, Daniel J. *The Americans: The National Experience.* New York: Vintage Books, 1965.

Borus, Jonathan F. "Strangers Bearing Gifts: A Retrospective Look at the Early Years of Community Health Center Consultation." *American Journal of Psychiatry* 141 (July 1984):868–71.

Bradbury, Anna R. *History of the City of Hudson, New York.* Hudson: Record Printing and Publishing Co., 1908.

Bremner, Robert H. *American Philanthropy.* Chicago: University of Chicago Press, 1960.

Brown, Richard. *Modernization: The Transformation of American Life.* New York: Hill & Wang, 1976.

Burdett, Henry C. *Hospitals and Asylums of the World: Their Origin, History, Construction, Administration, Management, and Legislation.* 4 vols. London: J. & A. Churchill, 1891.

Burnham, John Chynoweth. "Psychiatry, Psychology, and the Progressive Movement." *American Quarterly* 12 (Winter 1960):457–65.

———. *Psychoanalysis and American Medicine, 1894–1918: Medicine, Science, and Culture.* Psychological Issues, vol. 5, no. 4, monograph 20. New York: International Universities Press, 1967.

Bushman, Richard. *From Puritan to Yankee.* New York: W. W. Norton, 1970.

———. "The Great Awakening in Connecticut." In *Colonial America,* edited by Stanley N. Katz and John M. Murrin, pp. 487–97. New York: Alfred A. Knopf, 1983.

Butler, Caleb. *History of the Town of Groton, including Pepperell and Shirley*. Boston: Press of T. R. Martin, 1848.

Calhoun, Daniel H. *The American Civil Engineer*. Cambridge, Mass.: Harvard University Press, 1960.

————. *Professional Lives in America, 1750–1850*. Cambridge, Mass.: Harvard University Press, 1965.

Calvert, Monte A. *The Mechanical Engineer in America, 1830–1910*. Baltimore: Johns Hopkins Press, 1967.

Campbell, Jno. P. *The Nashville, State of Tennessee, and General Commercial Directory*. Nashville: Daily American Book and Job Printing, 1853.

Carlson, Eric T. "Amariah Brigham: I. Life and Works." *American Journal of Psychiatry* 112 (April 1956):831–36.

————. "Amariah Brigham: II. Psychiatric Thought and Practice." *American Journal of Psychiatry* 113 (April 1957):911–16.

————. "Edward Mead and the Second American Psychiatric Journal." *American Journal of Psychiatry* 113 (December 1956):561–63.

————. "The Influence of Phrenology on Early American Psychiatric Thought." *American Journal of Psychiatry* 115 (December 1958):535–38.

————. "Theodric Romeyn Beck, M.D." *American Journal of Psychiatry* 114 (February 1958):754–55.

————. "The Unfortunate Dr. Parkman." *American Journal of Psychiatry* 123 (December 1966):724–28.

Carlson, Eric T., and Chale, May F. "Dr. Rufus Wyman of the McLean Asylum." *American Journal of Psychiatry* 116 (May 1960):1034–37.

Carlson, Eric T., and Dain, Norman. "The Psychotherapy that was Moral Treatment." *American Journal of Psychiatry* 117 (December 1960):519–24.

Carlson, Eric T., and Wollock, Jeffrey L. "Benjamin Rush and His Insane Son." *Bulletin of the New York Academy of Medicine* 51 (December 1975):1312–30.

Carlson, Eric T.; Wollock, Jeffrey L.; and Noel, Patricia S., eds. *Benjamin Rush's Lectures on the Mind*. Philadelphia: American Philosophical Society, 1981.

Caulkins, Frances Manwaring. *History of Norwich, Connecticut*. N.p.: Published by the Friends of the Author, 1874.

Chapman, George T. *Sketches of the Alumni of Dartmouth College*. Cambridge, Mass.: Riverside Press, 1867.

Chase, Benjamin. *History of Old Chester from 1719–1869*. Auburn, N.H.: Published by the Author, 1869.

Cochrane, W. R., and Wood, George K. *History of Francestown, N.H.* Nashua, N.H.: James H. Barker, Printer, 1895.

Coleman, S. *The Portland Directory*. Portland, Me.: n.p., 1830.

Collins, G. *The Louisville Directory for 1838–9*. Louisville, Ky.: J. B. Marshall, 1838.

————. *The Louisville Directory for 1841.* Louisville, Ky.: Henkle, Logan & Co., 1841.

Commemorative Biographical Record of Wayne County, Ohio. Chicago: J. H. Beers & Co., 1889.

The Concord Directory. Concord, N.H.: Printed at the Observer Office, 1834.

Couper, William. *History of the Shenandoah Valley.* 3 vols. New York: Leur's Historical Publishing, 1952.

Craig, Thomas; Goodman, Ann; Siegel, Carole; and Wanderling, Joseph. "The Dynamics of Hospitalization in a Defined Population During Deinstitutionalization." *American Journal of Psychiatry* 141 (June 1984):782–85.

Craven, Avery O. *The Coming of the Civil War.* Chicago: University of Chicago Press, 1957.

————. *The Growth of Southern Nationalism, 1848–1861.* New Orleans: Louisiana State University Press, 1953.

Creech, Margaret. *Three Centuries of Poor Law Administration: A Study of Legislation in Rhode Island.* Chicago: University of Chicago Press, 1936.

Cross, Whitney R. *The Burned-over District.* New York: Harper & Row, 1965.

Cutter, Daniel B. *History of the Town of Jaffrey, New Hampshire, 1749–1880.* Concord, N.H.: Republican Press Association, 1881.

Dain, Norman. *Clifford W. Beers: Advocate for the Insane.* Pittsburgh: University of Pittsburgh Press, 1980.

————. *Concepts of Insanity in the United States, 1789–1865.* New Brunswick, N.J.: Rutgers University Press, 1964.

————. *Disordered Minds.* Williamsburg, Va.: Colonial Williamsburg Foundation, 1971.

Dain, Norman, and Carlson, Eric T. "Milieu Therapy in the Nineteenth Century: Patient Care at the Friends' Asylum, Frankford, Pennsylvania, 1817–1861." *Journal of Nervous and Mental Disease* 131 (October 1960):277–90.

Daniels, George H. *American Science in the Age of Jackson.* New York: Columbia University Press, 1968.

————. "The Process of Professionalization in American Science: The Emergent Period, 1820–1860." *Isis* 58 (Summer 1967):151–66.

Davies, John D. *Phrenology: Fad and Science.* New Haven, Conn.: Yale University Press, 1955.

Davis, David Brion. *Antebellum American Culture.* Lexington, Mass.: D. C. Heath, 1979.

Demos, John. *A Little Commonwealth.* New York: Oxford University Press, 1970.

Desilver, Robert. *Desilver's Philadelphia Directory and Stranger's Guide, for 1835 & 1836.* Philadelphia: n.p., 1834.

Deutsch, Albert. "The History of Mental Hygiene." In *One Hundred Years of American Psychiatry, 1844–1944,* edited by J. K. Hall, pp. 367–84. New York: Columbia University Press, 1944.

––––––. *The Mentally Ill in America.* New York: Doubleday, Doran, 1937.

Dexter, Franklin Bowditch. *Biographical Notices of Graduates of Yale College.* New Haven, Conn.: n.p., 1913.

––––––. *Biographical Sketches of the Graduates of Yale College.* 6 vols. New Haven, Conn.: Yale University Press, 1912.

Dictionary of American Biography. New York: Charles Scribner's Sons, 1828–1959.

"The Discharged: Mental Patients and the Community." *New York Times,* 18, 19, 20 November 1979.

Duffy, John. *The Healers.* New York: McGraw-Hill, 1976.

Dunne, Nancy Feys. "The Era of Moral Therapy at Western State Hospital." M.A. thesis, DePaul University, 1968.

Eaton, Leonard K. *New England Hospitals, 1790–1833.* Ann Arbor: University of Michigan Press, 1957.

Ebaugh, Franklin. "The History of Psychiatric Education in the United States from 1844–1944." *American Journal of Psychiatry* 100 (April 1944):151–60.

Elliott, Clark A. "The American Scientist in Antebellum Society: A Quantitative View." Ph.D. diss., Case Western Reserve University, 1970.

––––––. "The American Scientist in Antebellum Society: A Quantitative View." *Social Studies of Science* 5 (January 1975):93–108.

Ellyson, H. K. *Ellyson's Business Directory, and Almanac for the year 1845.* Richmond, Va.: n.p., 1845.

Ensign, Ariel. *Hartford City Directory, for 1828.* Hartford, Conn.: n.p., 1828.

Environs of Boston. An Almanac and Business Directory of the Cities of Cambridge, Charlestown, and Roxbury, and the Towns of Chelsea, Dorchester, Brighton and Brookline. Boston: David Clapp, Printer, 1848.

Everhart, J. F. *History of Muskingum County.* Columbus, Ohio: J. F. Everhart & Co., 1882.

Fairbanks, Edward T. *The Town of St. Johnsbury, Vt.* St. Johnsbury, Vt.: Cowles Press, 1914.

Farmer, John. *The Concord Directory.* Concord, N.H.: Hoag & Atwood, 1830.

Foster, Charles I. *An Errand of Mercy.* Chapel Hill: University of North Carolina Press, 1960.

Foucault, Michel. *Madness and Civilization.* Translated by Richard Howard. New York: Pantheon Books, 1965.

Fowler, William Chauncey. *History of Durham, Connecticut.* Hartford, Conn.: Press of Wiley, Waterman & Eaton, 1866.

Fox, Richard. *So Far Disordered in Mind*. Berkeley: University of California Press, 1978.

French, J. H. *French's Auburn City Directory for 1857*. Syracuse, N.Y.: n.p., 1857.

Frost, J. Robert. *The Quaker Family in Colonial America*. New York: St. Martin's Press, 1973.

Gardner's Hartford City Directory. Hartford, Conn.: Case, Tiffany, 1838, 1839, 1840.

Garraty, John. *The New Commonwealth*. New York: Harper & Row, 1968.

Gay, Peter. *The Enlightenment: An Interpretation*. 2 vols. New York: Alfred A. Knopf, 1969.

General Catalogue of Bowdoin College and the Medical School of Maine. 1794–1850. Portland, Maine: Anthoensen Press, 1950.

Gilb, Corinne Lathrop. *Hidden Hierarchies*. New York: Harper & Row, 1966.

Goffman, Erving. *Asylums*. Garden City, N.Y.: Doubleday, 1961.

Goldstein, Jan E. "French Psychiatry in Social and Political Context: The Formation of a New Profession, 1820–1860." Ph.D. diss., Columbia University, 1978.

Goode, William J. "Community Within a Community: The Professions." *American Sociological Review* 22 (April 1957):194–200.

———. "Encroachment, Charlatanism, and the Emerging Profession: Psychology, Sociology, and Medicine." *American Sociological Review* 25 (December 1960):902–914.

Gordon, Maurice B. *Aesculapius Comes to the Colonies*. Ventnor, N.J.: Ventnor Publishers, 1949.

Gordon, Michael, ed. *The American Family in Social-Historical Perspective*. New York: St. Martin's Press, 1983.

Greene, Evarts B. *The Revolutionary Generation*. New York: Macmillan, 1943.

Greven, Philip J., Jr. *Four Generations*. Ithaca, N.Y.: Cornell University Press, 1970.

———. *The Protestant Temperament*. New York: New American Library, 1977.

Griffin, C. S. *The Ferment of Reform, 1830–1860*. New York: Thomas Y. Crowell, 1967.

———. *Their Brothers' Keepers*. New Brunswick, N.J.: Rutgers University Press, 1960.

Grob, Gerald N. *Edward Jarvis and the Medical World of Nineteenth-century America*. Knoxville: University of Tennessee Press, 1978.

———. Introduction to *Insanity and Idiocy in Massachusetts* by Edward Jarvis. Boston: William White, 1855. Reprint. Cambridge, Mass.: Harvard University Press, 1971.

———. *Mental Illness and American Society*. Princeton, N.J.: Princeton University Press, 1983.

————. *Mental Institutions in America: Social Policy to 1875*. New York: Free Press, 1973.

————. "Rediscovering the Asylum." In *The Therapeutic Revolution*, edited by Morris J. Vogel and Charles E. Rosenberg, pp. 135–57. Philadelphia: University of Pennsylvania Press, 1979.

————. "The Social History of Medicine and Disease in America: Problems and Possibilities." *Journal of Social History* 10 (Summer 1977): 391–409.

————. *The State and the Mentally Ill*. Chapel Hill: University of North Carolina Press, 1966.

Gross, Samuel D., ed. *Lives of eminent American physicians and surgeons of the nineteenth century*. Philadelphia: Lindsay & Blakiston, 1861.

Gusfield, Joseph R. *Symbolic Crusade*. Chicago: University of Illinois Press, 1963.

Gutman, Herbert. *The Black Family in Slavery and Freedom*. New York: Vintage Books, 1977.

Hale, Nathan. *Freud and the Americans: The Beginnings of Psychoanalysis in the United States, 1896–1917*. New York: Oxford University Press, 1971.

Hall, Courtney R. "The Rise of Professional Surgery in the United States, 1800–1865." *Bulletin of the History of Medicine* 26 (Summer 1952): 231–62.

Hall, J. K., ed. *One Hundred Years of American Psychiatry, 1844–1944*. New York: Columbia University Press, 1944.

Hall, William S. "John Waring Parker, M.D." *Journal of the South Carolina Medical Association* 69 (October 1973): 381–89.

Hartman, Mary, and Banner, Lois, eds., *Clio's Consciousness Raised*. New York: Harper & Row, 1974.

Haskell, Thomas L. *The Emergence of Professional Social Science*. Urbana: University of Illinois Press, 1977.

Hatch, Nathan. "The Origins of Civil Millennialism in America." In *Colonial America*, edited by Stanley N. Katz and John M. Murrin, pp. 497–518. New York: Alfred A. Knopf, 1983.

Hays, Samuel P. *The Response to Industrialism*. Chicago: University of Chicago Press, 1957.

Henretta, James A. *The Evolution of American Society*. Lexington, Mass.: D. C. Heath, 1973.

————. "Families and Farms: *Mentalité* in Pre-Industrial America." *William and Mary Quarterly* 35 (January 1978): 3–32.

Herrick, Wm. D. *History of the Town of Gardner, Worcester County, Mass.* Gardner, Mass.: Published by the Committee, 1878.

Higham, John. *Strangers in the Land*. New York: Atheneum, 1971.

Himelhoch, Myra, and Shaffer, Arthur. "Elizabeth Packard: Nineteenth-Century Crusader for the Rights of Mental Patients." *Journal of American Studies* 13 (December 1979): 343–75.

Historical Catalogue of Brown University, 1764–1904. Providence, R.I.: Published by the University, 1905.

Hofstadter, Richard. *Anti-Intellectualism in American Life.* New York: Vintage Books, 1963.

Holbrook, Stewart H. *Yankee Exodus.* Seattle: University of Washington Press, 1968.

Hooper, Osman Castle. *History of the City of Columbus, Ohio.* Columbus, Ohio: Memorial Publishing, 1920.

Howard, Walker E., and Prentiss, Charles E. *Catalogue of the Officers and Students of Middlebury College in Middlebury, Vermont.* Middlebury, Vt.: Published by the College, 1901.

Hugins, Walter, ed. *The Reform Impulse, 1825–1850.* New York: Harper & Row, 1972.

Hunter, Richard, and Macalpine, Ida, eds. *Three Hundred Years of Psychiatry, 1535–1860.* London: Oxford University Press, 1963.

Hurd, Henry M., ed., *The Institutional Care of the Insane in the United States and Canada.* 4 vols. Baltimore: Johns Hopkins Press, 1916.

Hyde, C. M. *The Centennial Celebration and Centennial History of the Town of Lee, Mass.* Springfield, Mass.: Clark W. Bryan & Company, Printers, 1878.

Isaac, Rhys. "Evangelical Revolt." In *Colonial America,* edited by Stanley N. Katz and John M. Murrin, pp. 518–40. New York: Alfred A. Knopf, 1983.

James, Sydney V. *A People among Peoples.* Cambridge, Mass.: Harvard University Press, 1963.

Jewitt, Nathaniel G. *The Portland Directory & Register.* Portland, Maine: Todd & Smith, 1823.

Jimenez, Mary Ann. "Changing Faces of Madness: Insanity in Massachusetts, 1700–1850." Ph.D. diss., Brandeis University, 1980.

Johnson, Paul. *A Shopkeeper's Millennium.* New York: Hill & Wang, 1978.

Johnson, William R. "Education and Professional Life Styles: Law and Medicine in the Nineteenth Century." *History of Education Quarterly* 14 (Summer 1974):185–207.

Jones, Douglas Lamar. "The Strolling Poor: Transiency in Eighteenth-Century Massachusetts." *Journal of Social History* 8 (Summer 1975): 28–54.

Jones, James H. Review of *The Willowbrook Wars,* by David J. Rothman and Sheila M. Rothman. *New York Times Book Review,* 25 November 1984, p. 32.

Jones, Kathleen. *Lunacy, Law and Conscience.* London: Routledge & Kegan Paul, 1955.

———. *Mental Health and Social Policy, 1845–1959.* London: Routledge & Kegan Paul, 1960.

Kasson, John. *Civilizing the Machine: Technology and Republican Values, 1776–1900.* New York: Penguin, 1977.

Katz, Michael. *The People of Hamilton, Canada West: Family and Class in a Mid-Nineteenth Century City.* Cambridge, Mass.: Harvard University Press, 1975.

Katz, Stanley N., and Murrin, John M., eds. *Colonial America.* New York: Alfred A. Knopf, 1983.

Keller, Charles R. *The Second Great Awakening in Connecticut.* New Haven, Conn.: Yale University Press, 1942.

Kelly, Howard, and Burrage, Walter. *American Medical Biographies.* Baltimore: Norman Remington, 1920.

Kett, Joseph F. *The Formation of the American Medical Profession.* New Haven, Conn.: Yale University Press, 1968.

Klebaner, Benjamin J. "Poverty and Its Relief in American Thought, 1815–1861." *Social Service Review* 38 (December 1964):382–99.

Kleppner, Paul. *The Cross of Culture.* New York: Free Press, 1970.

Kriegman, George; Gardner, Robert D.; and Abse, D. Wilfred, eds. *American Psychiatry: Past, Present, and Future.* Charlottesville: University Press of Virginia, 1975.

Landrum, J. B. O. *History of Spartanburg County.* Atlanta, Ga.: Franklin Prtg. and Pub. Co., 1900.

Lee, Alfred E. *History of the City of Columbus, Capital of Ohio.* 2 vols. New York: Munsell & Co., 1892.

Leigh, Denis. *The Historical Development of British Psychiatry. Vol. I. 18th and 19th Century.* London: Pergamon Press, 1961.

Levy, Brian. " 'Tender Plants.' " In *Colonial America,* edited by Stanley N. Katz and John M. Murrin, pp. 177–203. New York: Alfred A. Knopf, 1983.

Lockridge, Kenneth A. *A New England Town.* New York: W. W. Norton, 1970.

Lubove, Roy. *The Professional Altruist.* Cambridge, Mass.: Harvard University Press, 1965.

Ludlum, David M. *Social Ferment in Vermont, 1791–1850.* Montpelier: Vermont Historical Society, 1948.

McCabe, Julius P. Boliver. *Directory of the City of Lexington & County of Fayette for 1838 & '39.* Lexington, Ky.: J. C. Noble, 1838.

McGovern, Constance M. "The Early Career of Pliny Earle: A Founder of American Psychiatry." M.A. thesis, University of Massachusetts, 1971.

———. "The Insane, the Asylum, and the State in Nineteenth-Century Vermont." *Vermont History* 52 (Fall 1984):205–24.

———. " 'Mad Doctors': American Psychiatrists, 1800–1860." Ph.D. diss., University of Massachusetts, 1976.

McGuire, H. M., and Fay, T. C. *Mobile Directory. For 1837.* Mobile, Ala.: n.p., 1837.

McIlhany, Hugh Milton, Jr. *Some Virginia Families being Genealogies of the Kinney, Stribling, Trout, McIlhany, Milton, Rogers, Tait, Snickers, McCormick, and other families of Virginia.* Staunton, Va.: Stoneburner & Prufer, 1903. Reprint. Baltimore: Genealogy Publishing Company, 1962.

Maddox, John. *The Richmond Directory, Register, and Almanac, for 1819.* Richmond, Va.: n.p., 1819.

Malamud, William. "The History of Psychiatric Therapies." In *One Hundred Years of American Psychiatry, 1844–1944,* edited by J. K. Hall, pp. 273–323. New York: Columbia University Press, 1944.

Marcos, Luis R., and Gil, Rosa M. "Psychiatric Catchment Areas in an Urban Center: A Policy in Disarray." *American Journal of Psychiatry* 141 (July 1984):875–77.

Marshall, Helen. *Dorothea Dix: Forgotten Samaritan.* Chapel Hill: University of North Carolina Press, 1937.

Martin, Abijah P. *History of the Town of Lancaster, Massachusetts.* Lancaster, Mass.: Published by the Town, 1879.

Martin, John H. *Columbus, Geo., from its Selection as a "Trading Town" in 1827, to its Partial Destruction by Wilson's Raid, in 1865.* 2 vols. Columbus, Ga.: Thos. Gilbert, Book Printer and Binder, 1874.

Martin, William T. *History of Franklin County.* Columbus, Ohio: Follett, Foster & Company, 1858.

Mathews, Donald G. "The Second Great Awakening Considered as an Organizing Process, 1780–1830, An Hypothesis." *American Quarterly* 21 (Spring 1969):23–43.

Mattingly, Paul. *The Classless Profession: American Schoolmen in the Nineteenth Century.* New York: Springer, 1963.

Mead, Sidney E. "Denominationalism: The Shape of Protestantism in America." *Church History* 1 (December 1954):291–320.

Meade, William. *Old Churches, Ministers and Families of Virginia.* 4 vols. Baltimore: Genealogical Publishing Company, 1966.

Menard, Russell. "From Servant to Freeholder." In *Colonial America,* edited by Stanley N. Katz and John M. Murrin, pp. 290–313. New York: Alfred A. Knopf, 1983.

Meyers, Marvin. *The Jacksonian Persuasion.* Stanford, Calif.: Stanford University Press, 1957.

Miller, Stephen B. *Historical Sketches of Hudson.* Hudson, N.Y.: Bryan & Webb Printers, 1862.

Morgan, Edmund. *The Puritan Family.* New York: Harper & Row, 1966.

Morton, Thomas G. *The History of the Pennsylvania Hospital, 1751–1895.* Philadelphia: Times Printing House, 1895.

Mower, Walter Lindley. *Sesquicentennial History of the Town of Greene, Androscoggin County, Maine, 1775–1900.* Auburn, Maine: Press of Merrill & Webber, 1937.

Nash, Gary B. "Up from the Bottom in Franklin's Philadelphia." In *The Private Side of American History,* edited by Gary B. Nash, pp. 163–78. New York: Harcourt Brace Jovanovich, 1983.

———. "Urban Wealth and Poverty." In *Colonial America,* edited by

Stanley N. Katz and John M. Murrin, pp. 447–83. New York: Alfred A. Knopf, 1983.

The National Cyclopaedia of American Biography. London: James T. White and Company, 1892.

Niebuhr, H. Richard. *The Social Sources of Denominationalism.* New York: H. Holt, 1929.

North, Douglass. *The Economic Growth of the United States.* New York: W. W. Norton, 1966.

North, Douglass; Anderson, Terry; and Hill, Peter. *Growth and Welfare in the American Past.* Englewood Cliffs, N.J.: Prentice-Hall, 1983.

Norton, A. Banning. *History of Knox County, Ohio, from 1779 to the present Inclusive.* Columbus, Ohio: Richard Nevins, Printer, 1862.

Norton, Benjamin H. *The Pocket Register for the City of Hartford.* Hartford, Conn.: n.p., 1825.

Norton, Mary Beth. *Liberty's Daughters.* Boston: Little, Brown, 1980.

Norwood, William F. *Medical Education in the United States before the Civil War.* Philadelphia: University of Pennsylvania Press, 1944.

Nourse, Henry S., ed. *The Birth, Marriage and Death Register, Church Records and Epitaphs of Lancaster, Mass.* Clinton, Mass.: W. J. Coulter, Printer, 1890.

Obituary Record of Graduates of Yale College. New Haven, Conn.: Tuttle, Morehouse, and Taylor, 1860–1910.

Oleson, Alexandra, and Voss, John, eds. *The Organization of Knowledge in Modern America, 1860–1920.* Baltimore: Johns Hopkins University Press, 1979.

O'Malley, C. D. *The History of Medical Education.* Berkeley: University of California Press, 1970.

Orcutt, Samuel. *History of Torrington, Connecticut.* Albany, N.Y.: J. Munsell, Printer, 1878.

The Origins of the State Mental Hospital in America. New York: Arno Press, 1973.

Owen, David. *English Philanthropy, 1660–1960.* Cambridge, Mass.: Harvard University Press, 1964.

Packard, Francis R. *History of Medicine in the United States.* 2 vols. New York: Hafner, 1963.

Palmer, Joseph. *Necrology of Alumni of Harvard College: 1851–52 to 1862–63.* Boston: John Wilson and Son, 1864.

Parke, John E. *Recollections of Seventy Years and Historical Gleanings of Allegheny, Pennsylvania.* Boston: Rand, Avery, & Company, 1886.

Parker, Edward L. *The History of Londonderry, comprising the towns of Derry and Londonderry, N.H.* Boston: Perkins and Whipple, 1851.

Parry-Jones, William L. *The Trade in Lunacy.* London: Routledge & Kegan Paul, 1972.

Pessen, Edward. *Jacksonian America.* Homewood, Ill.: Dorsey Press, 1969.

Peterson, M. Jeanne. *The Medical Profession in Mid-Victorian England.* Berkeley: University of California Press, 1978.

Pitts, John A. "The Association of Medical Superintendents of American Institutions for the Insane, 1844–1892: A Case Study of Specialism in American Medicine." Ph.D. diss., University of Pennsylvania, 1979.

"A Plan for Discharged Mental Patients." *New York Times,* 6 July 1981.

Platman, Stanley R., and Booker, Thomas C. "The New Long-term Patient in the Public Mental Health Hospital." *American Journal of Psychiatry* 141 (June 1984):794–95.

Power, J. L. *Professional & Business Directory of the City of Jackson, Miss.* Jackson, Miss.: n.p., 1860.

Poynter, F. N. L. *The Evolution of Hospitals in Britain.* London: Pitman Medical Publishing, 1964.

Quen, Jacques M. "Asylum Psychiatry, Neurology, Social Work, and Mental Hygiene: An Exploratory Study in Interprofessional History." *Journal of the History of the Behavioral Sciences* 13 (January 1977): 3–11.

Quen, Jacques M., and Carlson, Eric T., eds. *American Psychoanalysis: Origins and Development.* New York: Brunner/Mazel, 1978.

Rabb, Theodore K., and Rotberg, Robert I., eds. *The Family in History.* New York: Harper & Row, 1971.

Reader, W. J. *Professional Men.* London: Weidenfeld and Nicolson, 1966.

Richards, Leonard L. *The Advent of American Democracy.* Glenview, Ill.: Scott, Foresman, 1977.

———. *"Gentlemen of Property and Standing."* New York: Oxford University Press, 1970.

Riznik, Barnes. "The Professional Lives of Early Nineteenth-century New England Doctors." Typescript. Old Sturbridge Village Library, Sturbridge, Massachusetts.

———. "The Professional Lives of Early Nineteenth-century New England Doctors." *Journal of the History of Medicine and Allied Sciences* 19 (January 1964):1–16.

Roseboom, Eugene H., and Weisenburger, Francis P. *A History of Ohio.* New York: Prentice-Hall, 1934.

Rosen, George. *Fees and Fee Bills.* Baltimore: Johns Hopkins Press, 1946.

———. *Madness in Society.* Chicago: University of Chicago Press, 1968.

Rosenberg, Charles E. "And Heal the Sick: The Hospital and the Patient in Nineteenth Century America." *Journal of Social History* 10 (June 1977):428–47.

———. *The Cholera Years.* Chicago: University of Chicago Press, 1962.

———. *No Other Gods.* Baltimore: Johns Hopkins Press, 1976.

———. "The Practice of Medicine in New York a Century Ago." *Bulletin of the History of Medicine* 41 (Summer 1967):223–53.

———. "The Therapeutic Revolution." In *The Therapeutic Revolution,* edited by Morris J. Vogel and Charles E. Rosenberg, pp. 3–25. Philadelphia: University of Pennsylvania Press, 1979.

————. *The Trial of the Assassin Guiteau*. Chicago: University of Chicago Press, 1968.

Rosenberry, Lois K. Mathews. *The Expansion of New England*. New York: Russell & Russell, 1962.

Rosenkrantz, Barbara G. "The Search for Professional Order in Nineteenth-Century American Medicine." *Proceedings of the Fourteenth International Congress of the History of Science*, no. 4, pp. 113–24. Tokyo and Kyoto, 1974.

Rothman, David J. *Conscience and Convenience*. Boston: Little, Brown, 1980.

————. *The Discovery of the Asylum*. Boston: Little, Brown, 1971.

Rothstein, William G. *American Physicians in the Nineteenth Century*. Baltimore: Johns Hopkins Press, 1972.

Rowe, William Hutchinson. *Ancient North Yarmouth and Yarmouth, Maine, 1636–1936, A History*. Yarmouth: Southampton-Anthoensen Press, 1937.

Russell, William. *The New York Hospital*. New York: Columbia University Press, 1945.

Ryan, Mary. *The Cradle of the Middle Class*. Cambridge: Cambridge University Press, 1981.

Sanborn, Franklin B. *Memoirs of Pliny Earle, M.D.* Boston: Damrell & Upham, 1898.

Scheff, Thomas. *Mental Illness and Social Processes*. New York: Harper & Row, 1967.

Schneider, David M. *The History of Public Welfare in New York State*. Chicago: University of Chicago Press, 1938.

Scott, Donald. *From Office to Profession*. Philadelphia: University of Pennsylvania Press, 1978.

Scott, Harvey W. *History of the Oregon County*. 6 vols. Cambridge, Mass.: Riverside Press, 1924.

Scull, Andrew, ed. *Madhouses, Mad-doctors, and Madmen*. Philadelphia: University of Pennsylvania Press, 1981.

————. *Museums of Madness*. New York: St. Martin's Press, 1979.

Sedgwick, Charles F. *General History of the Town of Sharon, Litchfield County, Conn.* Amenia, N.Y.: Charles Walsh, Printer and Publisher, 1891.

Semelaigne, René. *Les Pionniers de la psychiatrie française avant et après Pinel*. 2 vols. Paris: Librairie J.-B. Baillière et Fils, 1930–32.

Shafer, Henry B. *The American Medical Profession, 1783–1850*. New York: Columbia University Press, 1936.

Sheehan, Susan. *Is There No Place on Earth for Me?* Boston: Houghton Mifflin, 1982.

Shryock, Richard H. *Medical Licensing in America, 1650–1965*. Baltimore: Johns Hopkins Press, 1967.

————. *Medicine and Society in America, 1660–1860.* New York: New York University Press, 1960.

————. *Medicine in America.* Baltimore: Johns Hopkins Press, 1966.

————. "Public Relations of the Medical Profession in Great Britain and the United States." *Annals of Medical History,* n.s. 2 (1930):308–39.

Sicherman, Barbara. "The Paradox of Prudence: Mental Health in the Gilded Age." *Journal of American History* 62 (March 1976):890–912.

"Sketch of the Life and Work of Dr. Horace A. Buttolph." Typescript. Trenton State Hospital, Trenton, N.J.

Smith, Daniel Blake. "Autonomy and Affection." In *The American Family in Social-Historical Perspective,* edited by Michael Gordon, pp. 209–28. New York: St. Martin's Press, 1983.

Smith, Daniel Scott. "Family Limitation, Sexual Control, and Domestic Feminism in Victorian America." In *Clio's Consciousness Raised,* edited by Mary Hartman and Lois Banner, pp. 119–36. New York: Harper & Row, 1974.

————. "Parental Power and Marriage Patterns." In *The American Family in Social-Historical Perspective,* edited by Michael Gordon, pp. 255–68. New York: St. Martin's Press, 1983.

Solomon, Harry C. "The American Psychiatric Association in Relation to American Psychiatry." *American Journal of Psychiatry* 116 (July 1958):1–9.

Steele, Alden B. *The History of Clark County, Ohio.* Chicago: W. H. Beers & Co., 1881.

Stiles, Henry R. *The History of Ancient Wethersfield, Connecticut.* 2 vols. New York: Grafton Press, 1904.

Stilwell, Lewis D. *Migration from Vermont.* Montpelier: Vermont Historical Society, 1948.

Stookey, Byron. "Origins of the First National Medical Convention." *Journal of the American Medical Association* 177 (15 July 1961):133–40.

"Streets Called 'Asylums of the '80s' at Conference on Homeless." *Washington Post,* 26 April 1984.

Studer, Jacob H. *Columbus, Ohio: Its History, Resources, and Progress.* Columbus, Ohio: W. Richies, 1873.

"Suffering in the Streets." *New York Times,* 16 September 1984.

Szasz, Thomas. *The Age of Madness.* New York: Jason Aronson, 1974.

————. *Law, Liberty, and Psychiatry.* New York: Macmillan, 1963.

Taber, Merlin. *The Social Context of Helping: A Review of the Literature on Alternative Care for the Physically and Mentally Handicapped.* Rockville, Md.: National Institute of Mental Health, 1980.

Talbott, John A. "Response to the Presidential Address: Psychiatry's Unfinished Business in the 20th Century." *American Journal of Psychiatry* 141 (August 1984):927–30.

Thistlewaite, Frank. *The Anglo-American Connection in the Early*

Nineteenth Century. Philadelphia: University of Pennsylvania Press, 1959.

Tocqueville, Alexis de. *Democracy in America.* 2 vols. Translated by Henry Reeve. New York: Dearborn, 1838. Reprint, revised and edited by Phillips Bradley. 2 vols. New York: Vintage Books, 1945.

Tomes, Nancy. *A Generous Confidence: Thomas Story Kirkbride and the Art of Asylum-Keeping.* Cambridge: Cambridge University Press, 1984.

Trumbull, James Russell. "Genealogies of Northampton." Typescript. Forbes Library, Northampton, Massachusetts.

Tyler, Alice Felt. *Freedom's Ferment.* New York: Harper & Row, 1962.

Vogel, Morris J., and Rosenberg, Charles E., eds. *The Therapeutic Revolution.* Philadelphia: University of Pennsylvania Press, 1979.

Vollmer, Howard M., and Mills, Donald L., eds. *Professionalization.* Englewood Cliffs, N.J.: Prentice-Hall, 1966.

Waddell, Joseph A. *Annals of Augusta County, Virginia.* 2d ed. Bridgewater, Va.: C. J. Carrier, 1958.

Walker, Charles M. *History of Athens County, Ohio.* Cincinnati, Ohio: Robert Clarke & Co., 1869.

Wallace, Anthony. *Rockdale.* New York: W. W. Norton, 1981.

Waller, William. *Nashville in the 1890s.* Nashville, Tenn.: Vanderbilt University Press, 1970.

———. *Nashville: 1900–1910.* Nashville, Tenn.: Vanderbilt University Press, 1972.

Walters, Ronald G. *American Reformers.* New York: Hill & Wang, 1978.

"Wards Without Walls." *Burlington Free Press,* 2, 9 December 1984.

Waters, Wilson. *History of Chelmsford, Massachusetts.* Lowell, Mass.: Courier-Citizen Company, 1917.

Watson, David. *A Directory containing the Names, Occupations, and Residence of the Inhabitants of Concord Centre Village.* Concord, N.H.: Morrill, Silsby, and Co., 1844.

Weibe, Robert. *The Search for Order.* New York: Hill & Wang, 1967.

Weir, Robert. " 'The Harmony We Were Famous For.' " In *Colonial America,* edited by Stanley N. Katz and John M. Murrin, pp. 421–46. New York: Alfred A. Knopf, 1983.

Wells, Robert V. "Demographic Change and the Life Cycle of American Families." In *The Family in History,* edited by Theodore K. Rabb and Robert I. Rotberg, pp. 85–94. New York: Harper & Row, 1971.

———. "Family History and Demographic Transition." *Journal of Social History* 9 (Fall 1975):1–19.

Williams Brothers. *History of Franklin and Pickaway Counties.* N.p.: n.p., 1880.

Williams, David. "The Small Farmer in Eighteenth-Century Virginia Politics." In *Colonial America,* edited by Stanley N. Katz and John M. Murrin, pp. 410–21. New York: Alfred A. Knopf, 1983.

Williams Lexington Directory, City Guide and Business Mirror. Lexington, Ky.: Hitchcock & Searles, 1859.

Wilson, James G., and Fiske, John, eds. *Appleton's Cyclopaedia of American Biography.* New York: D. Appleton and Company, 1887.

Wood, T. Outterson. "The Early History of the Medico-Psychological Association." *Journal of Mental Science* 42 (April 1896):241–60.

Woods, Evelyn A., and Carlson, Eric T. "The Psychiatry of Philippe Pinel." *Bulletin of the History of Medicine* 35 (January-February 1961):14–25.

Woollen, William Wesley. *Biographical and Historical Sketches of Early Indiana.* Indianapolis, Ind.: Hammond & Co., 1883.

Wyman, Morrill, Jr. *A Brief Record of the Lives and Writings of Dr. Rufus Wyman and His Son Dr. Morrill Wyman.* Cambridge, Mass.: privately printed, 1908.

Wynkoop, Henry M. *Picturesque Lancaster: Past and Present.* Lancaster, Ohio: Republican Printing Company, 1897.

Yasuba, Yasukichi. *Birth Rates of the White Population in the United States, 1800–1860.* Baltimore: Johns Hopkins Press, 1962.

Young, James Harvey. *The Toadstool Millionaires.* Princeton, N.J.: Princeton University Press, 1961.

Zainaldin, Jamil S., and Tyor, Peter L. "Asylum and Society: An Approach to Industrial Change." *Journal of Social History* 13 (Fall 1979): 23–48.

Zilboorg, Gregory. *A History of Medical Psychology.* New York: W. W. Norton, 1941.

Index

Thompson, Austin W., 180
Thomson, Samuel, 50–52
Thrall, William, 180
Tilden, W. P., 180
Tocqueville, Alexis de, 30
Todd, Eli: curability statistics of, 3;
and familiarity with ideas of Tuke
and Pinel, 41; and interest in blind
and deaf, 34; as mentor of Rock-
well, 14, 50; and relationship with
Woodward, 81–82; role of in Con-
necticut Medical Society, 80–81; as
superintendent of Hartford Retreat
for the Insane, 80–81, 176
Tomes, Nancy, 119
Torbett, George A., 180
Tourtellott, L. A., 180
Trenton (N.J.), 65
Trimble, Isaac, 180
Truman, Harry, 169
Tuke, Samuel, 39–40, 57
Tuke, William, 39–40, 41, 56
Turner, Philip, 46
Tyler, John, 14, 141, 176

University of Maryland Medical
School, 46
University of Pennsylvania School of
Medicine, 45, 47–48

Vail, Jackson, 145
Van Anden, Charles, 51–52, 176
Van Deusen, Edwin, 14, 100, 176
Vermont, 82, 146, 169
Vermont Asylum for the Insane, 173,
174, 176, 177, 178, 179, 180; exposé
of, 145; and patients' newspaper,
11–12; Rockwell as superintendent
of, 11–12, 14, 114–15; size of patient
population at, 115; use of family
image at, 114–15
Vermont Phoenix, 145
Virginia, 2, 3, 7, 25, 31, 43, 62, 69–70,
99–100, 122; Augusta County, 74,
82; Staunton, 1, 2, 6, 7, 51, 69, 70,
130; Williamsburg, 44, 69, 70, 74,
93, 122, 123, 124

Walker, Clement: as medical student,
31, 47; on psychiatric experts, 14;
role of in AMSAII meetings, 14; and

service at house of industry, 34, 56;
as superintendent of Boston Lunatic Hospital, 14, 176; youthful experiences of, 31
Washington, D.C., 98, 104
Weeks, F. C., 180
West Virginia Hospital for the Insane, 175
Western Lunatic Hospital, 2, 174, 176,
177, 178; authority of board of directors of, 123–24; modeled on
Worcester State Lunatic Hospital,
82; moral treatment at, 71–73; and
rivalry with Eastern Lunatic Hospital, 69–70; Stribling as superintendent of, 69–74, 122–24
White, Daniel (father of Samuel
White), 32
White, George, 136, 137, 176
White, Samuel, 137, 176; death of,
14; as founder of AMSAII, 5, 136;
medical training of, 32; and mo-
tivations for choice of asylum ad-
ministration, 44; as owner of private
asylum, 5, 136; role of in founding
of New York State Lunatic Asylum,
5; as vice-president of AMSAII, 89;
youthful experiences of, 32
White, William Alanson, 154, 164
Wilbur, Hervey B., 156
Willard Asylum for the Chronic In-
sane (N.Y.), 153
Willey, Samuel, 180
William and Mary College, 45
Williamson, W. B., 177
Wilson, William, 121, 180
Winchell, Martin E., 177
Wines, Frederick, 153, 156
Winslow, Forbes, 131
Wisconsin, 132
Wisconsin State Hospital for the In-
sane, 175, 176, 178
Wood, Thomas, 180
Woodstock Clinical School of Medi-
cine (Vt.), 146
Woodward, Rufus, 84, 180
Woodward, Samuel: and Connecticut
Medical Society, 80–81; and Con-
necticut State Prison, 80; corre-
spondence of about founding of
AMSAII, 1–2, 83; criticism of, 83–